The Russians Are Coming, Again

THE RUSSIANS ARE COMING, AGAIN

The First Cold War as Tragedy, the Second as Farce

by JEREMY KUZMAROV *and* JOHN MARCIANO

MONTHLY REVIEW PRESS
New York

Library of Congress Cataloging-in-Publication Data
available from the publisher

ISBN: 978-1-58367-694-3 paper
ISBN: 978-1-58367-695-0 cloth

Typeset in Minion Pro

Monthly Review Press, New York
monthlyreview.org

5 4 3 2 1

Contents

To the millions of victims of the Cold War,
and those who have struggled valiantly for a lasting friendship
between the American and Soviet/Russian people

Acknowledgments

WE WISH TO THANK David Gibbs, Jerry Lembcke, and Michael Parenti for their careful reading and comments. Thanks also go to Philip Bennett for his reading of the manuscript; Chuck Churchill for his comradeship throughout; Michael Yates of Monthly Review Press for his editorial support and encouragement; Erin Clermont for her fine copy editing; and Leslie Dwyer, always strong, keeping her eyes on the prize. Jeremy would also like to thank the staff of the McFarlin Library at the University of Tulsa for assisting him, and to Kate Blalack and the staff at the Woody Guthrie Archive for permission to quote from Woody's songs. In addition, he thanks his lovely daughters, Chanda and Olivia, for their patience while he typed away in his office, and his wife, Ngosa, and parents. We trust that everyone mentioned will find this book worthy of their solidarity.

The Russians Are Coming, Again

The 1966 Academy Award–winning film *The Russians Are Coming, The Russians Are Coming*, directed by Norman Jewison, parodies the Cold War paranoia pervading the United States as the war in Vietnam was heating up, depicting chaos that seizes a small coastal New England town after a Soviet submarine runs aground.

Half a century later, U.S. citizens are again being warned daily of the Russian menace, with persistent accusations of Russian aggression, lies, violations of international law, and cyber-attacks on U.S. elections, as reported in leading outlets such as the *New York Times* and the *Washington Post*.

The charges are many and relentless: the Russians invaded neighboring Georgia; the Russians attempted to subvert and overthrow the Ukrainian government; the Russians shot down Malaysian Flight MH17 in July 2014 over eastern Ukraine or supported rebel forces that did so; the Russians annexed Crimea in 2014 in an aggressive move reminiscent of the Soviet Union's postwar actions in Eastern Europe; the Russians have threatened smaller NATO nations in that region; and, most recently, the Russians engaged in cyber warfare by attempting to interfere in the U.S. presidential election and then tried to manipulate the president through connection to key figures in his inner circle.

A prime example of the new Russian hysteria comes from a 2016 report in the *New York Times* by national security correspondents David Sanger, Eric Schmitt, and Michael R. Gordon:

> For his part, Mr. Putin is counting the days until Mr. Trump is in the Oval Office. Despite a failing economy, the Russian president has been pursuing for the past four years what most Western analysts see as a plan to reassert Russian power throughout the region. First came the annexation of Crimea and the shadow war in eastern Ukraine. Then came the deployment of nuclear-capable forces to the border of NATO countries, as Moscow, working to fracture the power structures in Germany and France and promote right-wing parties, sent a reinvigorated military force on patrol off the coasts of the Baltics and Western European nations.[1]

Possessing some unproven assertions masquerading as fact, such as that Putin was working to fracture the power structures in France and Germany and promote right-wing parties, the article fails to acknowledge that a verbal agreement was made in late 1990 between Mikhail Gorbachev and U.S. Secretary of State James Baker. According to the Russians, whose version is corroborated by hundreds of memos and transcripts at the George H. W. Bush Presidential Library, Baker made a pledge to Gorbachev that NATO would not expand east toward their border, in return for Russian support for German reunification.[2] Since then, of course, the United States has armed and funded NATO's eastward advance to include states that share common borders with Russia.

The United States also provocatively increased its naval presence in the Black Sea, carried out military exercises in former Warsaw Pact countries, forged ties with former Soviet republics like Azerbaijan, built oil pipelines to bypass Russia with the involvement of major Western oil companies, and covertly supported Putin's opponents through the National Endowment for Democracy (NED) along with Islamic terrorists in Chechnya as the British had done a century and a half earlier.[3]

In 2014, the State Department fanned protests that led to the overthrow of Ukraine's semi-autocratic but democratically elected pro-Russian government, prompting the Russian annexation of Crimea, which was voted on by a 95 percent majority of Crimeans. The United States then provided over a billion dollars in security assistance to a newly installed Western-friendly right-wing regime that suppressed a pro-Russian uprising in the eastern Donbass region.[4]

By omitting these aggressive U.S. actions, the *New York Times* and other media sources failed to provide proper context for many of Putin's policies, hence furthering the impression that he alone is a major danger to world peace.

In summer 2016, the Obama administration announced the construction of a future U.S. missile defense site in Poland and the activation of a missile defense system in Romania.[5] This came on top of a previously announced trillion-dollar nuclear modernization program, prompted in part by lobbying undertaken by the Bechtel Corporation, that includes the development of new nuclear-tipped weapons whose size and "smart" technology, according to a leading general, ensures that the use of nuclear arms is "no longer unthinkable."[6]

Russia, not surprisingly, has viewed these policies with alarm, putting five new strategic nuclear missile regiments into service in 2016, intensifying development of long-range precision-guided weapons and a galaxy of surveillance drones, and stepping up support for the Bashar al-Assad government in Syria. Former secretary of defense William J. Perry is among those who believe that the danger of nuclear catastrophe stemming from the renewed arms race is "greater today than during the Cold War."[7]

As during the original Cold War, U.S. arms manufacturers have fueled the escalation by lobbying Washington and NATO to maintain high levels of military spending, aided by hired-gun think tanks and professional experts. As retired Army General Richard Cody, a vice president at L-3 Communications, the seventh-largest U.S. defense contractor, explained to shareholders in December 2015, the industry faces a historic opportunity. Following the end of the Cold War, peace had "pretty much broken out all over the world," with Russia in decline and NATO nations celebrating. "The Wall came down," he said, and "all defense budgets went south."[8]

Reversing this slide toward peace required the creation of new foreign enemies including the perception of a revived Russian imperialism, even though U.S. military spending, totaling $609 billion in 2016, dwarfs that of Russia, which spent $65 billion that year.[9]

Tragedy, Then Farce

Karl Marx famously wrote in *The Eighteenth Brumaire of Louis Bonaparte* that history repeats itself "first as tragedy, then as farce."[10] If the First Cold War (1917–1991) was a tragedy, the Second Cold War is playing out as Marx predicted: a farce. During the First Cold War, there was at least some semblance of legitimacy in that the Soviets had infiltrated at least one verifiable spy in the Manhattan Project (Klaus Fuchs) even if the fear of domestic subversion was ultimately grossly overblown, and some aspects of the "evil empire" lived up to this moniker. However, in the New Cold War, the Democrats, backed by most of the media have accused Donald Trump, a U.S. capitalist original and an arch-imperialist, of being a "Manchurian Candidate" surrounded by disloyal agents, which is preposterous. The agents include Trump's wealthy son-in-law and his attorney general, who is a living monument to the Confederacy.

The charge of election interference has been accepted by most of the media even though intelligence agencies—whose legitimacy was already at a low point following the Weapons of Mass Destruction (WMD) debacle in Iraq—released a report so bereft of actual evidence they could only make an "assessment." Forensic specialists working with dissenting intelligence veterans asserted that the hack on the email server of the Democratic National Committee chairman was the result of a leak by someone on the inside carried out in the eastern time zone.[11]

The greatest irony of the Second Cold War is surely the importance of former Communist Party USA leader Earl Browder's grandson, William, a hedge fund manager in Russia sentenced in absentia to nine years in prison for failing to pay 552 million rubles in taxes ($16 million), in leading the lobby for economic sanctions. Browder has spread what appears to be a misleading story about a man he said was his lawyer, Sergey Magnitsky, who was actually an accountant, dying suspiciously after exposing a $230 million Russian government tax scam (the first blacklisted film of the Second Cold War, a documentary blocked from commercial distribution, has unearthed evidence that Browder made up the Magnitsky story to cover up his own orchestration of the scam).[12] To make matters worse, one of the primary villains of the new Cold War, WikiLeaks founder Julian Assange, is an Australian national, so no one can accuse him of treason like the Rosenbergs or Alger Hiss. And there is no Whittaker Chambers who has emerged with a hidden cache of documents to aid the government's case or savvy political opportunists like Richard Nixon to exploit the situation. All we have now is the childish Trump-Comey (former FBI director) standoff and a Senate investigation seizing on any connection between Trump supporters and the Russian government as a sign of disloyalty, which has exposed almost nothing.[13]

No figure has driven the new Cold War frenzy more than Russia's ex-KGB president, Vladimir Vladimirovich Putin, who earned the ire of the American establishment with his dreams of restoring Russia's greatpower status. Putin, however, is unlikely to be hiding any gulags or show trials that could inspire moral purpose behind U.S. foreign policy at a time when the post–Second World War victory culture has receded. Furthermore, Putin is a conservative traditionalist who improved Russia's economy from the damage done by the "Harvard Boys" and other shock therapists in the 1990s and reasserted Russian power without the bloodshed of Stalin.[14] Public opprobrium may thus be hard to sustain this time around, though the scapegoating of Russia functions as a distraction for a ruling class that has otherwise lost its legitimacy.

THE RUSSIANS ARE COMING, AGAIN provides a historical perspective on contemporary U.S.-Russian relations that emphasizes how the absence of historical consciousness has resulted in a repetition of past follies. The first chapter discusses the new Cold War, with a focus on the Russophobic discourse and demonization of Putin in the *New York Times* and its political implications. The second chapter goes back in history to uncover the forgotten U.S. invasion of Soviet Russia in 1918–1920, which was carried out without the consent of Congress, and was opposed by the military commander in Siberia, William S. Graves, who considered it a violation of Russia's sovereignty.

The next four chapters provide a panoramic history of the Cold War, showing how it was an avoidable tragedy. Included in our discussion are the imperatives of class rule that drove the United States to expand its hegemony worldwide, the warping of the American political economy through excessive military spending, the purges and witchhunts, and the Cold War's adverse effect on the black community and unions. The final chapter delves into the Cold War's effect on Third World nations, which suffered from proxy wars and ill-conceived regime change operations. We also spotlight the era's victims and dissidents, whose wisdom and courage may yet inspire a new generation of radicals.

The alarmism about Russia today has served to reinvigorate a traditional Soviet-phobia that draws on a deeper European tradition in which Russian perfidy and aggression have been used to rationalize imperialistic policies.[15] Bill Browder, a key figure lobbying for the new Cold War, depicts Russia in his book *Red Notice: A True Story of High-Finance, Murder and One Man's Fight for Justice* as a hopelessly corrupt, violent, and lawless country that supposedly enlightened Western entrepreneurs like himself could not save and now had to punish.[16] Two generations earlier, President Harry S. Truman explained Stalin by referring to a forged document purporting to show that Russian tsar Peter the Great had developed a blueprint for conquering Europe.[17] The "Father of Containment" doctrine, George F. Kennan, argued that those who wanted to extend goodwill to the Soviets had no real understanding of the malicious Russian character, which he said had been shaped by geography and a history of invasion by "Asian hordes." According to Kennan, the "return of Stalin, a native of the Asiatic country of Georgia holding court in the barbaric splendor of the Moscow Kremlin," confirmed that the "Bolshevik revolution had stripped Russia of its brittle veneer of European culture," embraced since the reign of Peter the Great. "The technique of Russian diplomacy," adopted by Stalin, "like that of the Orient . . . is concentrated in impressing an adversary with the terrifying strength of Russian power while keeping him uncertain and confused as to the exact channels of most of its applications."[18]

This prejudicial attitude and suspicion made peaceful cooperation impossible then as now. Stalin, like Putin, did not actually act too aggressively or irrationally if we consider the history of U.S. invasion, coupled with the Soviet experience in the Second World War, and the fact that the United States virtually encircled the Soviet Union with military bases after the war. In the late 1940s, CIA director Walter Bedell Smith was so confident that the Soviets would *not* "undertake a deliberate military attack on . . . our concentrations of aircraft at Wiesbaden [Germany]" that he would "not hesitate to go there and sit on the field myself."[19]

Following the 1917 Russian Revolution, U.S. congressional hearings first helped create the impression that "Soviet Russia was a kind of bedlam inhabited by abject slaves completely at the mercy of an organization of homicidal maniacs whose purpose was to destroy all traces of civilization and carry the nation back to barbarism"—a depiction that was repeated after the Second World War.[20] Almost no publicity was given to atrocities committed by Admiral Kolchak, a key U.S. ally in Soviet Russia's civil war, whose men burned villages and, according to U.S. intelligence, executed 30,000 people in one year in Siberia as part of actions that would have been considered "shameful in the Middle Ages."[21] Atrocities perpetrated by American-backed regimes like the Nazi-tainted government in Greece, Guomindang in China, or Latin American national security states were similarly sugarcoated or ignored by the "patriotic press," whose foreign correspondents maintained symbiotic relations with the State Department and CIA.[22]

The media's role in hyping the Soviet threat was epitomized by a 1951 *Collier's* magazine special issue that fantasized about the U.S. overthrow of the Soviet government after the Soviets attacked U.S. cities with atomic weapons. Arthur Koestler, author of *Darkness at Noon*, wrote in one of the *Collier's* essays that "in the Soviet slave state, human evolution" had "touched the bottom."[23] This prejudicial assessment ignored some of the major accomplishments of the Communist revolution, including its facilitation of greater economic independence, industrial growth, social equality, cultural brilliance as seen in Sergei Eisenstein's films, Dmitri Shostakovich's music, Boris Pasternak and Andrei Voznesensky's poetry, and "the slave state's" total mobilization to defeat Nazi Germany.

The Woodrow Wilson Foundation and the National Planning Association were perceptive in describing the actual threat of Communism to U.S. political and economic elites as being "the economic transformation of the communist power in ways which reduce their willingness and ability to complement the industrial economies of the West . . . their refusal to play the game of comparative advantage and to rely primarily on foreign investment for development."[24] General Douglas MacArthur, of all people, asserted that to sustain the Cold War the

[United States] government has kept us in a perpetual state of fear—kept us in a perpetual stampede of patriotic fervor—with the cry of a grave national emergency. Always there has been some terrible evil at home or some monstrous foreign power [Russia or China] that was going to gobble us up if we did not blindly rally behind it by furnishing the exorbitant funds demanded. Yet, in retrospect, these disasters seem never to have happened, seem never to have been quite real.[25]

Social conditioning combined with Russophobic prejudice thus enabled the skewed priorities in which the federal government spent an estimated $904 billion, or 57 percent of its budget, for military power from 1946 to 1967, and only $96 billion, or 6 percent, for social functions such as education, health, labor, and welfare programs. Congress rubber-stamped an arsenal of horror that included multi-megaton hydrogen bombs, intercontinental bombers with unmanned missiles, and chemical and biological weapons that had to be made operational to justify taxpayer expense.[26] To contain Soviet Russian power, the U.S. further waged "limited wars" in Korea and Vietnam where it splashed oceans of napalm, defoliated the landscape, killed millions of civilians, supported drug trafficking proxies in Southeast Asia and Latin America, and unleashed chemical and likely biological warfare, while training repressive police forces in dozens of countries. The Cold War also devastated communities of leftists and activists in the United States as a result of McCarthyite witchhunts, eroding the prospects for social democracy.[27]

Suppressing the truth, popular commemorations of the Cold War have fixated almost exclusively on the crimes of Communism. In 1993, a bipartisan bill was passed by Congress and signed into law by Bill Clinton establishing a foundation to educate the public about the crimes of Communism and honor its victims.[28] In 2007, Senator Hillary Clinton introduced legislation to establish the Cold War Medal Act to honor Cold War military veterans. Her speech referenced "our [great] victory in the Cold War" and ability to "defeat the threat from the Iron Curtain."[29] Clinton, not coincidentally, has been at the forefront promoting a confrontational policy and demonized view of Putin and Russia, and, in the style of the First Cold War, redbaited Bernie Sanders during the 2016 Democratic Party primary. She in turn is a key figure epitomizing how the distortion of public memory surrounding the first Cold War is fueling its reinvigoration today, a story this book aims to tell.

CHAPTER 1

Anti-Russian Hysteria in Propaganda and Fact

I n the first part of this chapter, we will look at the new Cold War, reviewing recent accusations about Russia and its president Vladimir Putin as found in the *New York Times*, the "Newspaper of Record" and the most influential paper in the country. This virtually monolithic attack on Russia and its president by the *Times'* leading columnists, feature writers, and editorial board has been part of "one of the biggest fake news operations in U.S. history" according to best-selling author Dan Talbot, "comparable to the yellow journalism promoted by the Hearst papers, which sold military intervention in the Spanish American War."[1]

Re-invoking a historical Russophobia, the *Times* and media counterparts have consistently warned about a "new Russian imperialism" while casting Putin as a veritable "red devil," as columnist Maureen Dowd termed him.[2] Like all effective propaganda, there is a grain of truth to some of the allegations. However, many are unfounded or taken out of context. The U.S. role in provoking some of Putin's actions is ignored, and inflated metaphors have been used, such as comparisons of the Russian annexation of Crimea to the German blitzkrieg and Anschluss during the Second World War.

The second part of the chapter will challenge the dominant narrative by presenting dissenting views from independent analysts who have placed the contemporary crisis with Russia in proper perspective. Unfortunately, their commentary has been confined to alternative media and hence has not been able to contain the growth of a dangerous "moral panic" that has helped precipitate the outbreak of a new Cold War.

PART I: THE OFFICIAL STORY IN THE *NEW YORK TIMES*

Owned since 1896 by the Ochs-Sulzberger family, which enjoys close relations with many elements of the U.S. power elite, the *New York Times* relies on revenues from corporate advertisers and loans from banking firms, neither of which would be pleased if the *Times* took positions hostile to their interests or that of the corporate community at large. Though nominally liberal in its support for environmental and financial regulation, as well as social issues, the "Newspaper of Record" quite blatantly supports the centrist wing of the Democratic Party. During the 2016 election, even its most liberal columnist, Paul Krugman, frequently ridiculed Bernie Sanders, the progressive dissident. The *Times* has also supported CIA covert operations and U.S. military power abroad. Its Putin-bashing, defense of NATO, and fomenting of anti-Russian hysteria can thus be placed in the larger context of the paper's history in "manufacturing consent," often by playing up the alleged atrocities of official government enemies while whitewashing those of its allies.[3]

After Putin was elected in March 2000, the *Times* mixed reservations about his KGB background with reassurance that he "seemed to harbor no nostalgia for the suffocating ideology of communism or the terrors carried out in its name." It noted that he was "smart and articulate" and appeared to be "a skillful, pragmatic manager" with "some democratic credentials."[4] A June 2003 editorial stated that "Putin had done a lot to end the chaos of the Yeltsin years" and bring stability to his country and that he was a "sober, Westernizing leader" who was "prepared to cooperate with the United States and Europe."[5]

Subsequent editorials encouraged "[President] Bush's instinct to befriend Mr. Putin" and to "write a positive new chapter in relations with Moscow." Former national security adviser and Iran-Contra felon Robert "Bud" McFarlane urged cooperation in the War on Terror, suggesting that the United States didn't have to "choose between Russia and Europe. It [was] in America's interest to cooperate with both."[6]

When Putin opposed the Iraq war and U.S.-Russian relations soured, the *Times* predictably became more hostile. Columnist William Safire, who characterized Russia as "authoritarian at heart and expansionist by habit," launched the first shot in the anti-Putin movement with his December 10, 2003, editorial, "The Russian Reversion," which urged resistance against the budding "cult of Putin" and his "one-party rule."[7] The *Times* subsequently denounced Putin's "old-style KGB tactics" when he arrested oligarch Mikhail Khodorkovsky before he was to sell a majority of shares of his Yukos oil company to Exxon-Mobil.[8] Columnist Nicholas Kristof suggested that the West had been "suckered" into believing "Putin was a sober version of Boris Yeltsin," when he was a "Russified Pinochet or Franco" leading Russia to fascism. According to Kristof, a "fascist Russia was [actually] much better than a communist Russia, since communism was a failed economic system while Franco's Spain, General Pinochet's Chile and the others generated solid economic growth, a middle class and international contacts" and "lay the groundwork for democracy." The United States, nevertheless, needed to take its cue from the Baltic states and Ukrainians and "stand up to Putin" and his "bullying tactics."[9]

In February 2007, Putin delivered what *Times* correspondent Steven Lee Myers termed an "acerbic assault on American unilateralism" at the Munich Conference on Security Policy, which roiled feathers in Washington.[10] When Russia subsequently sent troops to defend secessionists in South Ossetia and Abkhazia, which were invaded by the Georgian government of Mikheil Saakashvili with U.S. military support, *Times* Foreign Affairs columnist Thomas L. Friedman wrote that Putin "deserved a gold medal for brutish stupidity." Many observers blamed Saakashvili, however, for starting the war, and the Russian intervention (orchestrated actually by President Dmitri Medvedev, whom Friedman called "Putin's mini-me") prevented South Ossetia's absorption into a future NATO member state, restored pride in the Russian army, and prevented threatened ethnic cleansing.[11]

Anti-Putin Invective Grows in the Obama Years

The anti-Putin invective escalated throughout the Obama years, peaking in Obama's second term during the Ukraine crisis when the *Times* supported the U.S.-backed Maidan "revolution" of February 2014 that resulted in the toppling of pro-Russian President Victor Yanukovych.[12] An article by C. J. Chivers and Patrick Reveel alleged Russian intimidation, military occupation, and electoral manipulation ahead of the March 16, 2014, referendum in which 95 percent of Crimeans voted to rejoin Russia. The authors wrote that the referendum had the "trappings of the election-season carnivals that have long accompanied rigged ballots across the old Soviet world."[13] These claims ignored that Moscow had thousands of troops in an agreement to protect its naval base at Sevastopol, and that the referendum results stemmed from longstanding ambivalence to Kiev and disdain for the post-coup regime among a majority of Crimeans, especially the many ethnic Russians.[14]

In April 2014, the *Times* published photos of Russian fighters in the Donbass and Luhansk regions that purportedly "proved" the charge of Russian aggression in the civil war that broke out in eastern Ukraine, though the photos were proven to be fakes and the *Times* had to issue a retraction. The *Times* editorial board still referred to Russia as the aggressor in Ukraine nevertheless, saying Putin's actions revealed his "arrogance and contempt for international law," which justified the levying of sanctions and possibly expelling Russia from the G-8 nations.[15]

The *Times* further violated journalistic standards when it published an unsubstantiated allegation by a conservative Russian oligarch that Putin had been provided advance warning of the pro-Russian Yanukovich government's collapse, and planned in advance to exploit the ensuing chaos by annexing Crimea with the underlying goal of maintaining the gas supply routes that help Russia dominate European supplies.[16] The *Times* subsequently helped cover up the massacre of thirty-eight pro-Russian demonstrators in Odessa after right-wing Nazi sympathizers burned the Trade Union House where they were taking refuge after their tent encampment had been ransacked.[17]

When Malaysia Airlines Flight MH17 was shot down over eastern Ukraine in July 2014, *Times* columnist Roger Cohen mimicked Secretary of State John Kerry in claiming there was "an enormous amount of evidence" pointing to Russian culpability, including "damning audio and images that capture the crime." Putin has been "playing with fire," Cohen wrote, as the shooting down of the airplane "amounts to an act of war," with "193 innocent Dutch souls dishonored by the thugs of the Donetsk People's Republic." The only viable response was to help "transform Ukraine's army into a credible force," which "won't happen. Europe is weak [and] Obama's America is about retrenchment, not resolve. Putin must be appeased." At the time of these statements, however, no major criminal investigation had been conducted and Senator Saxby Chambliss (R-GA), a member of the Senate Select Committee on Intelligence privy to all the relevant evidence, said there was "no smoking gun."[18] Cohen's column was thus pure hyperbole and an incitement for war.

In August 2015, Andrew Higgins and Michael Gordon reported that "Russia had escalated tensions with Ukraine to the highest levels since its stealthy invasion of Crimea in the spring, sending more than 200 trucks from a long-stalled aid convoy into rebel-held eastern Ukraine over the objections of Kiev and, NATO said, conducting military operations on Ukrainian territory."[19] The latter operations, however, were unverified and the aid convoy was designed to assist local populations devastated from missile and other attacks by Ukrainian government forces. The *Times* furthermore omitted the United States, European Union (EU), and Canadian role in providing weapons, intelligence support, and training to Ukrainian regiments, which were led in some cases by neo-Nazi militias.[20]

Times writers Michael D. Shear, Allison Smale, and David Herszenhorn had invoked the Nazi blitzkrieg in referencing Putin's "invasion" and "lightning annexation" of Crimea, which, they said, "shocked" the NATO countries because it revealed Russia's "abrupt abandonment of the rules of cooperation and territorial integrity that have governed East-West relations for decades."[21]

Amy Chozick and Ian Lovett reported uncritically on Secretary of State Hillary Clinton's comparisons between Russia's issuing of passports "to Ukrainians with allegiances to Russia" to what Adolf Hitler did before Germany began invading bordering countries." Though differentiating Putin from Hitler, the assertion that he had to go into Crimea to protect the Russian minority there was said to be "reminiscent of claims made back in the 1930s" when the Nazis asserted they had to invade Eastern European countries to "protect German minorities."[22] In Crimea, however, Russians are the majority at 65 percent, while Ukrainians and Tatars are the minority. Crimea was historically part of Russia and sacred as the place where Vladimir the Grand Prince of Kiev brought Christianity to Russia and Russian troops heroically fought Britain, France, and Turkey during the nineteenth-century Crimean War.[23]

Supporting NATO Expansion

Just as the British press whipped up fear about Russian aggression on the eve of the Crimean War, the "Newspaper of Record" is creating a new Red Scare by echoing U.S. government officials warning about the "re-Sovietization" of Central Asia and Russia's "resurrection [under Putin] as a global disrupter."[24] Strong offense has been taken at Russia's "furious" opposition to NATO's expansion on its borders, despite the fact that Russia had been promised NATO would not expand there. In early 2017, the *Times* editorial board critiqued President Trump and Defense Secretary James Mattis for calling NATO "obsolete" and suggesting the United States might not support NATO members that have not met their financial obligations at a "time the Western alliance was again facing an assertive and aggressive Russia," an "especially worrisome" trend "given Mr. Trump's possible links to Moscow." In the *Times* version of history, these are "fraught times for the Western alliance, which even after the Cold War remains a critical unifying bond among the democracies of North America and Europe and whose members have worked together to confront terrorism in Afghanistan and promote stability in several Middle Eastern countries."[25]

Russian Interference in the Presidential Election

The official indictment against Putin holds that he ordered an "influence campaign aimed at the U.S. election," with the goal of "undermining faith in the U.S. democratic process, denigrating Hillary Clinton, and harming her electability and potential presidency." The Office of the Director of National Intelligence (DNI), representing seventeen intelligence agencies, and the Department of Homeland Security (DHS) determined with "high confidence" that Russia hacked the Democratic National Committee (DNC) and leaked documents to WikiLeaks that showed efforts to undermine Bernie Sanders and exposed some of Clinton's speeches to Wall Street high-rollers. DNI James Clapper testified that "Russia's alleged meddling in the 2016 campaign went beyond hacking, and included disinformation and the dissemination of fake news often promoted on social media," with Putin being said to have "personally directed" the operation.[26]

Like the good soldiers they are, the *Times* commentators reported the allegations as fact when conclusive evidence was lacking. Columnist Charles M. Blow asserted that Russian hacking made it "more . . . clear that . . . Trump's victory [is] tainted beyond redemption." He wrote: "A hostile power stole confidential correspondence from American citizens . . . and funneled that stolen material to a willing conspirator, Julian Assange [WikiLeaks founder]." Then the hostile foreign action "had its desired result." Blow later characterized Putin "as the man whose thumb was all over the scale that delivered Trump's victory," and likened Trump's effort to set up a cybersecurity working group with the Russians to "inviting the burglar to help you design your alarm system."[27]

Thomas L. Friedman said we did not "take seriously from the very beginning [that] Russia hacked our election. That was a 9/11-scale event. They attacked the core of our democracy. That was a Pearl Harbor scale event. . . . This goes to the very core of our democracy."[28] For Nicholas Kristof, the truth was absolutely clear: while some foreign leaders want to steal billions of dollars, Putin "may have wanted to steal something even more valuable: an American presidential election." The fundamental issue is that a "foreign dictatorship [apparently made an effort] to disrupt an American presidential election." Kristof ended on a small note of caution, however, since the "intelligence community' is sometimes an oxymoron," pointing to the alleged Russian "yellow rain" chemical warfare in Southeast Asia decades ago, saying that it may have actually been excrement.[29]

Yale University history professor Timothy Snyder wrote baselessly in the *Times* that Putin is a "fascist," influenced by Ivan Ilyin, "a prophet of Russian fascism." He has "consciously worked to hollow out the idea of democracy in [his] own country [and] also [seeks] to discredit democracy" in the United States [by meddling in the election].[30] Nobel Economics Laureate Paul Krugman agrees, asserting that the "post-election CIA declaration that Russia had intervened on behalf of the Trump campaign was a confirmation, not a revelation (although we've now learned that Mr. Putin was personally involved in the effort)." Precisely how Putin was involved, however, he does not say. Krugman reveals his support for Hillary Clinton when he writes that the hacked emails "mostly revealed nothing more than the fact that the Democrats are people," when in reality they revealed unethical plans to influence the primary outcome, something from which the Russian hacking charge helped divert attention.[31]

"The Kind of Person Sister Mary Ingrid Warned Us About"

According to a June 2017 Pew Research Center poll, 87 percent of Russians have confidence in Putin and think their country has gained stature on the world stage. Some 58 percent of Russians also said they were satisfied with their country's direction.[32] The *New York Times*, however, has depicted Putin as a threat to global stability and "The New Tsar," to quote the title of a book by Steven Lee Myers, and by implication an embodiment of the backward traits of Russian society long held in the American imagination.[33]

The prize for the most juvenile commentary goes to Gail Collins, who informed *Times* readers that during the Cold War her Catholic schooling prepared her "to die for our faith in the event of a Communist takeover; things [now] were getting scary again as Putin invaded Ukraine, bombed the hell out of Aleppo [and] tried to interfere with our election. He's just the kind of person that Sister Mary Ingrid warned us about."[34]

This imbecilic chattering and levying of accusations without proof are from a columnist for the most prestigious paper in the country. To put this in historical perspective, one simply needs to recall the propaganda that drenched the media, including the *Times*, prior to the invasion of Iraq in March 2003 about the evil incarnate Saddam Hussein.[35] It's as if he has been reincarnated in the body of Vladimir Putin. There are no nuances and subtleties, no historical context in the pages of the *Times* that can help us intelligently explain Putin's appeal among Russians or how the United States bears considerable responsibility for rising hostilities and can hence play a critical role in defusing them.

Roger Cohen characteristically called Putin a "pure Soviet product [who] traffics in lies," such as "the supposed Western encirclement of Russia." It is "inevitable, given what he represents, that Trump looks to Putin." Paul Krugman reminds readers that Putin is "an ex-KGB man—which is to say, he spent his formative years as a professional thug." In another column, he writes that Russia has very little to offer anyone except those rightists who find "macho posturing and ruthlessness attractive."[36] Krugman treats Barack Obama respectfully by contrast, even though Obama ordered the deaths of thousands in the drone war.

Michael McFaul, ambassador to Russia under Obama, blames Putin for increased U.S.-Russian tension, writing that "this new era crept up on us, because we did not fully win the Cold War. . . . But the collapse of the Soviet order did not lead smoothly to a transition to democracy and markets inside Russia"—a telling juxtaposition clearly not intended. An autocrat at heart, Putin "needed an enemy—the United States—to strengthen his legitimacy." His "propagandists rolled out clips on American imperialism, immoral practices and alleged plans to overthrow the Putin government," with the "shrill anti-Americanism reaching fever pitch" during the annexation of Crimea. Putin "embraces confrontation with the West, [and] no longer feels constrained by international laws and norms." Just like the Cold War, an "ideological struggle between autocracy and democracy has returned to Europe," and democracies "need to recognize . . . Putin's rule for what it is—autocracy [with which] there can be no compromise."[37]

Failing to give adequate context for Putin's rise, McFaul sounds like George Kennan in differentiating the supposedly progressive, democratic West from the backward, autocratic, and expansionist Russia, whose strongman only understands the language of force. According to Swiss journalist Guy Mettan, Russophobic discourse has its roots in the Middle Ages when Charlemagne competed with Byzantium for the title of heir to the Roman Empire, and anti-Orthodox Catholic propaganda followed the schism between the West and East of which Russia was associated. Russophobia, Mettan says, resembles both anti-Semitism and Islamophobia in that it "exists first in the head of the one who looks not in the victims' alleged behavior or characteristics. [It is] a way of turning specific pseudo-facts into essential one-dimensional values, barbarity, despotism and expansionism in the Russian case in order to justify stigmatization and ostracism."[38]

What popular demonology leaves out is that many of Russia's problems are structural and linked to the predatory actions of Western financial interests in the 1990s, and that Mr. Putin has a base of popular support because he has revived Russian self-respect and power from the Yeltsin era. In his time in office, Putin has ordered the oligarchs to pay taxes and jailed or exiled some, regained national control over oil and gas deposits sold to ExxonMobil and other Western oil companies under Yeltsin, and asserted control over the Russian Central Bank. Putin has further prevented Russia's disintegration while implementing policies that improved infrastructure, living standards, and led to a decrease in corruption and crime, something the *Times* has admitted. Inflation, joblessness, and poverty rates have declined while wages have improved. Putin has overcome Western sanctions by improving trade relations with China and other "BRIC" nations (Brazil, Russia, India, China) and advanced his vision of a Eurasian Union uniting Kazakhstan and Belarus in a regional trading bloc.[39]

The *Times* and other media outlets promote a double standard in singling out Putin for his authoritarian style when the United States supports murderous tyrants around the world like the Saudi royal family and Rwanda's Paul Kagame, and authoritarian leaders in the former Soviet republics whose abuses are rarely highlighted or exposed. Putin's predecessor, Boris Yeltsin, was characterized as "the father of Russian democracy" and compared to Abraham Lincoln when he used tank cannons to storm the parliament following a constitutional crisis he precipitated, resulting in around five hundred deaths, killed thousands in invading Chechnya, and imposed disastrous "shock therapy" economic policies pushed by American advisers—dubbed "the Harvard Boys"—that resulted in an unprecedented rise in the mortality rate. Yeltsin also allied with oligarchs who essentially bought him the presidency in 1996.[40]

Paul Craig Roberts, assistant secretary of the treasury under President Ronald Reagan, points out that "the initial collapse of the USSR worked very much to the West's advantage. The [United States and its allies] could easily manipulate Yeltsin, and various oligarchs were able to seize and plunder the resources of the country. Much . . . American money was part of that. When Putin came along and started stopping this and trying to put the country back in place, he was demonized."[41]

There is a gap in quality between at least some of the *Times* reporting and the opinion pieces. In April 2016, for example, the *Times* ran an informative article by William J. Broad and David E. Sanger discussing the race for the latest class of nuclear weaponry between Russia, China, and the United States. They pointed out that while American officials have largely blamed escalating tensions on Putin and the Chinese for their apparent aggressive drives in the South China Sea, these two "adversaries look at what the United States expects to spend on nuclear revitalization—estimated up to a trillion over three decades—and use it to lobby for their own sophisticated weaponry."

The article went on to point out that President Obama himself had recognized that his nuclear weapons modernization program could undermine his own previous record of progress on arms control.[42] From this example we see that *Times* journalists are capable of first-rate analysis. However, in our assessment, instances of quality reporting have been overshadowed by the barrage of pieces painting Putin and Russia in the darkest of hues, which contribute in turn to the popular impression that the Russians are coming, again.

PART II: FURTHERING OUR CRITIQUE

In a December 2016 interview with David Barsamian on *Alternative Radio*, a weekly public affairs program that provides analyses and views that are often ignored or distorted in the corporate media, Stephen Cohen, the noted scholar on the Soviet Union and Russia, reminded listeners that the Russian people have a long memory of the staggering loss of human life and physical destruction brought on by the Nazi invasion during the Second World War. Their celebration of V-E Day (Victory in Europe) on May 9 is their "most sacred secular holiday." Vivid memories of the war "awakened . . . ferocious reactions in Russia" over what was unfolding in Ukraine. "When you get guys who look and smell like neo-Nazis running around burning up people, as they did in Odessa in 2014, it awakens memories of World War Two and the Nazi occupation." It was greater because the United States helped bring about the coup in Ukraine, the result of years of U.S. intervention there, aided by the Soros Foundation and the National Endowment on Democracy (NED), which worked to undermine the existing regime. Victoria Nuland, undersecretary of state under Hillary Clinton, admitted before Congress that the United States spent $5 billion "building democracy" there before the crisis.

What does it mean to "build democracy"? It is "to create a country aligned with us, because there's probably less democracy in Ukraine today . . . than there was when they overthrew" the former president Victor Yanukovych, in February 2014.

Cohen says it is a misnomer to claim that Putin invaded Ukraine when what he did was "react" to a Western encroachment that was part of a "long-term effort to bring Ukraine into NATO. The documents are there to be read." Putin was given intelligence information stating that there "was going to be a march on the Russian historical and strategic naval base on the Crimean peninsula" and this possibility presented "a grave danger. . . . We could argue that he overreacted; you can make a case. But he was reacting." After the United States helped "to overthrow the government there or abetted the overthrow of a legally elected leader—and it was recognized that the Ukrainian election of Yanukovych had been fair—and bringing an unelected regime to power," why wouldn't Russia react? "Taking Ukraine over, recognizing the new government immediately, bringing these guys to Washington, with McCain and the others in the streets egging them on, did we think Russia wouldn't react? Why is that Russian aggression?"[43]

Russian filmmaker Andrei Nekrasov, who supported the Maidan protests and produced a film investigating the death of Russian defector Alexander Litvinenko, concurs with Cohen's assessment, pointing out that Putin is not a threat to world security any more than the United States, which is much more powerful. Nekrosov further stated in an interview that "there is simply no evidence of Putin's excessive riches [as the media has reported]; not even a single evidence of some bank accounts, or a bribe he or his wife for example got from an industry or such thing [whereas] there was such evidence in Yeltsin's case, quite specific and direct." Though not personally enamored of Putin, Nekrosov says that he gets "elected and is hugely popular in Russia and doesn't need to suppress democracy very much, even if he were able to. . . . The media apart from the big national TV channels is relatively free."[44]

Robert Parry of *Consortium News* suggests that the broad demonization of Putin has set the groundwork for a potential "regime change" and program of isolation designed to punish Putin for blocking American machinations in Syria and Iran and to ensure control over the Eurasian heartland. The first phase of this plan was the Ukraine coup where Victoria Nuland "was caught on an unsecure phone line telling U.S. Ambassador Geoffrey Pyatt" how they "would 'midwife' a change in government that would put Nuland's choice . . . in power." Parry has raised doubt about Russia's culpability in the shooting down of Malaysia Airlines Flight MH17, based on the fact that the State Department refuses to make public radar information that Secretary of State Kerry said points to the location of the offending missile. Parry spoke to an intelligence agent who indicated that as U.S. "analysts gained more insights from technical and other sources, they came to believe the attack was carried out by a rogue element of the Ukrainian military" with ties to hardline oligarch Ihor Kolomoyskyi, who may have been intending to bring down Putin's plane which was flying nearby.[45]

In September 2016, a Dutch-led investigation provided evidence suggesting that the missile used in the shoot-down was fired from a field controlled by pro-Russian fighters in Ukraine and was brought in from Russian territory. The investigation relied heavily on Ukrainian intelligence sources with a vested interest in blaming Russia, however, and failed to mention that the Ukrainian military controlled all anti-aircraft missile batteries in eastern Ukraine. It also did not have access to U.S. radar data and said it was still trying to establish who the perpetrators were.[46] The truth thus remains elusive.

Like the British and French press did in the nineteenth century, the *New York Times* alleges without substantiation that Russia financed political parties throughout Western Europe in an effort to infiltrate and destabilize the region. Putin also reportedly killed many of his rivals, pilfered millions in state funds and armed the Taliban, though the director of the Defense Intelligence Agency told the Senate he had "not seen any physical evidence."[47] Putin was further accused of covering up Syrian chemical attacks, though it now appears it was not the source of these attacks. The Syrians struck a weapons cache that released toxic clouds of fertilizers that were magnified by dense morning air, as veteran journalist Seymour Hersh reported in a story published only by a German newspaper.[48]

According to Edward S. Herman, the *Times* from January 1 to March 21, 2014, had twenty-three articles on the Pussy Riot group to signify alleged Russian limits on free speech, and gave one member of the group op-ed space to denounce Putin. The group had been arrested after disrupting a church service and were given a two-year sentence. Around the same time, eighty-four-year-old Sister Megan Rice was given a four-year jail sentence for protesting a nuclear weapons site in Tennessee, but she was mentioned only in the back pages and not given an opportunity to publish an op-ed. Nor could she meet with the *Times* editorial board as Pussy Riot did. Another double-standard was the great indignation at Assad-Putin inhumanity in Aleppo compared to the relative silence about rebel atrocities in Syria and civilian casualties in Fallujah and Mosul under U.S.-allied attacks, which were significant.[49]

The *Times* meanwhile refused to characterize the Maidan protests that resulted in the overthrow of Yanukovych as a coup when even Maidan protestors in Kiev characterized it as such since they could not pass a referendum for impeachment. The *Times* in turn sugarcoated the new regime led by Petro Poroshenko, who was described in a WikiLeaks cable from the American embassy as a "disgraced oligarch . . . tainted by credible corruption allegations," and appointed as deputy prime minister a member of the far-right Svoboda Party who told the EU parliament that a "fascist dictatorship is the best way to rule a country."[50]

The *Times* further failed to report on the CIA and George Soros Foundation's role in financing the Maidan protests, and on the humanitarian crisis that resulted from brutal "anti-terrorist" operations directed by Kiev against pro-Russian separatists in the eastern Donbass region who were falsely labeled "pawns of Putin" (the region is, in fact, Russian-speaking and has strong interests in remaining tied to Russia). Warning about the plight of over a million displaced children whose schools had been destroyed, UNICEF referred to "an invisible emergency which most of the world has forgotten." This was thanks largely to the blackout in the *Times* and other media that also ignored the machinations of the Biden wing of the Obama administration in undermining efforts by John Kerry to promote the Minsk peace agreements, possibly because of Biden's son Hunter's business interests in the Ukraine. Hunter was named to the board of a Ukrainian Natural Gas company in April 2014—just three months after the coup.[51]

Lessons Not Learned

The similarities between the blitz in 2002–2003 for war against Iraq and for action against Russia and Putin are striking. Many readers will recall how the CIA under George W. Bush leaked phony intelligence to Michael Gordon and Judith Miller of the *Times*, claiming that Iraq was procuring aluminum tubes to enrich uranium for its nonexistent weapons of mass destruction (WMD). James Carden, a former adviser to the U.S.-Russia Presidential Commission at the State Department, pointed out in 2017 that something eerily similar was taking place regarding Russia, in which "assurances from the intelligence community and from anonymous Obama administration 'senior officials' about the *existence* of evidence [regarding alleged election hacking] is being treated as . . . *actual* evidence."[52]

As a sign of continuity, Michael Gordon, a chief culprit in "helping to scam the USA into occupation and invasion of Iraq," is among those who have reported disinformation about Ukraine. Fellow Iraq War cheerleaders have been among the loudest to demonize Putin. Charles Krauthammer told Fox News: "Of course it all [DNC hacks] came from the Russians, I'm sure it's all there in the intel." David Frum in *The Atlantic* stated that Trump "owes his office in considerable part to illegal clandestine activities in his favor conducted by a hostile, foreign spy service." Jacob Weisberg agrees, tweeting: "Russian covert action threw the election to Donald Trump. It's that simple." This is the same Weisberg who wrote back in 2008, "The first thing I hope I've learned from this experience of being wrong about Iraq is to be less trusting of expert opinion and received wisdom."[53] Lesson not learned.

Placing the Election Hysteria in Context

When U.S. intelligence agencies finally released a declassified version of its report on the election, the *New York Times* and the *Washington Post* quoted from it verbatim, supporting the conclusion that Putin and Russia were behind the DNC hacks. Close reading of the report, however, shows that it barely supports such a conclusion. Devoting considerable attention to the Russia Today (RT) news network, which was impugned for offering critical analysis of U.S. politics, the report merely provided an "assessment," which journalist Robert Parry notes is an "admission" that the classified information was "less than conclusive because, in intelligence-world-speak" to "assess" actually means "to guess."[54]

Historian Gareth Porter writes that the intelligence community never obtained evidence to prove Russia was behind WikiLeaks' publication of the DNC emails, "much less that it had done so with the intention of electing Trump." After the U.S. election, DNI James Clapper testified twice before Congress that "the intelligence community did not know who had provided the emails to WikiLeaks and when they were provided." The NSA further considered the idea that the Kremlin was working to elect Trump as merely plausible, not actually supported by reliable evidence.[55]

Half of Clinton voters nevertheless believe that Russia not only leaked emails but tampered with vote tallies. A more plausible scenario is that either Clinton blamed Russia to try to save her campaign, or that CIA director John Brennan, appointed by President Obama, initiated the election-hacking scandal and Russia-Gate investigations in order to preserve a belligerent policy toward Russia to which the CIA and other national security organizations were committed. Brennan issued a public warning to Trump about his Russian policy on Fox News. "I think Mr. Trump has to understand that absolving Russia of various actions that it's taken in the past number of years is a road that he, I think, needs to be very, very careful about moving down."[56]

In December 2016, twenty intelligence, military, and diplomatic veterans who had formed Veteran Intelligence Professionals for Sanity

(VIPS) sent an open letter to President Obama calling on him to release the evidence that proves Russia aided the Trump campaign—or to admit that it does not exist. They wrote that the alleged Russian interference in the election has been called "an act of war" and Mr. Trump a "traitor"; the "intelligence," however, to support these assertions, "does not pass the smell test." Obama never responded.

The VIPS wrote that media attacks against Trump and Putin were lacking journalistic standards as top intelligence officials "published what we found to be an embarrassingly shoddy report purporting to prove Russian hacking in support of Trump's candidacy," and a *Times* banner headline said: "PUTIN LED SCHEME TO AID TRUMP, REPORT SAYS." The paper claimed that the revelations in "this damning report . . . undermined the legitimacy" of the President-Elect, and "made the case that Mr. Trump was the favored candidate of Mr. Putin," but a back-page article in the same issue stated: "What is missing from the public report is what many Americans most eagerly anticipated: hard evidence to back up the agencies' claims that the Russian government engineered the election attack. . . . [There was] no discussion of the forensics used to recognize the handiwork of known hacking groups, no mention of intercepted communications between the Kremlin and the hackers, no hint of spies reporting from inside Moscow's propaganda machinery."[57]

For VIPS, the key question was how the material from "Russian hacking" got to WikiLeaks, because WikiLeaks published the DNC and Podesta emails (John Podesta was chairman of Hillary Clinton's election campaign). William Binney, former technical director of the NSA, pointed out it "would almost certainly have yielded a record of any electronic transfer from Russia to WikiLeaks." If Obama could not make public any evidence, he probably did not have any.[58]

A forensics study undertaken by a retired IBM program manager, Skip Folden, found that DNC data were copied onto a storage device at a speed that exceeds the Internet capability for a remote hack. The operation was performed on the East Coast of the United States, suggesting an inside leak, which was later doctored to incriminate Russia. Folden's study was ignored by the *Times* and other media, along with the curious fact that the FBI never sought access to the DNC computers as part of its investigation or bothered to interview a British diplomat who claims to have met the leaker outside Washington.[59] Months after the fact, when the government's own investigation stalled, the *Times* kept publishing sensational front-page exposés purporting to unearth secret hackers in Ukraine, and a diabolical plot by Russia to set up fake social media accounts to spread stories critical of Clinton and U.S. foreign policy, which the *Times* baselessly claimed helped sway the election.[60]

Russia-Gate in Context: Trump and His Pro-Kremlin Cabinet

Times writers have routinely lambasted Donald Trump for his alleged "slavish devotion to the Russian strongman" as Max Boot put it in an op-ed calling for a get-tough policy, and cast him as beholden to Russian interests. Paul Krugman on July 22, 2016, predicted that "Mr. Trump would, in office, follow a pro-Putin foreign policy, at the expense of America's allies and her own self-interest." Maureen Dowd later advised Trump to "stop fawning over his new BFF [Best Friend Forever] whose eyes flash KGB" and to stop "adopting a blame America First attitude when it comes to the Russians."[61]

Following on the heels of the Senate Russia-Gate investigations, the *Times* published numerous articles trying to show collusion between Trump advisers and Russia, insinuating some had committed treason.[62] However, thus far the only proof is that they had financial dealings in Russia or communications with Russian officials they failed to disclose, or expressed some interest in obtaining political dirt on Clinton from people with vague ties to the Kremlin. There is no evidence they, or Trump, colluded with the Russians, as a number of key figures including former CIA directors have acknowledged.[63]

Even Michael Flynn, who was forced to resign his position after intelligence officials leaked that he had discussed Obama's last round of sanctions with the Russian ambassador before he took office, appears to have simply said, when the Russian ambassador brought it up, that the sanctions would be reviewed upon taking office. This statement by Flynn violated the 1799 Logan Act prohibiting individuals outside the administration from influencing foreign governments in disputes by the United States. However, critical commentators have pointed out that if this is a crime, there are far worse precedents, including Obama's top Russian adviser Michael McFaul visiting Moscow on the campaign trail in 2008 for talks, and treason committed by Richard Nixon when he sabotaged the Vietnamese peace talks to secure his election in 1968. The underlying agenda behind the Russia-Gate is apparent in that Flynn's replacement, Lt. Gen. H. R. McMaster, has a strongly hawkish view on Russia, suggesting Russia-Gate was succeeding in pushing Trump away from his one sensible campaign pledge for détente.[64]

A Broken Promise: NATO Expansion and the New Cold War

American policymakers were deceitful at the end of the Cold War as they privately made plans for U.S. and NATO dominance in Eastern Europe while promising Soviet premier Mikhail Gorbachev and foreign minister Eduard Shevardnadze that if they agreed to German reunification and Germany's becoming a member of NATO, the latter would not "expand one inch to the east." When Russian political analyst Alex Duggan asked Zbigniew Brzezinski how the West managed to persuade Gorbachev to withdraw Russia's troops from East Germany, Brzezinski smiled and said, "We tricked him."[65]

Gorbachev had proposed a pan-European security agreement and raised the idea of having the Soviet Union join NATO, which then Secretary of State James Baker refused, leaving Russia on the periphery of post–Cold War Europe. According to historian Marie Elise Sarotte, a "young KGB officer serving in East Germany in 1989 offered his own recollection of that era in an interview a decade later in which he remembered returning to Moscow full of bitterness at how 'the Soviet Union had lost its position in Europe.' His name was Vladimir Putin and he would one day have the power to act on that bitterness."[66]

In 1999, Poland, Hungary, and the Czech Republic were admitted to NATO amid Russian opposition, followed over the next decade by seven Central and Eastern European countries including Georgia and Estonia, which is just sixty miles from St. Petersburg. Stephen Cohen points out that the use of NATO for offensive military purposes following the end of the Cold War represented a "radical departure from its original defensive mission, particularly in Russia's traditional backyard." Coming on the heels of the first NATO expansion, the U.S.-led bombing of Yugoslavia in 1999 inflicted "'a deep psychological wound' on Russian political life." The U.S.-NATO war against Russia's fellow Slav nation "played a major role in bringing the country's security forces back to the center of the political stage. . . . It even aroused the fear that Russia itself might be NATO's next victim—'Yugoslavia yesterday, Russia tomorrow.'" Since Russia could not "match the U.S. conventional air weapons it had observed over Serbia," the Kremlin fell back on a frightening conclusion: "There remained nothing else but to rely on nuclear weaponry."

In the face of misleading media coverage, Cohen pleads with citizens to "imagine how this encroachment . . . is seen from Moscow. Coupled with NATO's movement toward the country's western borders, it has revived the specter of a 'hostile encirclement of Russia.' Among the worst legacies of Stalinism, that fear played a lamentable Cold War and repressive role in Soviet Russian politics for four decades."[67]

Heading a state that has collapsed twice within eighty years, Putin's main focus has always been to ensure that the Russian state endures; not so it can conquer the world but so it can protect its people. After the collapse of the Soviet Union, GDP in Russia plunged by forty percent, people lost their social benefits, 75 percent were plunged into poverty, longevity for men dropped to about fifty-seven years and disease epidemics revived. The 1990s was a horrible decade, though the *New York Times* extolled Boris Yeltsin as a "key defender of Russia's hard-won democratic reforms" and "enormous asset for the U.S."[68]

In a rekindled Cold War atmosphere, those who try to explain Putin's motives today are subjected to neo-McCarthyite attacks, branded as Putin apologists, or worse. To sustain respectability, even progressive commentators go out of their way to demonize the

Russian leader. Matt Taibbi, for example, called Putin a "gangster-spook-scum of the lowest order . . . capable of anything" in a *Rolling Stone* article critical of Russia-Gate.[69]

The net effect of all the media coverage is to entrench the belief that Putin is an aggressor and menace to the United States like Stalin during the Cold War. Critical scrutiny into U.S. conduct is ignored and the bipartisan consensus remains one of promoting confrontation. The House Republican most critical of the Magnitsky Act promoting economic sanctions tellingly called for investigation into Hillary Clinton's involvement with Russian financiers who donated heavily to the Clinton Foundation, and an alleged clandestine Russian campaign, backed by U.S. environmental groups, aimed at undermining the American fracking industry and construction of oil and gas pipelines.[70] Russophobia and the scapegoating of Russia, we can see, is a political tactic adopted on both sides of the aisle.

An ominous manifestation of the new Cold War is the growing competition to control the Arctic, where the thaw facilitated by climate change has facilitated access to raw materials. The U.S. Navy has announced plans to expand its presence and deployed its submarine-launched ballistic missile (SLBM) third of the U.S. nuclear triad there. This is another provocative act from the Russian viewpoint that counteracts the *New York Times* Manichaean view of world affairs in which Russia is always the aggressor.[71]

For over a decade, the "Newspaper of Record" has been competing with other major media outlets to place Putin on the same stage as Saddam Hussein, Kim Jong-Un, Bashir al-Assad, Muammar Qaddafi, and other "rogue state" leaders. These efforts have clearly succeeded; in 2015, polls showed that only 13 percent of citizens here had a favorable opinion of Mr. Putin, and 24 percent a favorable opinion about Russia, an all-time low. A 2017 poll found that 42 percent viewed Russia as a critical threat, up from 23 percent in 2002, while 53 percent think the United States should work to limit Russia's international influence rather than cooperate. Fifty-two percent would support using U.S. troops to defend a Baltic NATO member if attacked. In a stark reflection of the partisan divide, 61 percent of

Democrats view Russia as a major threat compared to only 36 percent of Republicans.[72] These figures, worse even than the Cold War years, exemplify the success of the elite media-orchestrated demonization campaign and allegations of election-meddling, and bode ominously for the prospect of future cooperation and peace.

CHAPTER 2

"The Time You Sent Troops to Quell the Revolution": The True Origins of the Cold War

> Did we declare war upon Russia
> when we took a hand in the game
> I know that we hopped onto Prussia
> And Austria got the same.
> But still I have no recollection
> Of breaking with Russia, I swear
> And cannot help making objection,
> To having our boys over there
> What quarrel have we with that nation?
> Just how did it tread on our toes?
> —GEORGE SMITH, "What About Bringing Them Home," 1919

Why are you fighting us, American? We are all brothers. We are all working men. You American boys are shedding your blood away up here in Russia and I ask you for what reason? My friends, and comrades, you should be back home for the war with Germany is over and you have no war with us. The co-workers of the world are uniting against capitalism: Why are you being kept here, can you answer that question? No. We don't want to fight you. But we do want to fight the capitalists and your officers are capitalists.

—BOLSHEVIK ORATOR, near Kadish in northern Russia, January 1919

As a new Cold War heats up today, it is no surprise that the history of the First Cold War has been distorted to fit a triumphalist narrative about U.S. policy, its adverse consequences predominantly overlooked.[1] President Barack Obama, a key architect of the Second Cold War, in his book *The Audacity of Hope* (2006), praised the postwar leadership of President Harry S. Truman, Secretaries of State Dean Acheson and George Marshall, and State Department diplomat George Kennan for responding to the Soviet threat and "crafting the architecture of a new postwar order that married [Woodrow] Wilson's idealism to hard-headed realism." This, Obama says, led to a "successful outcome to the Cold War": an avoidance of nuclear catastrophe; the effective end of conflict between the world's great military powers; and an "era of unprecedented economic growth at home and abroad." While acknowledging some excesses, including the toleration and even aid to "thieves like Mobutu and Noriega so long as they opposed communism," Obama went on to praise Ronald Reagan's arms buildup in the 1980s when he himself came of political age, saying that when the "Berlin Wall came tumbling down, I had to give the old man his due, even if I never gave him the vote."[2]

Obama's remarks reflect a strong element of wishful thinking echoed in academic studies that blame Joseph Stalin principally for the outbreak of the Cold War and praise the visionary quality of America's "wise men" in saving the world from Communism.[3] Left out is how U.S. policymakers constantly exaggerated the Soviet threat to justify expanding a U.S. overseas network of military bases, caused serious economic problems through excessive military spending, waged violently destructive wars in Korea and Vietnam, and led the world close to the nuclear brink during the Cuban Missile Crisis.

Obama and others advancing a similar worldview meanwhile neglect the real reason the Cold War started and when it actually broke out, which was at the dawn of the November 1917 Bolshevik Revolution.

Showing what Wilsonian idealism was really all about, President Wilson deployed over ten thousand American troops to the European theater of the First World War, alongside British, French, Canadian, and Japanese troops, in support of White Army counterrevolutionary generals implicated in wide-scale atrocities, including pogroms against Jews. This "Midnight War" was carried out illegally, without the consent of Congress, and was opposed by the U.S. War Department and commander in Siberia, William S. Graves. He expressed "doubt if history will record in the past century a more flagrant case of flouting the well-known and approved practice in states in their international relations, and using instead of the accepted principles of international law, the principle of might makes right."[4]

The atrocities associated with this war and the trampling on Soviet Russia's sovereignty would remain seared in its people's memory, shaping a deep sense of mistrust that carries over into the present day. For Americans, the "Midnight War" is a non-event, however, because it does not fit the dominant triumphalist narrative of the Cold War or reflect well on a liberal icon and the tradition he invented.

As historian D. F. Fleming wrote:

> For the American people, the cosmic tragedy of the intervention in Russia does not exist, or it was an unimportant incident, long forgotten. But for the Soviet people and their leaders the period was a time of endless killing, of looting and raping, of plague and famine, of measureless suffering for scores of millions—an experience burned into the very soul of the nation, not to be forgotten for many generations, if ever. Also, for many years, the harsh Soviet regimentation could all be justified by fear that the Capitalist power would be back to finish the job. It is not strange that in an address in New York, September 17, 1959, Premier Khrushchev should remind us of the interventions, "the time you sent the troops to quell the revolution," as he put it.[5]

These comments suggest that the U.S. invasion helped poison U.S.-Russian/Soviet relations and contributed significantly to the outbreak of Cold War hostilities. It laid the seeds, furthermore, for all the destructive policies that were to come—including executive secrecy, the eschewing of diplomacy, burning of peasant villages, and arming of violent right-wing forces—which in turn mark the Cold War as a dark chapter in our history.

DURING THE NINETEENTH CENTURY, the Franklin Pierce administration sent a military delegation to assist Russia during the Crimean War, and Russia returned the favor by sending a naval fleet as a signal to the British and French to desist from their plans to intervene militarily on behalf of the Confederacy in the U.S. Civil War.[6] Popular stereotypes about Russia pervaded nevertheless, exemplified in Theodore Roosevelt's characterization of Russians as "utterly insincere and treacherous . . . [without] conception of the truth ... and no regard for others." He and his contemporaries feared that an independent Russia could not be counted on to acquiesce to American control in Southeast Asia and designs of opening up the fabled China market.[7]

The Bolshevik drive to nationalize industry and seize foreign assets was ideologically and economically anathema to the United States, which in 1917 held investments of over $658.9 million in the country, up from $26.5 million in 1913. Historian William Appleman Williams noted that almost all products of American industry were sold in Russia. Baldwin locomotives and U.S. Steel enabled the Trans-Siberian railway and Chinese eastern railways to run smoothly. International Harvester, which controlled the Russian market for agricultural machinery, even requested through the U.S. ambassador an intervention by the tsarist government to break a strike in Russia. The House of J. P. Morgan had given "great impetus to the rise of direct investments" after helping set up the American-Russian Chamber of Commerce in 1916. On the eve of the Revolution, Dean E. F. Gray of the Harvard Business School considered "Russia an inviting field for American business enterprise," that the Bolshevik takeover threatened.[8]

The Russian Revolution unfolded in two phases. In February 1917, the tsar was overthrown and Aleksander Kerensky established a liberal provisional revolutionary government. It was deeply unpopular because Kerensky kept Russian forces fighting in the Great War on the side of the Allies when they had begun to mutiny, and he refused to meet the demand for land and wealth redistribution. Following a counterrevolutionary putsch by Lavr Kornilov, whom the *New York Times* heralded as "the strong man who would deliver Russia from her tribulations," the Bolsheviks seized the Winter Palace in November 1917, led by Leon Trotsky and Vladimir Lenin, who envisioned the creation of a classless utopian society.[9]

Horrified by the Bolsheviks, American liberals, as Christopher Lasch detailed in *The American Liberals and the Russian Revolution* (1962), were enthusiastic about Kerensky's bourgeois revolution because it removed a stumbling block to Russia's effective participation in the Great War on the side of the Allies. The February revolution, Lasch notes, "purified the allied cause," making it easier for its supporters to conceive of it as a "conflict between the principle of democracy and the principle of autocracy," as the *Springfield, Missouri Republican* declared.[10]

To keep Russia in the war, the Wilson administration extended tens of millions in credits for armaments and military supplies to Kerensky's government, with J. P. Morgan also raising money in direct support of Kerensky's cause. The influential diplomat George Kennan Sr., author of an exposé of the tsarist criminal justice system that depicted Russia as an embodiment of Dante's *Inferno*, lost patience with Kerensky because of his unwillingness to undertake a thorough purge of the opposition. Kennan hoped for the emergence of a strongman who would forcibly suppress every trace of radicalism in Russia. He lamented the Bolsheviks' strong urging for peace, fearing they would use their popularity in ending the war to proceed with their "crazy plan" for "turning Russia upside down with the proletariat on top."[11]

Secretary of State Robert Lansing, a corporate lawyer married to the daughter of Secretary of State John Foster (making him the uncle of John Foster Dulles and Allen Dulles) was similarly skeptical of Kerensky, not because he was "incompetent, inefficient and worthless" as British General Alfred Knox considered him, or failed to "reach down roots into the life of Russia," as Raymond Robins, director of a Red Cross mission, recognized, but because he "compromised too much with the radical element of the revolution." Like Kennan Sr., Lansing considered Bolshevism a "despotism [born] of ignorance," that is, of the mob, and a menace that could trigger social unrest "throughout the world." Lansing asked: "Because wealth unavoidably gravitates toward men who are intellectually superior and more ready to grasp opportunities than their fellows, is that a reason for taking it away from them or for forcing them to divide with the improvident, the mentally inferior and the indolent?"[12]

Lansing's viewpoint reflected an engrained class prejudice among America's foreign policy elite that drove conservative, anti-radical policies. Charles S. Crane, another influential adviser to President Wilson, and who later urged FDR to support Nazi Germany as a "bulwark of Christian culture," spoke of the "futility of revolution as a means of progressing and the fearful disaster that may overtake a state and all of its citizens if it does not progress in orderly fashion."[13]

Releasing its decision to the press weeks after the fact, the Wilson administration initially justified sending troops from the European theater of the First World War into Russia as an extension of the war against Germany. Edgar Sisson, the Petrograd representative of the Committee on Public Information, a propaganda agency set up to promote U.S. involvement in the war, produced a series of sixty-eight documents purporting to prove that Lenin and Trotsky were German agents. Later, however, these were proven to have been fabrications. When the Bolsheviks withdrew from the war, the military campaigns continued with backing from prominent intellectuals, moderate labor leaders like Samuel Gompers, who considered the Bolsheviks to have "used every means to throttle freedom by joining Germany in its efforts to enslave the world," and business executives like R. D. McCarter, president of Westinghouse and a later associate of President Herbert Hoover who considered armed intervention in

Russia "absolutely necessary . . . as a prerequisite for building grain elevators . . . refrigerator plants and cars . . . railway improvements and new railways."[14]

Raymond Robins, chairman of the Progressive Party Convention in 1916, became a dissenting voice urging accommodation alongside State Department envoys William Bullitt and William Buckler, who reported the Soviets' willingness to compromise on foreign debt and protection of existing enterprise and to offer amnesty to Whites and cease foreign propaganda if peace were to be secured. Recognizing that "revolutions never go backward," Robins proposed an economic program designed to tie the Soviet economy to that of the United States, persuading Lenin to exempt the International Harvester Company, Singer Sewing Machine Company, and Westinghouse Brake Company from his nationalization decree. For these efforts, he was recalled and shadowed by agents of the Bureau of Investigation (later the FBI), a victim of the mounting anti-communist hysteria of the first Red Scare.[15]

Robins nevertheless influenced congressional anti-imperialists such as Senators William Borah (R-ID), Robert La Follette (R-WI), and Hiram Johnson (R-CA), who wondered whether in attempting to destroy Bolshevism the Wilson administration was bent on putting "the Romanovs [back] on the throne? Do we seek a dictator for this starved land?" Johnson continued: "I warn you of the policy, which God forbid this nation should ever enter upon, of endeavoring to impose by military force upon the various peoples of the earth the kind of government we desire for them and they do not desire for themselves."[16]

President Wilson had long believed in a strong executive, which he considered the only bulwark against the "clumsy misrule of Congress."[17] He was also a vigorous proponent of U.S. expansion, having previously sent forces to help suppress revolution in Mexico. At one point, he acknowledged that the October Revolution was a "desperate attempt on the part of the dispossessed to share in the bounty of industrial civilization" and that the Russian people had grown impatient with the slow pace of reform, though he fretted about the revolutionary effort to "make the ignorant and incapable mass dominant in the world." The only remedy for "class despotism in Petrograd," as Wilson and Lansing saw it, was for a "strong commanding personality to arise . . . and gather a disciplined military force [capable of] restoring order and maintaining a new government."[18] Great hope in fulfilling this role was placed with Admiral Aleksandr Vasilevich Kolchak, a famed Arctic explorer and commander of the Russian Black Sea Fleet. Kolchak was known for a rash temper that often led him "beyond the limits of the law." James Landfield of the State Department was among those "greatly heartened" by the November 1918 coup Kolchak launched, with British backing, in Omsk, Siberia, believing that at last real military power might emerge in Russia that could "restore orderly existence."[19] Wilds P. Richardson, commander in northern Russia, claimed that "the Russian mind generally speaking [was] several hundred years behind the mind of Western Europe and the United States in the matter of free or democratic government and that [it would] take some generations to develop it."[20]

Declaring himself "Supreme Ruler of Russia," Kolchak received thousands of machine guns, hand grenades, and explosives from the Allied stock. His cause was championed by, among others, Winston Churchill, the *New York Times*, the U.S. consul general in Irkutsk, and J. P. Morgan.[21] The Omsk group, however, represented the "minority and ancient imperialists who were obstinately impervious to the new Russia flaming in revolution against age-long abuses and tyrannies," as a lieutenant in the 339th Infantry put it. According to General Graves, "Kolchak did not possess sufficient strength to exercise sovereign powers without the support of foreign troops."[22]

The American ambassador to Japan, Rowland Morris, reported that all over Siberia under Kolchak's rule, there was an "orgy of arrests without charges; of executions without even the pretense of a trial; and of confiscations without the color of authority. Panic and fear has seized everyone. Men support each other and live in constant terror that some spy or enemy will cry 'Bolshevik' and condemn them to instant death." Among those killed were former members of the constituent assembly, and railroad workers who had struck for higher wages. In Ekaterinburg, where the Bolsheviks executed Tsar Nicholas II and his family, Kolchak allowed Cossacks to massacre at least two thousand Jews, part of a larger wave of pogroms.[23]

Unconcerned about these atrocities, President Wilson set up a "little war board" to expedite arms shipments to Admiral Kolchak. He provided military support without congressional sanction through Kerensky's former ambassador to the United States, Boris Bakhmetev, who controlled over $200 million in assets. Historian Robert Maddox wrote that "by conserving and augmenting the embassy's resources, the Wilson administration established what amounted to an independent treasury for use in Russia . . . [which was] immune from prying congressmen. The ambassador of the Russian people had now become the quartermaster for the Kolchak regime."[24] In short, the "Midnight War" was waged by executive power, setting an early precedent for today's imperial presidency.

To keep the Bolsheviks at bay, the State Department established an intelligence apparatus, headed by an American businessman of Greek-Russian extraction, Xenophon Kalamitiano, which infiltrated Soviet-controlled territory and promoted anti-Bolshevik propaganda. Under future president Herbert Hoover, head of the American Relief Administration (ARA), humanitarian aid was positioned to assist the anti-Bolshevik cause.[25]

The intervention in Russia was formative in the development of covert action. Two major figures in the history of American intelligence, "Wild" Bill Donovan, a Wall Street lawyer and future director of the Office of Strategic Services (OSS), and John Foster Dulles, whose brother Allen later headed the Central Intelligence Agency, served as military intelligence officers, with Donovan undertaking undisclosed missions in Siberia. He concluded that the "time for intervention had past [as] we were a year too late," though "we [could] prevent a shooting war [next time] if we take the initiative to win the subversive war."[26]

One of Donovan's colleagues, Major David P. Barrows, who went on to become president of the University of California, cultivated close relations with a Manchurian detachment headed by Cossack Ataman Gregori Semonoff, who according to Barrows "was capable of great severity" toward the Bolsheviks, whom he had "devoted his life to destroying."[27] A decorated veteran of the tsarist and Kerensky armies nicknamed "the Destroyer," Semonoff allegedly set up "killing stations," boasting that he could not sleep at night if he did not kill somebody that day. In Trans-Baikal, according to General Graves, his men shot the men, women, and children of an entire village as if they were hunting rabbits. U.S. Army intelligence estimated that Semonoff was responsible for 30,000 executions in one year, which earned him promotion by Kolchak to the rank of major general.[28]

Another Kolchak deputy, Ataman Ivan Kalmykoff, roamed the Amur territory robbing, burning, raping, and executing hundreds of Russian peasants without trial, including two Red Cross representatives and sixteen Austrian musicians who allegedly housed a Bolshevik one night. Lt. Col. Robert Eichelberger said Kalmykoff's "actions would have been considered shameful in the Middle Ages."[29] Graves referred to Kalmykoff as a "notorious murderer" and "the worst scoundrel" he had ever seen. He compared him unfavorably with Semonoff since he "murdered with his own hands," whereas Semonoff "ordered others to kill."[30] Third on the brutality scale was General S. N. Rozanoff, who would execute the male population and burn down villages that resisted Kolchak incursions.[31]

Congressional hearings ignored the White Terror, which General Graves predicted would "be remembered by, and recounted to, the Russian people for [the next] fifty years." Instead, as historian Frederick Schuman summarized, they depicted "Soviet Russia as a kind of bedlam inhabited by abject slaves completely at the mercy of an organization of homicidal maniacs [the Bolsheviks] whose purpose was to destroy all traces of civilization and carry the nation back to barbarism." Drawing from these hearings, the press became filled with screaming headlines, claiming the Bolsheviks had even nationalized women. Graves, however, wrote in his memoirs that he was "well on the side of safety" in saying that "the anti-Bolsheviks killed 100 people in Eastern Siberia to everyone killed by the Bolsheviks."[32]

A Texan with experience fighting in the Philippines and with the Pershing mission in Mexico, Graves had gone into Siberia believing his mission was to uphold Soviet Russia's neutrality and protect the Trans-Siberian railway. He became disheartened at how America's allies applied the word *Bolshevik* to "most of the Russian people," including peasants opposed to the Kolchak coup who were "kicked, beaten and murdered in cold blood by the thousands." This damaged the prestige of the "foreigner intervening" while serving as a "great handicap to the faction the foreigner was trying to assist."[33] Turning against the war, Graves was hounded by the Bureau of Investigation as a security risk when he came back. According to historian Benson Bobrick, "in the whole sad debacle, he may have been the only honorable man."[34]

Graves had conducted an investigation which found that Kolchak would force young men into the army. If any resisted, he would send troops into their village to torture men beyond military age through methods like pulling out their fingernails, knocking out their teeth, breaking their legs, and then murdering them.[35] Ralph Albertson, the Young Men's Christian Association secretary with the army in Archangel, said that wide-scale executions by Kolchak's forces created "Bolsheviks right and left. . . . When night after night, the firing squad took out its batches of victims, it mattered not that no civilians were permitted on the streets as thousands of listening ears [could] hear the rat-tat-tat of the machine guns, and every victim had friends who were rapidly made enemies of the military intervention."[36]

Albertson wrote that though he had heard many stories of alleged Bolshevik atrocities that told of rape, torture, and the murder of priests, the only Bolshevik atrocity about which he had any authentic information through the entire expedition was "the mutilation of the bodies of some of our men who had been killed in the early days of Ust-Padenga"—where an entire U.S. platoon was wiped out. U.S. prisoners of war were well treated and released, with the exception of two men who died in a Soviet hospital. Sgt. Glenn Leitzell described how he was allowed to walk around the nearest city dressed in a Russian overcoat and fur cap and encouraged to attend a club where he was "harangued in English on Marxist doctrine and the evils of capitalism," and then rewarded with plates of hot soups and horsemeat steak."[37]

Referring to them as "John bolo" or "bolos," a euphemism for wild men, American and British troops pioneered the use of nerve gas designed to incapacitate and demoralize the Red Army, and, according to Albertson, "fixed all the devil traps we could think of for them when we evacuated villages." He noted that we "shot more than thirty prisoners in our determination to punish these murderers. And when we caught the Commissioner of Borok, a sergeant tells me, we left his body in the street, stripped, with sixteen bayonet wounds."[38]

According to Lt. John Cudahy, U.S. soldiers let loose their firepower upon the "massed Bolsheviks, felling them like cattle in a slaughter pen." On the day of the First World War armistice, Toulgas, on the Northern Dvina river, where Leon Trotsky led the Bolshevik defense, was turned into a "smoking, dirty smudge upon the plain," as Capt. Joel Moore, Lt. Harry Meade, and Lt. Lewis H. Jahns described it in an eyewitness account.

Given three hours to vacate, the authors describe a "pitiful sight" in which the inhabitants of Toulgas turned "out of the dwellings where most had spent their whole simple, not unhappy lives, their meagre possessions scattered awry on the grounds." With their houses engulfed by roaring flames, "the women sat upon hand-fashioned crates wherein were all their most prized household goods, and abandoned themselves to a paroxysm of weeping despair, while the children shrieked stridently, victim of all the realistic horrors that only childhood can conjure." Sad as the situation was, the authors wrote, when "we thought of the brave chaps whose lives had been taken from those flaming homes, for our casualties had been very heavy, nearly one hundred men killed and wounded, we stifled our compassion and looked on the blazing scene as a jubilant bonfire."[39]

Such dehumanization in war and desire for revenge would go on to spawn the 'atrocity producing environment" that characterized the war in Vietnam and other Cold War conflicts.[40] Moore, Meade, and Jahns's history spotlights the "enormous" and "terrific" Red Army losses under bursts of "murderous" shelling and "dreadful trench mortars" that could shower the enemy at eight hundred yards with a "new kind of hell." The British contingent had many First World War vets who had been gassed or wounded and were prone to "homicidal excesses," as were the Japanese.[41] A Canadian platoon from rural Saskatchewan included "unpremeditated murderers who had learned well the nice lessons of war and looked upon killing as the climax of a day's adventure." They committed gratuitous acts with Americans such as closing a school for the storage of whiskey, and threw peasants out of their homes, looted personal property, stole rubles from dead Bolsheviks, and ransacked churches.[42]

British General Edmund Ironside said he was "overpowered by the smell" upon visiting the Archangel prison; suspected Bolsheviks were crowded into dank cells sometimes sixty to a room, with the windows sealed and baths closed.[43] Ralph Albertson concluded that the

> spoliation of scores of Russian villages and thousands of little farms and the utter disorganization of the life and industry of a great section of the country with the attendant wanderings and sufferings of thousands of peasant folk who had lost everything but life, was but the natural and necessary results of an especially weak and unsuccessful military operation such as this one was.[44]

In southern Soviet Russia, the British deployed tanks and bombed enemy transport vehicles, bridges, towns, and villages. For the first time, they deployed gas bombs that caused respiratory illnesses (one victim had his eyes and mouth turn yellow and then died). The British were supporting viciously anti-Semitic White Russians under the command of General Anton Denikin. Winston Churchill, then a minister in Lloyd George's government, urged Denikin to prevent the massacre of Jews in "liberated" districts—not out of concern for the Jews but because they were powerful in England and could impinge on his political career. He stated in 1953 that the day would yet come when "it will be recognized . . . throughout the civilized world that the strangling of bolshevism at birth would have been an untold blessing to the human race."[45]

Historian John T. Smith reports on the bombing of Grozny on February 5, 1919, with incendiaries that ignited a large fire. He later discusses the RAF's bombing of Tsaritsyn (Stalingrad) on the Volga, which had been defended by a Soviet committee led by the future dictator Joseph Stalin and Marshal Georgy Zhukov, deputy supreme commander during the Second World War. Allegedly a British DH9 dropped a huge missile on a building where eighty Soviet commissars were meeting, all of whom were killed.[46] Such incidents would remain seared in the minds of Soviet leaders, shaping a deep distrust for the West as the Cold War developed.

Coming mostly from Michigan ("Detroit's Own") and rural Wisconsin, American soldiers had to fight in frigid temperatures (40 below zero) without proper clothing or boots and against a motivated and disciplined enemy that adopted effective camouflages in the snow. Over four hundred "doughboys" died, hundreds more were wounded, and one committed suicide. Most U.S. forces were disdainful of Soviet society and culture. They considered Soviet Russia a "great international dump" and "land of infernal order . . . and national smell." One wrote that he would "rather be quartered in hell."[47]

Tommy Thompson told a reporter in the 1950s that he remembered Siberia as a cold and dirty place where he did not know whom to trust.[48] Capt. Joel Moore stated that "every peasant could be a Bolshevik. Who knew? In fact, we had reason to believe that many of them were Bolshevik in sympathy."[49] Lt. Montgomery Rice pointed out that the Bolsheviks were "inspired men even if their rifles were foul with rust, their clothing worn to rags, their bodies sour with filth, or their cheeks sunken from malnutrition."[50] Fighting with U.S. munitions captured from the tsar's armies, they adopted guerrilla methods centered on disrupting the local infrastructure and cultivating popular support in villages, from which guerrillas could carry out ambushes and sneak attacks on invading forces at night.[51] According to Moore, the Bolsheviks were assisted by "a system of espionage of which we could never hope to cope."[52]

"The Battle Hymn of the Republic" sung by U.S. troops, adapted to the Russian conflict, made a joke of the quagmire:

"We came from Vladivostok, to catch the Bolshevik; We chased them o'er the mountains and we chased them through the creek; We chased them every Sunday and we chased them through the week; But we couldn't catch a gosh darn one." The song continued: "The bullets may whistle, the cannons may roar, don't want to go to the trenches no more. Take me over the sea, where the Bolsheviks can't get me, Oh my, I don't want to die, I want to go home."[53]

Another poem, "In Russia's Fields," was modeled after the famous First World War poem "Flanders Field":

> In Russia's fields, no poppies grow
> There are no crosses row on row
> To mark the places where we lie
> No larks so grayly singing fly
> > As in the fields of Flanders.
>
> We are the dead. Not long ago
> We fought beside you in the snow
> And gave our lives, and here we lie
> Though scarcely knowing reason why
> > Like those who died in Flanders.[54]

At least fifty American soldiers deserted, including Anton Karachun, a coal miner originally from Minsk who had emigrated to the United States. After he deserted, he took up a post with the Red Army in Sunchon.[55] A Judge Advocate General report cited by Albertson specified that an unusually large number American soldiers were convicted by court-martial of having been guilty of self-inflicted wounds.[56] Lt. John Cudahy of the 339th regiment noted: "War shears from a people much that is gross in nature, as the merciless test of war exposes naked, virtues and weaknesses alike. But the American war with Russia had no idealism. It was not a war at all. It was a freebooter's excursion, depraved and lawless. A felonious undertaking for it had not the sanction of the American people."[57]

In February 1919, the British 13th Yorkshire Regiment under a Colonel Lavoi refused orders to fight, which inspired mutiny in a French company in Archangel. On March 30, I-Company in the 339th American infantry followed suit in refusing orders, asserting they had accomplished their mission defeating Germany and were by now "interfering in the affairs of the Russian people with whom we have no quarrel." Col. George Stewart allegedly responded that he had "never been supplied with an answer as to why they were there himself, but that the reds were trying to push them into the white sea and that they were hence fighting for their lives."[58] Though apparently satisfying, this response ran counter to the lies of the Wilson administration that the United States was only in Soviet Russia for defensive purposes and to safeguard war material and property.

Peter Kropotkin, the celebrated Russian writer, told a British labor delegation that progressive elements in the "civilized nations" should "bring an end to support given to the adversaries of the revolution" and refuse to continue playing the "shameful role to which England, Prussia, Austria and Russia sank during the Russian Revolution." Kropotkin was an anarchist opposed to the Soviet undermining of the worker and peasant councils that initially supported the revolution, but noted that "all armed intervention by a foreign power necessarily results in an increase in the dictatorial tendencies of the rulers. . . . The natural evils of state communism have been multiplied tenfold under the pretext that the distress of our existence is due to the intervention of foreigners."[59]

In the United States, critics of the intervention were prosecuted under the Alien and Sedition Acts passed under the Wilson administration that made it a crime to "willfully utter, print, write or publish any disloyal, profane, scurrilous or abusive language about the U.S. form of government, constitution, military or naval force or flag." Radical journalist John Reed and New York State Assemblyman Abraham Shiplacoff (the "Jewish Eugene V. Debs"), who said American troops were perceived by Russians as "hired murderers and Hessians," were among those jailed. Also imprisoned were six Socialist-anarchist activists—Jacob Abrams, Jacob Schwartz, Hyman

Rosansky, Samuel Lipman, Mollie Steimer, and Hyman Lachowsky—who were beaten, given long sentences, and deported for distributing antiwar leaflets condemning Wilson's hypocrisy and urging strikes in munitions plants. The jailings and deportations were upheld in a Supreme Court ruling.[60] This case shows how intervention in Soviet Russia not only helped sow conflict abroad, but also resulted in the suppression of domestic civil liberties in a pattern that would extend through the Cold War.

It is ironic that we in the United States have always been led to fear a Russian invasion when Americans were in fact the original invaders. In May 1972 on a visit to the Soviet Union promoting détente, President Richard Nixon boasted to his hosts about having never fought one another in a war, a line repeated by Ronald Reagan in his 1984 State of the Union address. A *New York Times* poll the next year found that only 14 percent of Americans said they were aware that in 1918 the United States had landed troops in northern and eastern Soviet Russia, a percentage probably even lower today.[61]

James Loewen in *Lies My Teacher Told Me: Everything Your American History Textbook Got Wrong* found that none of twelve high school history textbooks he surveyed mentioned the "Midnight War." In two cases, the U.S. troop presence in Russia was mentioned but only as part of U.S. war strategy and not as an effort to roll back the Russian Revolution. The National World War I Museum in Kansas City meanwhile has only a tiny backroom display, which claims that U.S. soldiers in Archangel "found themselves fighting the Bolshevik Red Guards as well as the anti-Bolshevists," which is inaccurate. A separate discussion of Siberia claims that U.S. soldiers performed guard duty and protected the railways from Bolshevik forces and that they "followed Wilson's policy of non-aggression closely, only fighting when provoked small-scale but fierce actions resulting in 170 American dead." These comments do not properly capture the nature of the war, with no mention at all of atrocities, the soldiers' poems, mutiny, nor General Graves's dissent.[62]

Deeper public awareness of history in the United States might force us to rethink the direction of our policies and the current slide toward renewed confrontation with Russia, and could enable us to see the world from Russia's perspective, potentially opening possibilities for engagement. During the Second World War conferences, Stalin is said to have referred to the Wilson administration's intervention.[63] His policies were not consequently based on paranoia, but a real security threat. George F. Kennan, the Father of the Containment Doctrine, was one of the few policymakers to acknowledge the importance of the "Midnight War," though it was after he had been removed from any position of power. In 1960, Kennan wrote:

> Until I read the accounts of what transpired during these episodes, I never fully realized the reasons for the contempt and resentment borne by the early Bolsheviki towards the Western powers. Never surely have countries contrived to show themselves so much at their worst as did the allies in Russia from 1917–1920. Among other things, their efforts served everywhere to compromise the enemies of the Bolsheviki and to strengthen the communists themselves [thus] aiding the Bolshevik's progress to power. Wilson said, "I cannot but feel that Bolshevism would have burned out long ago if let alone."[64]

These latter comments remain dubious. However, it is clear that after sending troops to quell the revolution, the Soviets would never again trust the United States, predominantly for good reasons, as later history would prove.

CHAPTER 3

Provoking Confrontation: The United States and the Origins of the Cold War

In his June 24, 2015, *Times* column, "Cold War Without the Fun," Thomas L. Friedman lamented that the new confrontation between the United States and Russia has so far lacked some of the drama of the twentieth-century version, such as "Nikita Khrushchev's shoe-banging, a race to the moon or a debate between American and Soviet leaders over whose country has the best kitchen appliances."

According to Friedman, the new "post-post-Cold War has more of a W.W.E.—World Wrestling Entertainment—feel to it, and I don't just mean President Vladimir Putin of Russia's riding horses bare-chested, although that is an apt metaphor. It's just a raw jostling for power for power's sake—not a clash of influential ideas but rather of spheres of influence."[1] Friedman's remarks promote a nostalgic view of the twentieth-century Cold War characteristic of the U.S. political establishment. Cast aside is the horrific human costs that led Mikhail Gorbachev to conclude that the Cold War "made losers of us all." These costs include the millions of deaths in Korea and Vietnam, the destabilization of Third World countries, the overmilitarization of the U.S. political economy, abuse of civil liberties, and wide inequality.

Carl Marzani, an Office of Strategic Services (OSS, forerunner of the

CIA) and State Department employee convicted of lying about involvement with the Communist Party, described in his 1952 book *We Can be Friends* how the United States became thrust into "semi-hysteria" amid a manufactured "war psychosis" with "dog tags on children, airplane spotters on twenty-four-hour duty . . . roads marked for quick evacuations, buildings designated as air raid shelters, air raid drills everywhere in streets, in stores, in schools."[2] The twentieth-century Cold War was not really fun at all if we consider all this. Certainly not for victims like Julius and Ethel Rosenberg, a Jewish couple unjustly executed as atomic spies, thousands of Americans who lost their jobs because of left-leaning political views, or political activists around the world who experienced torture or were "disappeared."

The next four chapters will provide a pocket history of the Cold War, showing how Gorbachev was sounder in his assessment than Friedman, America's "imperial messenger," as he is named in a book by Belen Fernandez, and others of his ilk. We will begin by looking at the breakdown of U.S.-Soviet relations following the Second World War, and the origins of a conflict that in hindsight we believe, like the current U.S.-Russian standoff, was avoidable.

While derided by critics as naïve and a communist sympathizer, FDR's vice president, Henry Wallace, had a sound vision for U.S. foreign policy after the Second World War, one in which the United States would promote the industrialization of newly decolonizing nations absent any military or economic imperialism, and would pursue peaceful rapprochement with the Soviet Union. Unfortunately, Wallace was the target of political machinations that ousted him from any position of power and led to his being red-baited.[3] This marked an important watershed in the origins of the Cold War, the history of which needs to be remembered as a cautionary lesson and not the object of nostalgia.

"HOLDING THE LEG FOR STALIN TO KILL THE DEER": U.S.-SOVIET RELATIONS IN THE SECOND WORLD WAR

The seeds of the Cold War lay in the uneasy U.S-Soviet alliance during the Second World War. After withdrawing troops from Soviet Russia in 1920, the United States had promoted "Open Door" expansion as part of an effort to penetrate Russia economically, holding off on recognition until 1933. When the Nazis broke the Ribbentrop-Molotov Pact, a temporary alliance between the Soviet Union and Germany, and invaded the USSR in 1941, Roosevelt aide Harry Hopkins was sent to meet with Stalin and the United States began extending Lend-Lease aid, amounting to over $10 billion during the war. In popular cultural depictions the treacherous "Reds" were transformed at this time into "the brave Russians," whose resistance to the Nazis "amazed the world."[4]

American elite opinion had been divided in the 1930s and early 1940s over the Soviet Union. The State Department favored support for right-wing dictatorships that repressed the political left and kept an open door to foreign investment, including in Eastern Europe.[5] Wall Street firms like Sullivan and Cromwell, employers of the Dulles brothers, provided a cloak of respectability for the Nazis before the war, acting as counsel for financiers who bankrolled Hitler while supporting the FDR–Neville Chamberlain "appeasement" policy enabling Hitler's early conquests. According to Joseph E. Davies, U.S. ambassador to Russia from 1936 to 1938, they were among the influential classes of people in the United States and elsewhere "who abhor the Soviets to the extent they hope for a Hitler victory in Russia."[6]

The Soviets had built up a powerful military through a centralized political economy. The Red Army faced the majority of the Reich military on the Eastern Front when the Allies faced a dramatically smaller force on the Western Front, making it clear that without the Soviet Union, the Nazis would have ruled all of Europe.[7] General Douglas MacArthur stated in February 1942 that during his lifetime, he had

> participated in a number of wars and witnessed others, as well as studying in great detail the campaigns of outstanding leaders of the past. In none have I observed such effective resistance to the heaviest blows of a hitherto undefeated enemy, followed by a smashing counterattack which is driving the enemy back to his own land. The scale and grandeur of this effort marks it as the greatest military achievement in all history.[8]

The most important battle was at Stalingrad in February 1943, where the Soviets fought the Nazi invaders to the last basement in frigid temperatures after the city had been reduced to rubble by Luftwaffe bombers. The epic victory—compared in the Soviet press to the ancient battle of Cannae in which Hannibal's Carthaginians routed Rome—was followed by the Battle of Kursk, in which the Red Army turned back the last major German offensive three days before the Anglo-American landing in Italy.[9]

Historian Richard Overy, in his book *Why the Allies Won*, credits Soviet planning and central direction for providing the "weapons and food and labor to sustain the deep war." He wrote that "the [Soviet] success in 1943 was earned not just by the tankmen and gunners at the front, but also by the engineers and transport workers in the rear, the old men and the women who kept farms going without tractors or horses, and the Siberian workforce struggling in bitter conditions to turn out a swelling stream of simply constructed guns, tanks and aircraft."[10]

In December 1941, the State Department had rejected Stalin's proposal for an agreement in which the United States and Britain would recognize the Soviet Union's existing boundaries and acquisition of the Baltic States and Eastern Poland after the war, forcing Stalin to "trust to the power of the Red Army to win the guarantees the West rejected."[11] Even more troublesome from the USSR's point of view was the diversionary strategy of fighting in Northern Africa in 1942–43, leaving it to absorb the full brunt of Germany's fury. This is when the United States was urging the Soviet Union to take the risk of having to fight on a second front—in the Far East. The United States invaded Italy in September, 1943 and then on June 6, 1944, landed at Normandy, France, where nine thousand American soldiers died. By that point, the Soviets had reversed the Nazi blitzkrieg at a cost of over seven million military and five to six million civilians killed, with shattered towns and villages destroyed by fire. And they were occupying much of Central Europe.[12]

Secretary of War Henry Stimson wrote to Dean Acheson on May 17, 1943, that "the British are trying to arrange this matter so that the British and Americans hold the leg for Stalin to kill the deer and I think that will be dangerous business for us at the end of the war. Stalin won't have much of an opinion of people who have done that and we will not be able to share much of the postwar world with him."[13] These comments capture the essence of a military policy that forced the Soviets to shoulder a huge portion of the military burden, which added to the legacy of the Wilson administration's "Midnight War" in sowing Soviet mistrust for the West. This mistrust was also deepened with proposals by military leaders like George Patton for preventive war, and the exclusion of Soviet influence and repression of the political left during the Allied occupation of Italy, which intensified Stalin's urge to consolidate his own sphere of power in Eastern Europe.[14]

The Promise of Yalta and Its Breakdown

"Russia hands" in the U.S. State Department and British Foreign office considered the Soviets to display Asian features, which made them inclined toward tyranny, adopting a mix of Russophobia and anti-Communism tinged at times with anti-Semitism. Nevertheless, during wartime conferences, President Roosevelt established a good rapport with Stalin and recognized the Soviets' need for a security buffer in Eastern Europe to protect the country from renewed German aggression. Stalin in a November 1944 speech had called for creation of an organization akin to the United Nations to "defend peace and ensure security" and would establish a military force that could be activated to "liquidate aggression and punish those guilty of aggression."[15] Even Dwight Eisenhower was hopeful about postwar cooperation, telling a group of congressmen, "Russia has not the slightest thing to gain by a war with the United States. There is in Russia a desperate and continuing concern for the lot of the common man and they want to be friends with the United States."[16]

At the Yalta Conference in February 1945, held at a resort town in the Crimea, a deal was brokered whereby the Big Three (Britain,

United States, and the USSR) agreed to accept Soviet influence in Romania and a pro-Soviet government in Poland, a provisional body consisting of leaders known as the Lublin Poles. By way of concession, Stalin agreed to enter the war against Japan and support the United Nations. He also accepted the addition to the Warsaw regime of some members of the anti-Soviet Polish government in exile, the London Poles whom writer and journalist Isaac Deutscher described as a "motley coalition who could not by any criterion, 'Eastern' or 'Western,' be labelled democrats." Elections would follow in due course. The Anglo-Americans, Diane Shaver-Clemens writes, had reason to trust Stalin because despite acts of perfidy such as the cover-up of the Katyn Forest massacre by Soviet troops in Poland, he had already allowed free elections in Austria and Finland, and he had recognized Charles de Gaulle as leader of France. Clemens regarded the Yalta Conference as an agreement among realists to maintain spheres of influence, though right-wingers in the United States considered it a form of appeasement by pro-Communist New Dealers (in 2005, George W. Bush compared it to Munich and the Ribbentrop-Molotov Pact). As part of the agreement, Stalin agreed to non-interference in the Greek civil war where Britain and the United States backed right-wing monarchists, many of them Nazi collaborators, against left-wing guerrillas advocating for socialism, land and wealth redistribution, and nationalization of industry.

After succeeding Roosevelt in April 1945, Harry S. Truman rejected the Lublin government in Poland that Stalin had helped impose, and created a separate West German government that denied the Soviets access to the Ruhr industrial heartland and provided only minimal reparations payments. Truman felt betrayed because the 1947 election in Poland was considered to be unfair and Stalin endorsed acts of political terror against the pro-Western opposition. Stalin felt the West was hypocritical in trying to interfere in Poland by supporting Stanislaw Mikolajczyk (pro-West candidate who got 10 percent of the vote) when the Soviets did not attempt to interfere in Belgium, Italy, or Greece. The Soviets in turn consolidated control over Eastern Europe with their support for Communist dictatorships, and thus the

Cold War commenced. "We are living with the problems of a world that did not benefit from the experience at Yalta," Clemens concluded from the perspective of the 1970s. "It is perhaps relevant to ask what the world would have been like if the spirit of Yalta had triumphed."[17] Perhaps it is still relevant.

THE PATH OF PEACE NOT PURSUED: THE REMOVAL OF HENRY WALLACE

A key turning point that may have influenced the entire history of the Cold War occurred at the 1944 Democratic Party national convention in Chicago when Harry S. Truman was nominated over Henry A. Wallace as vice president on the Roosevelt ticket.

Wallace was a progressive New Dealer who supported free trade, national health insurance, abolishing Jim Crow, and free public schooling and day care. Unique among American leaders, Wallace was sensitive to the conditions of grinding poverty and oppression that Lenin had seized upon, and to the accomplishments and appeal of Soviet Communism. He also questioned many aspects of U.S. foreign policy, such as the State Department's friendliness toward right-wing dictators.[18]

As an alternative to Henry Luce's vision of the "American Century," which demanded that the United States "accept wholeheartedly our duty and our opportunity as the most powerful and vital nation in the world and . . . exert upon the world the full impact of our influence, for such purposes as we see fit and by such means as we see fit," Wallace had proposed a "Century of the Common Man," in which "no nation will have the god-given right to exploit other nations. Older nations will have the privilege to help younger nations get started on the path to industrialization, but there must be neither military nor economic imperialism. The methods of the nineteenth century will not work in the people's century which is now about to begin."[19]

At the Democratic Party convention, California oilman, party treasurer, and chief fundraiser Edwin Pauley and chairman Robert Hannegan coordinated with Southern segregationists, big-city machine politicians, and business interests to remove Wallace from his nomination as vice president through a backroom arrangement supported by Congress of Industrial Organization (CIO) leader Sidney Hillman and an ailing FDR. When Wallace appeared poised to receive the nomination, the convention was adjourned and spotlights turned off just before Claude Pepper (D-FL), a Wallace supporter, could take the podium. Overnight, the bosses then worked to secure Truman's nomination by offering ambassadorships, postmaster positions, and cold cash to delegates, blocking Wallace supporters from entering the arena the next day.[20]

Wallace was subsequently fired as commerce secretary after proposing in a speech at Madison Square Garden, on September 12, 1946, that the United Nations assume control of the strategically located air bases with which "the United States and Britain [had] encircled the world." According to Wallace, "nations not only should be prohibited from manufacturing atom bombs, guided missiles and military aircraft for bombing purposes, but also prohibited from spending on its military more than 15 percent of its budget." The United States, he said, could easily ensure cooperation with the Soviets if they made clear "we are not planning for war against her," and had "no more business in the political affairs of Eastern Europe than Russia has in Latin America." Wallace ended the speech by calling on Americans "who look on this war-with-Russia talk as criminal foolishness . . . [to] carry our message direct to the people—even though we may be called communists because we dare to speak out."[21]

Wallace's words proved prophetic. When he mounted an independent campaign for the presidency in 1948 on the Progressive Party ticket, he and his supporters, who included folksinger Woody Guthrie and civil rights icon Paul Robeson, were smeared as Communists. Some of his supporters were also beaten up. Democratic Party presidential adviser Clark Clifford told Truman that "every effort must be made to . . . identify and isolate [Wallace] in the public mind with the communists." DNC chairman J. Howard McGrath said that a vote for Wallace was "a vote for the things for which Stalin, Molotov, and Vishinsky stand."[22]

Wallace himself had believed the alliance with the Communists was a hindrance to his campaign, but he had to set an example to show that cooperation was possible when thinking about U.S.-Soviet relations. His removal from the political scene along with others promoting peace like Harold Ickes, Secretary of the Interior from 1933 to 1946, who pointed out that "without Russia we would still be fighting a war," and James Roosevelt, FDR's eldest son, who said it was up to "every peace-loving man and woman in the world to stand up now and repudiate the words, the schemes and the political allies of the honorable Winston Churchill," paved the way for the catastrophe of the Cold War in which military budgets went through the roof and the threat of nuclear Armageddon was only narrowly averted.[23]

Nobel Laureate Linus Pauling wrote in 1970:

Who can say what the world [would] have been like if Wallace had remained as Vice President in 1944. . . . [There is] the possibility that he could have been successful in averting the Cold War. . . . There might have been no American involvement in a war in Korea, Vietnam, Cambodia or Laos. The military dictatorships sponsored by the U.S. in many countries might not have come into existence. Tens of thousands of people who are now political prisoners might have remained free. International treaties might have been made that would have saved the United States and Soviet Union hundreds of billions of dollars. . . . We might have a better world today.[24]

"No Serious Indication the USSR is Preparing for Hostilities"

The Stalinist Soviet Union experienced horrendous human rights atrocities, though most scholars on the Soviet Union conclude that its foreign policy was cautious and not bent on reckless conquest like that of Hitler.[25] The Soviet people were tired of war and grateful for U.S. Lend-Lease aid. Journalist Edgar Snow wrote that the legacy of the Second World War and the dangers of atomic attack "created in the mind and spirit of all the Russian people an unprecedented receptivity, and an unprecedented need for any proposals which offered mankind surcease from war, and permanent peace." Conscious of domestic opinion, the Stalin regime's main foreign policy goal was to establish a security belt in Eastern Europe to prevent another German invasion and to consolidate influence over Communist regimes there to help revitalize the Soviet economy which had lost much of its productive capacity.[26]

The Sovietization of Eastern Europe came at a high cost for the region's people; *however, the suppression of civil liberties before the war by dictatorships was never the subject of official criticism.* NATO chiefs tellingly concluded in 1950 that the Soviet armed forces had *not* increased since the end of the Second World War, and there were no serious "indications that the USSR is preparing for hostilities [with the West]." General Albert Greunther, Eisenhower's Chief of Staff in Europe, stated that Soviet "industrial production [was] not geared to an all-out war," and journalist Ernie Hill of the *Chicago Daily News* reported that "the people of Europe remain pretty well unconvinced of Russian plans for an aggressive war."[27] In April 1952, Gruenther and General Omar Bradley told Congress that there was little danger of a Russian attack. CIA analyst Harry Rositzke wrote: "The specter of a powerful Russia was remote from the reality of a country weakened by war, with a shattered economy, an overtaxed civilian and military bureaucracy and large areas of civil unrest."[28]

Historian Gabriel Kolko characterized Soviet foreign policy as "counterrevolutionary." Stalin ordered Soviet troops out of Azerbaijan, enabling the liquidating of the Communist regime of Jafar Pishevari, and failed to back the Greek leftist resistance movement. Stalin also urged Communist acquiescence with capitalist parties in Europe.[29] D. F. Fleming wrote that Stalin "scoffed at communism in Germany, urged the Italian Reds to make peace with the monarchy, did his best to induce Mao Zedong to come to terms with the Guomindang [Chinese Nationalist Party] and angrily demanded of Tito that he back the [Greek] monarchy, thus fulfilling Stalin's bargain with Churchill."[30]

The Soviets' main "threat" for Western interests was economic. They and allied Communist regimes sought to extract themselves from the world-capitalist system and forge an alternative, with Eastern Europe escaping its traditional status as a supplier of raw materials to the West. American and British investors, including those in the oil industry, lost out from nationalization policies. Historian James Peck points out that Communism's claim to be "scientific and infallible" and its invocation of the "predetermined pattern of world history" was also a great challenge to the universalistic claims of American civilization.[31] Walter Lippmann wrote presciently in 1959 that "we delude ourselves if we do not realize that the main power of the Communist state lies not in their clandestine activity but in the force of their example, in the visible demonstration of what the Soviet Union has achieved in forty years, or what Red China has achieved in about ten years."[32] He was referring to rapid industrialization and modernization, and a boost in economic productivity, as well as better living standards for the masses, free education, and improved health care. These achievements made the Communist model attractive in Third World countries, which the United States wanted to integrate into the world capitalist economy.

THE DOMINANT NARRATIVE OF THE COLD WAR

The official narrative of the Cold War blames its onset on the Soviet Union. According to President Harry S. Truman, Soviet Premier Joseph Stalin "want[ed] to dominate the world, spread Communism, build an empire; the Russians played President Roosevelt for a sucker; got a lot of concessions from him, gave nothing in return and all along" the United States got double-crossed. Political analyst Mike Lofgren notes that this story was put forth by an "American leadership class" that was composed of "government elites, top business executives, corporate media management, newspaper editorial boards, [and] 'opinion leaders' everywhere," including academic historians.[33] Historian John Lewis Gaddis argues that the Cold War "had been forced on a reluctant American government that did not want it, but wanted insecurity even less. Responsibility fell on [Stalin]. . . . American policy towards the world . . . had always been primarily defensive." After the Cold War ended in 1991, Gaddis characterized the essential nature of the conflict as "a battle of good against evil . . . in which American conceptions of collective security, embodied in a NATO alliance inspired by federal principles akin to those of the U.S. Constitution, had triumphed over narrow Soviet conceptions of unilateral security, and in doing so diffused democracy across the world."[34]

In 1947 diplomat George F. Kennan affirmed the guiding premise of the official story in his famous "Long Telegram" that became a basis for the Containment Doctrine. Kennan was a protégé of Robert F. Kelley, head of the State Department's Eastern European Division, where Kennan had worked since 1926. He held a deep suspicion of Russia and even occasionally the Russian character and viewed any effort at collaboration as akin to appeasement. According to Kennan, the Soviets rejected "every ethical value in their methods and tactics" while the Americans "negotiated in good faith." The Soviets "recognized no restrictions, either of God or man," while American leaders "kept their promises and honored their agreements." The Soviets believed in "aggression and domination, while the Americans were equated with peace and cooperation." Soviet politics "were abnormal, secretive, and driven by the 'doctrines and actions of a small ruling clique'"; on the other hand, American politicians "were normal, open, and responsive to the rule of public opinion." The Soviet system "was unnatural and ungodly, while the American system dovetailed with natural law and divine Providence."[35]

Like his mentor, Kennan embraced Russophobic beliefs that the Soviet Union was more oriented to the East and a natural haven for oriental despotism. This view was echoed by media commentators such as Martin Sommers, foreign editor of the *Saturday Evening Post*, who wrote that "if we pulled out of the competition anywhere in the world today, the Oriental-minded rulers of Russia would surely consider this as proof of our decadence and weakness."[36] National Security Council Document 68 (NSC-68, 1950), prepared for President Truman by Paul Nitze, a wealthy investment banker who helped formulate post–Second World War policy toward the Soviet

Union, followed up Kennan's report by advocating a huge expansion of U.S. military spending along with development of a hydrogen bomb and increased military aid to allies. The NSC-68 authors believed America's fundamental goal was to "assure the integrity and vitality of our free society, which is founded upon the dignity and worth of the individual."[37]

According to the renowned public intellectual Noam Chomsky, NSC-68 had "the tone of an unusually simple-minded fairy tale, contrasting ultimate evil (them) with absolute perfection (us)." The "compulsion" of the "slave state" Soviet Union was allegedly to subvert or destroy the machinery of government and structure of society everywhere in the world not already under Kremlin domination, and to gain absolute authority. Since "no accommodation or peaceful sentiment is even thinkable," the United States must act to "foster the seeds of destruction within the Soviet system." The innate evil of the Soviet Union is compared with the United States, "a nation of almost unimaginable perfection" marked by "marvelous diversity," "deep tolerance," and "lawfulness."[38]

Political leaders would repeat this guiding frame in mobilizing the American population throughout the Cold War. Secretary of Defense Robert McNamara characteristically informed Congress in 1961 that there was "no historical parallel to the drive of Soviet Communist imperialism to colonize the world. . . . Soviet Communism seeks to wipe out the cherished traditions and institutions of the free world with the same fanaticism that once impelled winning armies to burn villages and sow the fields with salt so they would not again become productive." In the spirit and recommendations of NSC-68, McNamara and the rest of Kennedy's "action-intellectuals" pushed forward a huge military buildup, "justifying their program on the basis of a 'missile gap' that they knew to [actually] favor the United States by a large margin." The United States at this time was committed to becoming the "greatest military power in human history," in a truly imperial undertaking that was packaged as a righteous struggle to contain the "evil empire."[39]

"The Truth is We Have Spent Trillions of Dollars on a Gigantic Hoax"

As brutal a leader as he was, Stalin cannot be held singularly responsible for starting the Cold War if we consider that the U.S. controlled
more than 2,000 bases and 30,000 military installations at the end
of the Second World War, virtually encircling the Soviet Union.[40]
These included bases along its southern rim in the Middle East and
northwest India. Lt. General Stanley D. Embrick, an army plan-
ner, acknowledged that "[American] bases in Iceland would arouse
Russian suspicion of Anglo-American intentions."[41] His voice was
marginalized alongside that of Henry Wallace, who noted that the
maintenance of "great American air bases in Okinawa and Greenland
comes perilously close to a declaration of war against Russia," and
that the Soviets looked on "Anglo-American oil development in the
Near East" as a "grave menace to her security. . . . The United States
would feel the same way if Russia were developing oil in Mexico and
training troops in Cuba."[42]

The dropping of the atomic bombs over Hiroshima and Nagasaki
in August 1945 can be considered a first strike in the Cold War, exemplifying its horrific human cost. Historian Gar Alperovitz showed
that the bomb was militarily unnecessary since Japan's air defense had
been crippled and its leadership had offered to surrender with the
caveat that the emperor would be retained. After the bomb exploded,
Truman allegedly said, "If it explodes as I think it will, I'll certainly
have a hammer on those boys [the Russians]." A main purpose besides
saving the lives of U.S. soldiers was to circumvent a Soviet invasion
of Japan, ensure an American sphere of influence in the Asia-Pacific
after the war, and send a powerful message to Stalin and the world,
similar to that sent by the fire-bombing of Dresden in February 1945,
about American military power.[43]

The 1947 Truman Doctrine pledged over $400 million to assist
"free peoples" fighting Communism. A prime recipient, the Greek
government, was led by a former spy for the Nazi regime in Hungary,
however, and U.S. military advisers assisted in the suppression of a

left-wing insurgency that had roots in the anti-fascist resistance. Secretary of State George C. Marshall wrote to Dwight Griswold, the chief of the American mission for aid to Greece, 1947–1948, that "stern and determined measures may be necessary to effect the termination of the activities of the guerrillas and their supporters as speedily as possible." These measures included torture in island prisons and death by firing squad.[44]

In April 1948, the Truman administration initiated the European Economic Recovery Program (ERP), known as the Marshall Plan, which provided $2 billion annually to avert economic, social, and political chaos in Europe, contain Communism (meaning not Soviet intervention but the success of indigenous Communist parties), prevent the collapse of U.S. export trade, and achieve the goal of multilateralism. Stalin viewed the Marshall Plan as an effort to form "a Western bloc and isolate the Soviet Union," and enrich Wall Street tycoons, prompting his creation of the Cominform, an alliance of Communist states that increasingly adopted a uniform party line.[45]

The Marshall Plan was coordinated by W. Averell Harriman, who had made a fortune in zinc mining in Poland and was a founding partner of Brown Brothers, Harriman & Co., whose client list had included one of Hitler's top financiers. It promoted an embargo of East-West trade, which set back industrialization plans in Eastern Europe by limiting its access to capital, and it imposed restrictions on the recipient countries through all manner of economic and fiscal criteria.[46] The ERP also helped maintain markets for U.S. oil companies, financing over 50 percent of oil supplied to provide the energy needed for Western Europe's recovery. According to historian and former U.S. State Department official William Blum, the United States controlled "not only how Marshall . . . dollars were spent, but also the expenditure of an equivalent amount of the local currency, giving Washington substantial power over the internal plans and programs of the European states." Social welfare programs for starving and homeless survivors of the war "were looked upon with disfavor by the United States; even rationing smelled too much like socialism and had to go or be scaled down; nationalization of industry was even more vehemently opposed." Blum also points out that the CIA appropriated "large amounts of Marshall Plan funds to covertly maintain cultural institutions, journalists, and publishers, at home and abroad while diverting further funding for covert operations designed to crush Left and pro-Communist unions in Europe."[47]

The Truman administration had initially promoted a less vigorous aid program than the Marshall Plan, one designed to restrict Germany's economic rehabilitation and rearmament and break the power of its prewar banking system that had served the Nazis (the Morgenthau-White Plan). Following Germany's division into separate zones, however, John Foster Dulles, Allen Dulles, and Eric McKittrick, a former OSS agent and director of the Bank of International Settlements (BIS) in Basel, Switzerland, which had handled looted Nazi gold and arranged deals with Nazi industrialists during the war, lobbied for the rebuilding of West Germany under the conservative Konrad Adenauer as a bulwark against the Soviet Union. Wall Street interests stood to profit from the Marshall Plan and revival of Germany's old economic order, even though it had twice led the country into disaster. The Dulles brothers accused Harry Dexter White, the IMF director and author of the Morgenthau-White Plan, of being a Communist spy, deflecting attention away from the BIS and other treasonable Nazi connections, while placing the U.S. left on the defensive. Denazification programs were implemented haphazardly, with ex-Nazi agents who were capable of assisting the Cold War rescued from displaced-person camps and prosecution. What is more, the United States kidnapped engineers, managers, and scientists from East Germany, whose resources had been looted at the end of the Second World War, in order to facilitate economic growth in the West. It also suspended reparations promised under Yalta as part of an effort to "retard postwar Russia economically."[48]

In 1949, after Truman approved National Security Council Memorandum 14 advocating military assistance, Congress passed the Mutual Defense Act, the first in a series of global arms bills through which the United States came to provide grants amounting to over

$90 billion in military equipment and training to some 120 countries during the Cold War, with Western Europe a primary recipient. In 1949, the North Atlantic Treaty Organization (NATO) was established as an integrated military defense system financed primarily by the United States. In 1953, Congress approved $5 billion in military assistance to NATO nations, having provided over 7,000 tanks, 28,000 transport vehicles, and 10,000 artillery pieces. A Military Advisory Assistance Group (MAAG) helped revive the West German military under the command of Lt. Gen. Adolf Heusinger, former chief of operations for Nazi Germany's Wehrmacht, and Lt. Gen. Hans Spiedel, Gen. Erwin Rommel's chief of staff in France. This couldn't have gone over well in Russia.[49]

Denouncing Henry Wallace as a "dreamer" who wanted "to disband our armed forces, give Russia our atomic secrets, and trust a bunch of adventurers in the Kremlin politburo," Truman surrounded himself with hawkish advisers with deep Wall Street connections. Defense Secretary James Forrestal was former president of the Wall Street investment bank Dillon Read & Co., whose hands, according to Wallace, were "stained with oil." His successor, Louis Johnson, held a directorship in the Consolidated Vultee Aircraft Company which created the B-36 bomber, called the "Peacemaker." Forrestal told the president to gather the heads of major newspapers and to stress to them "the need for making the country aware of the dangers of the U.S.S.R. and need for greater military preparedness."[50]

In September 1945, over 70 percent of U.S. adults said they wanted friendly relations with the Soviet Union.[51] To further reverse these numbers, Forrestal and Secretary of State Dean Acheson, a Europhile who held a nostalgic view of colonialism, warned of a "red tide of aggression" sweeping over countries like Greece "from the outside," when, as we know from writer Milovan Djilas, Stalin attempted to stop the civil war there. During the Berlin crisis of 1948, the public was told about a "wicked decision" by the Soviets, "the most barbarous in history since Ghengis Khan" according to the commandant of the American sector in Berlin, "to shut off the Eastern zone of Germany from the West" and induce starvation (which was heroically thwarted by an Anglo-American airlift). Americans were subsequently made to fear the Soviet Union's alleged conquest of China following the triumph of the Maoist revolution in 1949, and bomber and missile gaps that all proved to be fraudulent along with the notion of a monolithic Communist bloc.[52]

Intelligence veteran William Corson dates the origins of the Cold War, with its acceptance of the idea of "ten-foot tall Russians," to the destruction of the Office of Strategic Services (OSS) Research and Analysis (R&A) division headed by Alfred McCormack. R&A dismissed any Soviet threat inside the secret councils of government, and reported that the Soviets had uprooted a third of the entire German railway system despite being militarily dependent on rail transport, a measure inconsistent with the behavior of a power contemplating an attack. The politicization of intelligence, however, led the Truman administration to embrace alarmist claims by ex-Nazi spymaster and torturer Reinhard Gehlen (recruited by the CIA under Operation Paperclip), who, according to CIA agent Victor Marchetti, could only make money by "creating a threat that we were afraid of." Marchetti stated that "the agency [CIA] loved Gehlen because he fed us what we wanted to hear. We used his stuff constantly, and we fed it to everyone else: the Pentagon, the White House, the newspapers. They loved it too. But it was hyped up Russian bogeyman junk, and it did a great deal of damage to this country."[53]

Historian Frank Kofsky concludes that the Truman administration manufactured a war scare in 1948 to save the airlines industry from oblivion. The industry was dependent on government contracts, which had ended after the Second World War. Forrestal and other advisers feared that if the aircraft industry collapsed, it would be vulnerable to nationalization. In their view, it was "up to private industry" to avert a "Marxist takeover." Truman's approval numbers also were down, and advisers such as Clark Clifford felt that if a crisis developed, he could rally support.[54]

Independent journalist I. F. Stone summed it up best when he wrote, "The truth is that we have spent [over a] trillion dollars . . . on a gigantic hoax." The United States emerged from the Second World

War, as from the First World War, "virtually unscathed, enormously enriched and—with the atom bomb—immeasurably more powerful than any nation on earth had ever been. The notion that it was in danger of attack from a devastated Soviet Union, with 25 million war dead, a generation behind it in industrial development, was a wicked fantasy. But this myth has been the mainstay of the military and war machine."[55]

"Any Anti-Communist Bastard": Operation Rollback and Gladio

After the debacle of Wilson's "Midnight War," the United States never again formally invaded the Soviet Union, but it did infiltrate soldiers covertly behind the Iron Curtain in Eastern Europe and organized stay-behind armies in Western Europe under Operation Gladio. These operations were a clear provocation from the Soviet point of view, and would have aroused unprecedented hysteria in the United States if the Soviets had done something similar in Mexico, Canada, or South America.

Schooled in paramilitary and psychological warfare techniques, Gladio soldiers included ex-Gestapo agents and terrorists valued for their extreme anti-Communism. Molded in the image of the British Special Operations Executive (SOE) which during the Second World War parachuted into enemy-held territory, they possessed escape and evasion devices with concealed compasses, clandestine listening devices disguised as batteries, pistol silencers, and backlit maps. Part of the training exercises included "going out in the dead of the night and pretending to blow up trains in the railway stations without the stationmaster or the porters seeing you." An operative noted, "We laid bricks inside railway engines to simulate plastic explosives."[56]

The political left in Italy and other European countries at the time was strong because of the role it had played in the defeat of Nazism, economic circumstances, and the charismatic nature of leaders like Italy's Palmiro Togliatti.[57] To help suppress pro-Communist labor demonstrations in Italy, CIA officers distributed crowd-control equipment including colored tear gas and helped empower the Mafia-connected Christian Democratic Party, led by Alcide De Gasperi, which won elections the United States had a heavy hand in manipulating. Gladio armies later carried out terrorist attacks set up as false flag operations that were blamed on the political left as part of a strategy of tension designed to engender support for heightened state security measures. In the most notorious incident, the Italian secret service planted fragments from a bomb that had killed and wounded dozens of farmers at the Piazza Fontana in Milan inside the home of leftist newspaper editor Giangiacomo Feltrinelli. Gladio soldiers were implicated in more terrorist attacks in Spain and Portugal, which were under fascist regimes (Franco and Salazar) where "Gladio was the government," and against the Greek left during the country's civil war. CIA agents there trained secret paramilitary outfits called the Hellenic Raiders, and imported eavesdropping devices and IBM computers used by the intelligence services for amassing over 16 million political files.[58]

In Eastern Europe, the CIA and Britain's MI6 organized rollback missions designed to stir up rebellion against and overthrow the pro-Soviet governments taking shape there. George F. Kennan was among the major supporters of the operations, which were modeled on the Vlasov Army, an anti-Communist émigré campaign created by the SS and the Nazi foreign office during the Second World War. Scholars and propagandists who had once collaborated in formulating the Nazi political warfare program were brought into the United States to provide brains for the rollback operations, which fit a pattern of Western support for counterrevolution in Eastern Europe dating to the period of the Russian Revolution. They extended to Ukraine, where secret teams consisted of veterans of the Nazi SS Galizien Division who had been involved in "thousands of instances of mass murders of Jews and of families suspected of aiding Red Army partisans." The tactics of partisan warfare included sabotage of railroads and bridges and stealth raids upon villages to terrorize local civilians who failed to cooperate. CIA executive Frank Wisner admitted that thousands of Communist Party cadre and Soviet police troops were executed.[59]

Harry Rositzke, the former head of secret operations inside the USSR, later said, "We knew what we were doing. It was a visceral business of using any bastard as long as he was anti-Communist...[and] the eagerness or desire to enlist collaborators meant that sure, you didn't look at their credentials too closely."[60] One of the agency's most important agents in Ukraine, Mykola Lebed, had led the elite terror arm of the Ukrainian nationalists and been appointed home secretary and police minister in the Nazi quisling government in Lvov. Army counterintelligence reports referred to Lebed as a "well-known sadist and collaborator of the Germans," though a deal was cut after he provided intelligence on the Soviets.

Rollback agents like Lebed were viewed derisively by a local population that may have preferred Communist rule at this time. Others were tipped off by Russian double agents like Kim Philby of British MI6 or quickly discovered by the KGB and executed.[61] Halil Nerguti, who had been sent to overthrow Albanian dictator Enver Hoxha, said, "We were used as an experiment; a small part of a big game, pawns that could be sacrificed."[62] Despite their failure, rollback operations and Gladio became the prototype for hundreds of CIA operations in the Cold War aiming to exploit indigenous discontent, including the arming and training of the Hmong of Laos, anti-Castro Cubans, and the Nicaraguan Contras. The rationale for these operations has always been that U.S. arms and money for the rebel group will somehow provide a spark that will ignite popular support for democracy and resistance to totalitarian rule. However, as scholar-journalist Christopher Simpson pointed out, "the actual results have almost always produced serious backlash and been the exact opposite of what was originally intended even in instances where the U.S.-backed faction has succeeded in taking power."[63]

The one time some form of intervention might have benefitted progressive forces, the Eisenhower administration failed to support the revolution in Hungary led by Imre Nagy against Soviet-backed rule in 1956. As Soviet tanks were crushing Hungarian protestors demanding free elections, economic reform, and the withdrawal of Soviet troops, Secretary of State John F. Dulles lamely cabled the Soviets that the United States "did not see these states [Hungary] and [Poland] as potential military allies." The CIA at this time had but one single agent inside Hungary and he lost contact with the agency after the Soviet invasion, which exemplifies the failure of the earlier rollback operations.[64]

Speaking at the Churchill Memorial in Fulton, Missouri, on the fiftieth anniversary of Churchill's famous "Iron Curtain" speech, former British prime minister Margaret Thatcher praised Churchill for having provided "the first serious warning of what was afoot . . . [that] helped to wake up the entire West. . . . His speech bore rich fruit in the new institutions forged to strengthen the West against Stalin's assault." She was referencing the Marshall Plan, the Truman Doctrine, and the formation of NATO, which in her view "helped usher in what the Marxist historian Eric Hobsbawm has ruefully christened the 'Golden Age of Capitalism,' " while setting the groundwork for the "surrender and finally liquidation" of Communism.[65]

Thatcher's view, echoed by conservative and liberal commentators in the United States, helped reinforce the master narrative surrounding the Cold War, underlying the containment and rollback doctrines. This version of history, however, as we have sought to document, represents historical revisionism at its worst. It is a useable past, designed to reaffirm the status quo in the West, and is little different from Stalin's alteration of history in his *Short Course* on the Bolshevik Party and revolution.[66]

At the time Churchill gave his speech, conservative military figures including Dwight Eisenhower and ex-president Herbert Hoover were among those to point out that the Soviets had been decimated by the Second World War and were not planning for future conquest, apart from seeking a security buffer in Eastern Europe.[67] Donald Nelson, head of the War Productions Board in the Second World War, wrote in his 1946 book, *Arsenal of Democracy,* that he saw "no more reason why we should get into a fight with Russia than with the Planet Mars, as we have no fundamental conflicting interests [or] disputes."[68] Seen in this context, the policies that Thatcher praises were tactically unnecessary and served only to provoke a confrontation with the

Soviets when peaceful rapprochement was feasible, as true visionary leaders like Henry Wallace foresaw.

Filmmaker Oliver Stone and historian Peter Kuznick point out that Churchill was among those who "itched for a confrontation with the Soviet Union. A rabid anti-Communist and unabashed imperialist, Churchill had tried to draw the U.S. into military engagement with the Soviet Union as far back as 1918," successfully, as it were, since U.S. and British troops invaded that year.[69] The Cold War of the 1940s thus followed from an earlier era of confrontation that had decidedly negative consequences. Though more stable than the neoliberal era Thatcher helped inaugurate, the Golden Age of Capitalism was in reality marred by gross inequalities, a dangerous and futile arms race, and Third World proxy wars that left heavy collateral damage.

The Cold War, then, should be seen as an avoidable catastrophe provoked by one-dimensional leaders beholden mainly to their own class interests, prejudice, and hawkish proclivity. Its insanity was epitomized in a scene in which Defense Secretary James Forrestal was discovered in the street wearing his pajamas shouting, "The Russians are coming!" claiming they were about to invade Florida. *Washington Post* columnist Drew Pearson reported that President Truman had ordered a review of all of Forrestal's recent reports, recommendations, and decisions, wanting to ascertain whether he had "gone mad under the pressure of Cold War propaganda, which he himself had carried on for years, or . . . whether all that propaganda was the consequence of the insanity which had seized Mr. Forrestal a long time ago."[70]

CHAPTER 4

The Cold War and the Attack on U.S. Democracy

In its October 27, 1951, issue, *Collier's* magazine prophesied the outbreak of the Third World War after "Red Army hordes" staged a blitzkrieg offensive across Europe and the Far East, then suicide missions, and dropped atomic bombs on U.S. cities from bases in Alaska over Detroit, New York (near Grand Central Terminal), Washington, Philadelphia, and Chicago, yielding appalling destruction that included the White House. U.S. military forces backed by Douglas MacArthur's National Police Reserve in Japan were mobilized to stem the tide of Soviet aggression, using novel new weapons like the atomic artillery shell. U.S. B-36 bombers in turn delivered concentrated attacks of atomic bombs "the likes of which had never been dreamed of by the most fanciful author of scientific fiction," leading to the demise of the Soviet regime. The Soviet people were now liberated after years of tsarist and Communist tyranny and sought vengeance on the Communist leaders who survived. According to author Robert Sherwood, the light could now "shine in Russia and in all the other darkened places of the earth."[1]

This story reflects the Cold War alarmism, unabashed national exceptionalism, and Russophobia gripping the United States in the early 1950s that justified greater military preparedness. Sherwood tellingly credits air raid shelters with saving many American lives during the atomic attacks. He makes a point of emphasizing that the United States had less than ninety-seven operational B-36 bombers and that U.S. planes were outnumbered in the principal battle areas. Turning history on its head, the story also made reference to the roll-back missions behind the Iron Curtain using émigré commandos, which in this case were successful, and specified that U.S. bombing in contrast to the Soviets' was humane in targeting only strategic targets (which included *Pravda* and *Izvestiya* newspaper offices). It also pointed out American Communist traitors who assisted the Soviet attacks on American cities.[2]

The scenario presented by *Collier's* was wholly unrealistic but in line with the then dominant narrative about the Cold War and Soviet threat. It overlooked the evidence that the Soviet Union had been devastated by the Second World War and lacked the desire to ignite a new major world war, and it ignored U.S. actions that contributed to escalating tensions. Furthermore, *Collier's* lent support to policies that took money from vital social programs and contributed to the warping of democracy by fueling the growth of a gargantuan national security bureaucracy antithetical to professed U.S. principles of limited government and decentralized power.

Scott Nearing, an economist at the University of Pennsylvania fired for opposing the First World War and an early proponent of organic farming, was surely among those disturbed by *Collier's* war-game fantasy. Nearing characterized the Cold War in 1950 as a "mad adventure" that would "deplete natural resources, squander capital, divert human ingenuity and enterprise into destructive channels and deluge the human race with blood and tears." Pointing to suicidal programs driven by hysteria in which warplanes, guided missiles, and the hydrogen bomb were being developed, Nearing lamented how science and technology were mobilized to increase the destructive potential of explosives, incendiaries, chemical agencies, and bacteriological forces. Industrial and academic institutions had placed their facilities at the disposal, he said, of a government that aimed to destroy and kill

with maximum effectiveness through its military apparatus of "organized destruction" and "wholesale murder," which would be directed
most viciously against peasant societies in Korea and Vietnam.[3]

The Cold War also warped U.S. political culture by institutional-
izing a mindset that linked dissenting viewpoints and peace activism
with treason, and destroyed the prospects for a viable social democracy with attacks on organized labor and decimation of the ranks of
the progressive movement and political left. The Democratic Party
acquiesced to Trumanism and McCarthyism, becoming in effect a
conservative party for most of its subsequent history, apart from a
brief period when George S. McGovern was its presidential nominee.[4]

As part of our pocket history of the Cold War, this chapter and
the next one will profile many of its negative ramifications for U.S.
society. They include the warping of the U.S. political economy and
development of a permanent warfare state; the corruption of science,
U.S. universities, and the media; victimization of blacks; and the
abuse of civil liberties under McCarthyism and its lingering effects on
U.S. political culture, which can be seen in the hysteria about Putin.
Perhaps soon a major newspaper will develop a fantasy scenario like
Collier's in 1951, which contributed to a culture of fear undergirding
the waging of a war we did not need—then or now.

"A Permanent Arms Industry of Vast Proportions"

On January 17, 1961, President Dwight Eisenhower delivered his
Farewell Address to the nation about the threat to democracy represented by the military-industrial complex, a permanent armaments
industry of vast proportions that he had helped to enhance. He said:

> In the councils of Government, we must guard against the acqui-
> sition of unwarranted influence, whether sought or unsought, by
> the military-industrial complex. The potential for the disastrous
> rise of misplaced power exists and will persist. . . . Only an alert
> and knowledgeable citizenry can compel the proper meshing of
> the huge industrial and military machinery of defense with our

peaceful methods and goals, so that liberty and security may prosper together.[5]

Toward the end of the Second World War, Donald Nelson, head of the War Productions Board from 1942 to 1944, proposed a reconversion plan for war industries designed to transition back to a non-military based economy. He was opposed by Charles E. Wilson, the vice-chairman of the Board on leave from the presidency of General Motors, who was backed by wealthy defense contractors and a military propaganda campaign claiming that U.S. soldiers' lives would be endangered by equipment shortages. In a speech before the Army Ordinance Association, Wilson suggested an alliance of Big Business and the military in a permanent war economy, something that could only be sustained by drumming up public hysteria about the Soviet menace. Journalist Fred Cook pointed out that "the Pentagon line was that we were living in a state of undeclared emergency; that war with Russia was just around the corner; and that the safety of the nation was dependent upon the speedy rebuilding of the lower ranks of Army, Navy and Air [and Universal Military Training]."[6]

The Cold War led to enormous profits for military contractors like Lockheed, Boeing, General Dynamics, General Electric, Chrysler, and Hughes Aircraft. These corporations employed legions of former army officers, spent millions of dollars in lobbying, and increasingly financed the political campaigns of candidates from both major parties.[7] U.S. taxpayers were the ones who got fleeced. A 1959 congressional probe led by F. Edward Hébert (D-LA), a Southern conservative Democrat, found that major military contractors had defrauded the government of millions of dollars by pocketing excess profits and charging unnecessary overhead for no-bid contracts. They were given blank checks to produce weapons systems that often-proved to be faulty; they in turn got more money to correct the deficiencies, thus profiting from their own mistakes. The same probe found that the Army, Navy, and Air Force erected millions of dollars' worth of buildings on land owned by some of their favored contractors, who subsequently purchased them for "barely a nickel on the dollar."[8]

New York Times military editor Hanson Baldwin, ironically, given his contribution to the *Collier's* Third World War issue, asked his readers how the nation could prepare for new total war "without becoming a garrison state and destroying the very qualities and virtues and principles we originally set out to save." The United States indeed became far less "free" as a result of the Cold War. The Truman administration created a giant federal bureaucracy devoted to national defense, encompassed in the Defense Department, Central Intelligence Agency, Atomic Energy Commission, and National Security Council, each staffed by a new class of national security managers whose attitudes primarily reflected their class interests and backgrounds in corporate finance, Wall Street, and the Pentagon. As a cornerstone of what sociologist C. Wright Mills called the new "power elite," the military developed an increasingly visible presence in the State Department, resulting in the militarization of U.S. foreign aid. Schools built bomb shelters and conducted air raid drills, and youth were further imbued with military values through the expansion of ROTC, set up on university campuses, and universal conscription.[9]

The Cold War meanwhile tipped the balance in favor of the executive over the legislative and judicial branches, and enabled the expansion of "the imperial presidency" in which secrecy and deception, combined with efforts to spread disinformation, eroded democracy. The Tonkin Gulf fraud, Watergate scandal, and waging of secret wars exemplified the abuse of power manifesting from overweening executive authority. Deep state elements connected to the military-industrial complex could now skew the intelligence in support of wars that went against the national interest. These operatives could even help cover up the assassination of leaders promoting independent political policies, or individuals threatening to blow the whistle on secret, unethical programs.[10]

The late political analyst Chalmers Johnson noted that the Pentagon in the Cold War became "addicted to a black-budget way of life. . . . All funds for the CIA [are] secretly contained in the [Pentagon's] public budget under camouflaged names." In 1952, President Truman signed a then, and still secret, charter that created the National Security

Agency (NSA). In 1960, President Eisenhower set up the even more secret National Reconnaissance Office that runs our spy satellites. In 1961, President Kennedy launched the Defense Intelligence Agency, the personal intelligence organization of the Joint Chiefs of Staff and the secretary of war. In 1996, President Clinton combined several agencies into the National Imagery and Mapping Agency. "The budgets of all these ever-proliferating agencies are all unpublished and have not been challenged by either party since the creation of the National Security State in 1947."[11]

A disproportionate share of the defense budget went to politically conservative Western and Southern states constituting the so-called Gun Belt. Historian Ellen Schrecker notes that the Cold War consolidated the economic boom and aerospace infrastructure created during the Second World War in states like California and deepened the militarization of the South's economy. The "Gun Belt over time became self-perpetuating, creating its own powerful constituencies that pressed for increased military spending and the confrontationist foreign policies that bolstered it."[12]

"Corrupting the Last Citadels of Moral and Intellectual Integrity"

Though many citizens have heard of Eisenhower's warning about the military-industrial complex, not many are aware that later in the 1960s, Senator J. William Fulbright (D-AR) spoke out against the "militarization of academia." He warned that "in lending itself too much to the purposes of government [in the Cold War], a university fails its higher purposes," and called attention to the existence of what he termed the military-industrial-academic complex or what historian Stuart W. Leslie has termed the "golden triangle" of military agencies, the high-technology industry, and research universities.

Fulbright said that, though disappointing, the "adherence of the professors is not greatly surprising as no less than businessmen, workers and politicians, professors like money and influence and have hence welcomed the contracts and consultant-ships offered by the military establishment." The funds, he said, came at a high price, notably the "surrender of independence, the neglect of teaching and the distortion of scholarship. . . . The basic cause of the great trouble in our universities [referring to student protests] is the students' discovery of corruption in the last citadels of moral and intellectual integrity—the one place besides perhaps the churches which were supposed to be immune from the corruptions of our age."[13]

U.S. universities, to be accurate, had never been pure. In *The Goose-Step* (1923), Upton Sinclair wrote: "Our educational system is not a public service, but an instrument of special privilege; its purpose is not to further the welfare of mankind, but merely to keep America capitalist."[14] Integration with a permanent warfare state, however, was something bred by the Second World War and the Cold War. At many elite universities, area studies programs were started by Office of Strategic Services (OSS) operatives, receiving financing from foundations and agencies with covert CIA sponsorship. An example is the Russian Research Center at Harvard University, which was set up with a grant of $100,000 from the Carnegie Corporation to provide information about the Soviet Union that could be useful to the State Department and other government agencies. Stephen Cohen has noted that "university Sovietologists established many open and reasonable relations with government agencies, but also some that were covert and later troublesome."[15]

The CIA helped to place Nazi scientists recruited under Operation Paperclip on the faculty of universities, and used the cover of Michigan State University's criminal justice school to train the secret police in Vietnam. The FBI also solicited informants like Harvard University professor William Yandell Elliott and his protégé Henry Kissinger, who violated federal law by opening the mail of participants in his international relations seminar at Harvard to extract information about their political views in order to give them to the FBI.[16]

Those with the prestigious appointments and consultancies tended to favor authoritarian development models emphasizing the superiority of Anglo-Saxon traditions and neoliberal economics, giving primacy to foreign investment as a means of undercutting Communism. This often increased poverty and inequality and led to the clear-cutting of forests under the illusion that the world could be reshaped along the model of North America's petroleum-based culture.[17]

The fusion of social science and the Cold War reached its acme in the Special Operations Research office (SORO), an Army-funded institute managed by American University that studied the dynamics of insurgent and revolutionary movements as a means of assisting pacification and psychological warfare operations. By 1966, SORO boasted over a hundred researchers and an annual budget of well over $2 million. Project Camelot, "the Manhattan Project" of the social sciences, promised to create a computerized model capable of forecasting how and when any nation would undergo violent revolution, with the goal of undercutting insurgency and circumventing the volatility that led to Communism.[18]

Ithiel del Sola Pool, the chairman of MIT's Center for International Studies, which had been created to "bring to bear academic research on issues of public policy," was among the most enthusiastic proponents of a purported humanizing alliance between the social sciences and government, writing that "the social scientists have the same relationship to the traditional mandarins of the 20th century that the humanities have always had to the traditions of mandarins in the past. . . . The only hope for humane government in the future is through the extensive use of the social sciences by government."[19]

Student protestors of the 1960s disagreed with this logic, targeting university departments that undertook war-related research, including Columbia University's Institute for Defense Analysis (IDA), a weapons-related think tank that sponsored scientists who had developed a system of ground sensors to prevent North Vietnamese infiltration of the south, and MIT's Center for International Studies, whose faculty were involved with the interrogation of National Liberation Front prisoners.[20]

In August 1970, a physics graduate student was killed when antiwar activists bombed the University of Wisconsin's Army Mathematics Research Center (AMRC), which had developed equations used for war-gaming exercises, assisted in the development of infrared detection techniques for night bombing, and was connected with Project Michigan, which developed aerial photography techniques that were allegedly used to track Ché Guevara in Bolivia. Headed by J. Barkley Rosser, who was on a first-name basis with the Joint Chiefs of Staff, AMRC's research further assisted the military with methods of transporting weapons in the jungle, and undertook research into aerosol technology used to control clouds of CS gas that were dropped over the Vietnamese countryside, followed by napalm, which caused a chemical reaction producing lethal hydrogen cyanide.[21] The AMRC thus powerfully symbolized the militarization and corruption of higher education bred by the Cold War, which the antiwar movement aimed to reverse.

THE CORRUPTION OF SCIENCE

Albert Einstein considered the Cold War to have resulted in a "horrendous failure of Western civilization in its use of science and technology."[22] The groundwork was established in a report issued by General Dwight Eisenhower in April 1946, "Scientific and Technical Resources as Military Assets," which emphasized that the Cold War required "even greater contributions from science, technology and management than during the last war."[23] In 1948, Pentagon research activities accounted for 62 percent of all federal research and development expenditures, including 60 percent of federal grants to universities for research outside of agriculture.[24] Military research from 1947 to 1950 averaged over $500 million per year, with military contractors stockpiling scientific talent and establishing research labs subsidized by the government to fulfill the demand for new weapons systems. Many were adopted in Korea, including chemical warfare agents, mechanized flamethrowers, pilotless drone missiles called Matadors, and incendiary and large area cluster bombs.[25]

Look magazine reported in November 1950 that the Truman administration had "summoned scientists . . . as never before" from their "peacetime work-benches to the task of bettering the tools of war. In the Pentagon and in hundreds of labs and proving grounds from White Sands, New Mexico, to Aberdeen, Maryland, these scientists are engaged in a vast program, opening up awesome vistas of mass destruction and death."[26] Norbert Wiener, one of the world's foremost mathematical analysts who had developed theories of communications essential for winning the Second World War, was one of the few academics to lament with Einstein that scientists had become arbiters of life and death in the Cold War. He penned a letter in the *Atlantic Monthly* to the scientific community titled "A Scientist Rebels," in which he vowed not to publish any future work that would yield damage in the hands of "irresponsible militarists" who would use it to bomb or poison defenseless peoples. Guided missiles, he said, could only be used to "kill civilians indiscriminately; their possession can do nothing but endanger us."[27]

Under Operation Paperclip, which was supported by a wide spectrum of the political elite including even Henry Wallace, American intelligence services recruited over 1,600 Nazi scientists who helped the United States gain technological supremacy over the Soviets through development of rockets; chemical and biological weapons; electronic warfare capabilities including infrared, remote control, and jamming techniques; and aviation and space medicine (for enhancing military pilot and astronaut performance). Journalist Annie Jacobsen writes that Paperclip left a legacy of "ballistic missiles, Sarin gas cluster bombs, underground bunkers, space capsules and weaponized bubonic plague." Eight of the scientists had worked directly with Adolf Hitler, Heinrich Himmler, or Herman Goering, ten were part of the Nazi storm-troopers or SS, and six stood trial at Nuremburg, with another released under mysterious circumstances.[28]

The best-known Paperclip scientist, Werner von Braun, was instrumental to the development of guided missiles and the U.S. space program, which followed from a 1946 RAND Corporation report that advocated development of space-based vehicles in satellite orbits, pilotless missiles from satellites, and navigation satellites (Global Positioning System/GPS) that could provide prompt location and steering information for a variety of weapons systems.[29]

The corruption of members of the scientific-academic community in the Cold War was further exemplified in the army's biological
weapons program at Fort Detrick, Maryland, that led to the creation
of anthrax, pest-laden bombs, and herbicides like Agent Orange,
which resulted in birth deformities, cancers, and environmental
damage when applied in Vietnam.[30] Operation MK-ULTRA sponsored research in the behavioral sciences to counter alleged but never
proven Russian and Chinese brainwashing capabilities. It led to the
development of narcotic "truth" serums for use in interrogation,
which were tested on unwitting subjects, "harassment substances,"
and a fine hypodermic needle to inject drugs without piercing the
skin.[31]

The head of the CIA's Technical Services Division in the early
1960s, Dr. Sidney Gottlieb, was a California Institute of Technology–
trained biochemist and socialist in his youth. He developed a poison
handkerchief to kill Iraqi nationalist leader Karim Qassem, produced
toxic gifts for killing Fidel Castro, planted electrodes in the brains
of "Vietcong" prisoners in an experiment designed to stimulate violence, and prepared an "assassination kit" for Congolese nationalist
prime minister Patrice Lumumba containing lethal biological agents
(Lumumba would be killed by a Katangan warlord under the pay of
Belgium). During the Korean War, Gottlieb had instructed CIA operative Hans V. Tofte to obtain a selection of Korea's insect life and small
field animals like jungle rats that were used in the development of biological weapons, and he also spent time trekking in rain forests across
Latin America and Africa searching for botanical poisons. The *Times*
of London observed that "when Churchill spoke of a world made
darker by the dark lights of perverted science, he was referring to the
revolting experiments conducted on human beings by Nazi doctors
in the concentration camps. But his remarks might with equal justice
have been applied to the activities of the CIA's Sidney Gottlieb."[32]

After the Soviet launching of the Sputnik space satellite in 1957, the
Eisenhower administration founded the top-secret Defense Advanced
Research Projects Agency (DARPA), which financed advances in
rocketry and ballistic missiles, and awarded contracts to scientists for

development of fantasy weapons like radar death rays, magnetic missile shields in space, and particle beam weapons. The agency came to spawn an array of Frankenstein creations such as stealth bombers, which *Time* magazine characterized as a "death machine out of Darth Vader's workshop," as well as attack drones and robots. DARPA was also instrumental to the development of the electronic battlefield in Vietnam, a system of ground sensors promoted by Defense Secretary Robert S. McNamara that were connected to computers and used for bomb targeting.[33]

The elite JASON scientists associated with these DARPA projects became a focal point for antiwar protestors who felt they had "prostituted science for repression and murder." In Berkeley, Free Speech Movement (FSM) veterans held a mock war crimes tribunal in which they characterized the Livermore National Nuclear Weapons Laboratory—the site of development for the Multiple-Independent Targetable Reentry Vehicle (MIRV) used in Vietnam—as a "scientific whorehouse." They indicted Edward Teller, the father of the hydrogen bomb and later a science hero of the conservative New Right, as a "leading sparkplug . . . for an even greater military nuclear arsenal" and a "paranoid anti-communist."[34] Teller was subsequently awarded the second Dr. Strangelove Award at the American Association for the Advancement of Science (AAAS) national conference by Science for the People (the first was given to Livermore director M. M. May), which proclaimed that "Teller is recognized everywhere as a symbol of science in the service of war-makers."[35]

In a forum in *Science* magazine on the war in Vietnam, William Palmer Taylor of Hamilton, Ohio, wrote:

Our invasion of Vietnam has involved unprecedented mobilization of scientific resources. Scientists developed the gases which drive civilians and guerillas alike from their shelters; scientists developed the napalm and phosphorus and pellet bombs with which we wipe out the villages suspected of sheltering the Vietcong. Scientists developed the crop-spraying agents with which we are creating artificial famine. And scientists are now perfecting counterinsurgency techniques—the methods which are to make certain that a military dictatorship if once established can never be overthrown.[36]

These comments provide a vivid illustration about the misapplication of science in the Cold War, and its deadly consequences, which surely would have horrified Einstein had he lived to witness the war in Vietnam.

ARSENAL OF FOLLY: THE NUCLEAR ARMS RACE AND ITS PITFALLS

Under the mad logic of the Cold War, the United States developed a nuclear stockpile of 22,229 warheads (or 10,948 megatons of TNT) by 1961 compared to 3,320 Soviet warheads (3,420 megatons of TNT), which nonetheless did nothing to dispel anxiety on the U.S. side. In 1954, the Strategic Air Command (SAC) put forth a plan to attack the Soviet Union with hundreds of bombs, turning it into "a smoking, radiating ruin at the end of two hours. The plan involved killing 80 percent of the population in 118 major cities, or 60 million people." That same year the United States began to place nuclear weapons in Europe; by 1958, almost three thousand had been placed in Western Europe alone, a clear provocation and threat from the Soviet point of view, one that ignited their own escalation of the arms race.[37]

In August 1960, Eisenhower approved the "National Strategic Target List and Single Integrated Operational Plan" (SIOP), which was designed to use U.S. strategic nuclear forces "in a simultaneous strike against the Sino-Soviet bloc within the first twenty-four hours of a war." The Joint Chiefs of Staff estimated that 500 million people would be killed in the Soviet Union, China, Eastern and Western Europe, and bordering countries. These mind-numbing figures did not include the number who would be killed by Soviet nuclear weapons. "Nor did they include the then-unknown fact that an attack of this magnitude would almost certainly have triggered a nuclear winter, raising the possibility of extinction." Although Eisenhower was allegedly "horrified by the prospect of millions dying . . . [he] passed the plan, unaltered" to the Kennedy administration.[38]

General Lee Butler, a commander of the Strategic Air Command (SAC), issued a mea culpa upon his retirement in which he rebuked the "grotesquely destructive war plans" and "terror-induced anesthesia which suspended rational thought, made nuclear war thinkable, and grossly excessive arsenals possible during the Cold War." Butler added that "mankind escaped the Cold War without a nuclear holocaust by some combination of diplomatic skill, blind luck and divine intervention, probably the latter in greater proportion."[39] Whether the same luck will prevail in the Second Cold War is not worth leaving to chance.

In 1955, the Eisenhower administration rejected a Soviet offer to cut back its armed forces from 5.7 million to between one and 1.5 million and destroy its nuclear weapons stock in return for the United States doing the same.[40] The U.S. Air Force by this time had dropped radioactive material from planes or released it on the ground in at least a dozen nuclear tests. In at least four cases, radiation spread beyond the boundaries of the test, including at Dugway Proving Grounds in Utah where radiation bombs dropped at an Army site spread 50 percent further than expected.[41] The Pentagon also acknowledged thirty-two serious nuclear accidents, though a study by Eric Schlosser found that at least twelve hundred significant accidents occurred between 1950 and 1968. These included one where an atomic bomb blasted a home in Mars Bluff, South Carolina, in a failed test and a lethal fuel leak in Damascus, Arkansas, that resulted from a maintenance worker dropping a tool that pierced the shell of a Titan II Inter-Continental Ballistic Missile shell possessing a megaton thermonuclear warhead.[42]

Weapon production facilities, like the Hanford B Reactor in southeastern Washington State that produced plutonium for nuclear weapons during the Cold War, yielded hazardous radioactive waste with cancer-inducing effects that "will remain a risk to humans and the environment for tens or even hundreds of thousands of years," as the National Research Council concluded.[43] The explosion of a nuclear reactor at Chernobyl near Pripyat in Ukraine in April 1986 was one of the worst environmental disasters in modern history, resulting in the release of four hundred times more radioactive material than that caused by the atomic bombing of Hiroshima. An undisclosed number of people were killed or poisoned with radiation and approximately 100,000 square kilometers of land was significantly contaminated with fallout.[44]

Between 1945 and 1962, the United States conducted 105 nuclear tests in the Marshall Islands and other mid-Pacific locations involving highly radioactive hydrogen bombs. On March 1, 1954, the first U.S. hydrogen bomb test spread a cloud of radiation over 7,500 miles of ocean, leaving Bikini Island "hopelessly contaminated." The Rongelap and Utirik Atolls were also exposed to radiation.[45] Only a small percentage of the people were ever able to return. Lani Kramer, a councilwoman in Bikini's local government, noted that it was "not just their homes that were lost but an entire swathe of the islands' culture. As a result of being displaced we've lost our cultural heritage—our traditional customs and skills, which for thousands of years were passed down from generation to generation."[46] One could not think of a more tragic consequence of the arms race. The fate of the Bikinians was of little consequence to U.S. cold warriors, who also presided over the expulsion of the Chagossian people of Diego Garcia to make way for a military base in the Indian Ocean.[47]

"ECONOMY OF DEATH": MILITARY KEYNESIANISM AND ITS COST TO AMERICANS

The Korean War and related "war scares" raising fear of the Soviet Union helped save the aerospace industry from threatened nationalization, fueled economic booms in the "Gun Belt" states with large arms manufacturing, and led to military innovations in the realm of computers that spawned the growth of Silicon Valley. However, the Cold War could also be seen to have had a negative effect on the U.S. political economy overall. Economists have estimated that the United States spent over seven trillion dollars—equivalent to nearly ten trillion dollars in 1992 dollars—waging the Cold War from 1948 to 1991, with annual military budgets averaging over $168 billion per year.[48]

The war in Vietnam cost U.S. taxpayers at least $350 billion alone and around 5 trillion dollars was spent on nuclear weapons.[49]

Scholar-activist Richard Barnet observed in 1969:

> The economy of life in America has been starved to feed the economy of death. . . . The American people are devoting more resources to the war machine than is spent by all federal, state, and local governments on health and hospitals, education, old age and retirement benefits, public assistance and relief, unemployment and social security, housing and community development, and the support of agriculture. Out of every tax dollar there is about 11 cents left to build American society.[50]

From these comments, we see that, consistent with Gorbachev's viewpoint, the U.S. public lost out because of the Cold War. The United States evolved in that time as a highly unequal, over-militarized society with underfunded public schools, high crime rates, poor public transportation and infrastructure, no free health care, and an obscenely high homeless rate.[51]

The late Columbia University economist Seymour Melman emphasized in his 1970 book *Pentagon Capitalism* that the production of war material was parasitic because it was not useful for consumption and did not yield much outlying or further production (that is, no factory can use it for further production). According to Melman, in setting up a permanent warfare economy, buttressed by an alliance of business and the military, U.S. managers established a policy that would devastate U.S. manufacturing and its infrastructure, which in 2012 received a D+ rating by the American Society of Civil Engineers.

In 1968–69, ten million Americans suffered from hunger and thirty million Americans could be classified as an "economically underdeveloped sector of society." The United States at this time ranked 18th in infant mortality and had six million grossly substandard dwellings. Its railroads lagged behind those of the French and Japanese, and in 1967, for the first time, it imported more machine tools than it exported.[52]

In a 2010 posthumously published essay, "How the Pentagon Robs the People," Melman pointed to continuously expanding poverty rates as military spending levels remained astronomically high in the post-Vietnam era, with employment opportunities diminishing as civilian industrial technology deteriorated. Many Pentagon contractors reneged on paying taxes, further impoverishing the public sector. Gross inefficiency resulted from the fact that managers in state-subsidized firms, with cost-plus contracts, are under no pressure to minimize their costs, because new funds are made available each year with congressional allocations to the Pentagon. In 1984, a pulley puller for the F-16 fighter, essentially a steel belt two inches in length with three screws tapped in, was sold to the Pentagon by General Dynamics for $8,832 each. If the same equipment were custom-ordered in a private shop, it would cost $25. In the early 1960s, F-111s cost 3.25 times the initial estimate. Melman laments not only the depletion of America's manufacturing base but also the erosion of democratic standards owing to the institutionalized power lust of the Pentagon, which came to represent a state within a state.[53]

During Kennedy's presidency, Robert S. McNamara, who had won renown as an innovative organizer of Ford Motor Company, installed a central administrative office to oversee Pentagon operations. The top-down management was designed to control the activities of subsidiary management of firms that in 2003 produced $115 billion in goods purchased by the Department of Defense. "Never before in American experience," Melman writes, "has there been such a combination of economic and political decision-power in the same hands. The consequence of the establishment of the new state-management has been the installation within American society of an institutional feature of a totalitarian system."[54]

The deleterious effects of military Keynesianism were acutely felt in the 1980s when tax cuts were combined with the largest peacetime increase to that point of U.S. armed forces and weapons systems. The result was an escalation of the U.S. national debt to some $2 trillion in addition to a "stunning deterioration in distributional equity in the American economy." Accompanying this was the growth of an unprecedented penal system that was designed to warehouse America's poor, especially its black poor, for whom job prospects were bleak to nonexistent.[55]

Sheltered from reality in their ivory tower, conservative intellectuals boasted, following the end of the Cold War, that the "ideas of Adam Smith, Friedrich Hayek, Ludwig Von Mises and Milton Friedman have triumphed and workers are better off because of this," as one newly minted PhD in history lectured his colleagues.[56] Such analysis ignored the plight of America's dispossessed and the serious economic inequalities and problems that resulted in the 2008 financial crash and populist anger exploited by Donald Trump in the 2016 election. Furthermore, it ignored the fact that far from being a pure free market utopia, the U.S. political economy had evolved along militarist-state capitalist lines during the Cold War with heavy centralized planning by gargantuan bureaucracies, and an incestuous relationship between major military contractors and government officials that hindered functioning democracy.

"Getting Rid of the Communists": Labor and the Cold War

Right-wing attacks on organized labor during the Cold War resulted in a precipitous decline in union membership and labor union militancy, which was key to the surging social inequality that was facilitated by the rightward political drift. By the 1980s, the United States had the highest occupational fatality rate of any Western industrialized nation and the highest inequality rate, as union membership had plummeted to less than 23 percent of the workforce, markedly less than in the early 1950s. A key piece of legislation signaling the end of the New Deal era was the Taft Hartley Bill of 1947, or "Slave Labor Bill" as some called it, which forbade strikes in support of workers in other companies and made it illegal to honor the picket lines or refuse to work on goods made by scabs. Union members now also had to take loyalty oaths and purge Communists who had led some of the most dramatic strikes of the 1930s and 1940s and organized regional councils for the unemployed. In 1951, over a million trade unionists from twelve unions (one-fifth of the membership) were expelled from the Congress of Industrial Organization (CIO) following the investigation of Communism in New York City's distributive trades.[57]

For Joel Kovel, the principal object of the Cold War was not the Soviets but domestic radicals; it was really about this nation, not the Soviet Union. This changes the dominant perception of the Cold War from a professed fear about Soviet aggression and international tensions to U.S. "radicalism [that] was an ever-present threat to the order of things. At least it was perceived that way." The first step in domestic repression after the Second World War "was to neutralize workers' power, and nothing served this purpose better than to link insurgents with the 'foreign' doctrine of Communism." The labor militancy of the 1930s had "empowered the Communist Party and its thousands of sympathizers, who were positioned to play a major role in the golden era of labor that many saw ahead." A decade later, the Communist Party, Kovel notes, "was a ruined shell with more than one hundred of its leaders indicted and convicted under the Smith Act; and the CIO had rejoined the parent American Federation of Labor (AFL) in a reactionary alliance with the state and big business." A movement that was once based on "solidarity forever" now worked with the CIA "to crush labor insurgency wherever it appeared in the world," as the anti-Communism of the Cold War "proved an indispensable driving force in transforming labor and integrating it with capital."[58]

When Walter Reuther became president of the key CIO United Auto Workers (UAW), he had made it clear that "he intended to unite 90 percent of the autoworkers . . . against the 10 percent with 'outside loyalties,' meaning, explicitly, the Communists," whom he barred from holding union office. (Reuther believed from his travels that the structure of trade unionism in the Soviet Union was an elaborate fraud designed to impose the will of the Communist Party on a mass level.) Australian Harry Bridges, who had led the famous 1934 General Strike in San Francisco, was expelled from his post as Northern California director of the CIO on the grounds that he refused to endorse the Marshall Plan and supported Henry Wallace over Truman. This was part of a larger CIO campaign to deprive

Wallace of mass labor support by portraying him as a fellow traveler and by harassing his followers.[59]

George Meany, who served as AFL-CIO president from the 1955 merger until 1979, contributed to the trend toward top-down union management and expansive bureaucracy. The latter owed in large measure to the fact that American unions were "burdened with a set of servicing functions unknown in countries where either a labor party or a stronger welfare state assumed those responsibilities." Conservative in his political outlook, Meany stated that he "did not intend to abandon the capitalist system for some pipe dreams or some ideological fantasies invented by those who don't understand the worker's real needs and aspirations." At the 1965 convention, he instructed his underlings to "get these kooks out of the gallery," referring to activists chanting "Get out of Vietnam."[60]

Meany worked closely with Irving Brown, the AFL's representative in Europe, and Jay Lovestone, former head of the Communist Party USA, who "shared a mutual hatred of Communism and an ambitious plan to build a global network of pro-democratic unions under their control." These allegedly "pro-democratic" unions were actually pro-United States, pro-capitalist, and anti-Communist—*not pro-democratic*. Receiving a sizable slush fund from David Dubinsky, president of the International Ladies' Garment Workers, to purge the UAW of leftist activists, Lovestone became a key link for State Department and CIA funds that were secretly passed on to challenge left unions in key European countries. A key task was to disrupt Communist meetings and hire "squads of goons, many of them criminals, to wrest control of the docks" at French ports from Communist unions.[61]

AFL-CIO/CIA–supported Cold War actions in Latin America included efforts to overthrow the democratically elected Arbenz government of Guatemala and the establishment of the American Institute of Free Labor Development (AIFLD), headed by J. Peter Grace, head of United Fruit. It was the biggest foreign landowner in Latin America, and its underlying purpose was to make the hemisphere's impoverished countries safe for U.S. investors. In 1963, AIFLD backed the ouster of Dominican Republic's president Juan

Bosch who had cancelled Esso, Texaco, and Shell oil refinery contracts; pushed land reform and a 30 percent wage increase at the
South Puerto Rico Sugar Company; and negotiated a $150 million
line of credit with a Zurich-based consortium over U.S. banks. AIFLD
subsequently supported a military junta in Brazil and aided in the
overthrow of democratically elected socialist Salvadore Allende in
Chile, whose successor, General Augusto Pinochet, "outlawed traditional unions, eliminated long-established worker protections, and
jailed, abducted and killed many hundreds of unionists."[62]

Historian Ronald Radosh's *Labor and the Cold War* pointed out
that AFL-CIO leaders in the 1950s and 1960s envisioned unions as
junior partners to the large corporations, favoring counterrevolutionary policies along with the Pentagon's huge weapons program because
it helped secure good-paying union jobs. They "refused cooperation
with those workers who sought to end control of their countries by
local oligarchies," operating in the realm of foreign policy "without
consulting, and without obtaining the consent of . . . rank-and-file
workers."[63]

The undemocratic methods, purging of militants, growth of top-
heavy bureaucracy, uninspired and at times corrupt leadership, and
alignment with pro-corporate and imperialist foreign policies all
exemplified labor's retreat from progressive politics during the Cold
War. This in turn contributed to declining membership and political
influence, and an inability to withstand attacks from the right in the
post-Keynesian age of neoliberalism.

A key to the conservative backlash coinciding with the Red Scare
was a barrage of business propaganda, as discussed by Elizabeth Fones
Wolf in her book *Selling Free Enterprise: The Business Assault on Labor
and Liberalism, 1945–1950*. This was a coordinated effort to indoc-
trinate the public in the virtues of the "free market" and to promote
a pro-capitalist message—including in schoolbooks, media advertis-
ing, and classrooms, going hand in hand with the anti-Communism
of the Cold War. The U.S. corporate elite promoted a vision of freedom that stressed the homogenizing, advertising-based consumerism
of a business civilization. These campaigns were quite effective in

conditioning the public at a time when unions and the proletarian culture of the Depression era were in decline.[64]

Saving the Nation from Infection: The FBI's COINTELPRO

In his 1958 book *Masters of Deceit: What the Communist Bosses Are Doing Now to Bring America to Its Knees*, FBI Director J. Edgar Hoover wrote that "something utterly new has taken root in America during the past generation, a Communist mentality representing a systematic, purposive, and conscious attempt to destroy Western civilization and roll history back to the age of barbaric cruelty and despotism, all in the name of 'progress.'"[65] Hoover likened Communists to germs and political radicalism with "filth and licentiousness," suggesting that, like an epidemic, "a quarantine was necessary to keep it from infecting the nation."[66] Historian Ellen Schrecker points out that "had observers known in the 1950s what they have learned since the 1970s, when the Freedom of Information Act opened the bureau's files, 'McCarthyism' would probably be called 'Hooverism.'"[67]

According to Bill Sullivan, chief of FBI intelligence in the late 1960s and early 1970s, Hoover was "consistent in the things he hated all his life . . . he hated liberalism, he hated blacks, he hated Jews—he had this great long list of hates."[68] The Boss's career as a red hunter began during the first Red Scare in 1919 when he headed the newly formed Radical Division of the Bureau of Investigation under Attorney General A. Mitchell Palmer, which presided over the roundup, incarceration, and deportation of thousands of suspected subversives.

COINTELPRO, the FBI's counter-intelligence program, was formally established by Hoover in 1956 with the aim of "disrupting, harassing and discrediting" the U.S. Communist Party and Communist activists through "creative" and aggressive methods, which included disseminating false propaganda and hate mail attacks. It resulted in myriad constitutional violations, including illegal surveillance, blackmail, and collusion with local Chicago police in the 1969 murder of two Black Panther Party activists, Fred Hampton and Mark Clark, who were shot in cold blood while sleeping.

Benefitting from surveillance undertaken by "red squads," made up of local police, the targets of COINTELPRO included a wide spectrum of the American left, including civil rights activists like Martin Luther King Jr., the public and veterans' antiwar and student movements, as well as the Chicano movement and American Indian Movement (AIM). A program to disrupt the Ku Klux Klan (KKK) was less prioritized by Hoover, who considered the KKK patriotic, though extreme in their methods, and gave instructions not to develop high-level Klan informants.[69] COINTELPRO was exposed in 1971 after a break-in at FBI offices in Media, Pennsylvania, by antiwar activists and repudiated by the public. The 1975 Church Committee investigating covert actions directed against foreign countries and U.S. citizens characterized COINTELPRO as a "vigilante operation" involving fundamentally undemocratic techniques.

An early target was the leftist American Labor Party and radical East Harlem Congressman Vito Marcantonio, who, with over 6,000 pages of files, was placed on a list that would enable the U.S. attorney general to incarcerate him without trial during a national emergency.[70] In 1961, Hoover launched the Socialist Workers Party (SWP) disruption campaign, because, according to a secret memorandum, the party had been "openly espousing its line on a local national basis through running candidates for public office and strongly . . . supporting such causes as Castro's Cuba and integration in the South." The disruption campaign included breaking into the homes of SWP leaders, stealing their membership lists and internal party bulletins, planting fake evidence in order to jail them, or having them dismissed from their jobs. There were also attempts to influence boards of trustees at various universities to have socialist college faculty members dismissed. Numerous careers were ruined, and the universities were de-radicalized to a certain extent, with many afraid to promote left-wing views or causes.[71]

The House Pike Committee on illegal surveillance concluded in 1975 that the Socialist Workers Party was a legitimate political party kept under "intensive investigation for over thirty years without [the FBI] finding evidence for a single federal indictment against the party or any of its members."[72] This finding exemplifies the wide abuse of civil liberties under COINTELPRO, which was supported by both major parties. By adopting disruption, surveillance, harassment, infiltration, and intimidation tactics, the FBI was a decisive factor, along with the internal purges of the AFL-CIO, in the demise of leftist and radical movements during the Cold War.

"Creating a War Psychosis": The Cold War and Decline of Media Independence

In a landmark 1989 study, *Manufacturing Consent: The Political Economy of the Mass Media*, Noam Chomsky and Edward S. Herman examined the influence of corporate control of the mass media and the subtle rhetorical manipulations used to inculcate consent for existing U.S. policies in foreign affairs.[73] The Cold War fits perfectly within their model. Washington set out to create a "war psychosis," as Carl Marzani put it, and wage psychological warfare against the public with manufactured "war scares" in order to frighten the citizenry. U.S. newspapers and other media were "willing tools" in this process, because they published "rumors and malicious gossip as if they were facts."[74]

Life magazine complained as early as 1945 that "the fellow traveler is everywhere, in Hollywood, on college faculties, in government bureaus, in publishing companies, in radio offices, even on the editorial staffs of eminently capitalist journals."[75] *Look* magazine subsequently presented a scenario in which the Soviets invaded Detroit after arming prisoners in the Wayne County jail to assist in the "blitzkrieg-style attack." The essay warned that Detroit would then "know the chaos and horror that Bogotá Colombia knew [this spring] when a Red-inspired revolt unleashed a reign of terror and destruction."[76]

Many anti-Communist-themed stories were directly planted by the State Department and CIA, which had connections to prominent journalists like the Alsop brothers (Joseph and Stewart).[77] In the September 2, 1950, issue of *The Saturday Evening Post*, the Alsops wrote a characteristic piece, "The Lessons of Korea," suggesting that the United States had not done enough to deter Soviet aggression or contain Soviet imperialism. "The armed strength of the United States," the Alsops wrote, "was too slight to instill in the masters of the Kremlin any healthy fear of reprisals. Hence Korea was attacked." The story was buttressed by a photo of a bound American soldier who had been machine-gunned. The Alsops went on to warn that Korea was but the "first episode of an attempt to bring all Asia and all Europe within the Soviet empire." The real Soviet goal was not just South Korea, but to "make the living death of the slave society the universal condition of mankind, from the shores of the Atlantic to the islands of Japan, from the icy cliffs of Spitsbergen [in northern Norway] to the bright sands of cape common."[78]

Refuted by scholars who emphasize Stalin's cautious and pragmatic approach to foreign policy, such analyses helped engender public support not only for the Korean War but also for the massive military buildup that accompanied it. In August 1959, Joseph Alsop reported an invasion of Laos by the North Vietnamese, which was impossible because the roads were impassable during the rainy season. William Lederer wrote in *A Nation of Sheep* that "the people of the United States were led to believe that Laos physically had been invaded by foreign Communist troops from across its northern border. . . . The entire affair was a fraud. No military invasion of Laos had taken place."[79] In another classic example of how propaganda can work its magic, there was a dramatic shift in public opinion about Winston Churchill's famous "Iron Curtain speech" thanks to the relentless pro–Cold War message coming from the leading organs of the press. In a poll taken immediately after the speech, only 18 percent of the public was recorded as approving of it. A survey taken a month later showed 85 percent approval.[80]

According to historian Nancy Bernhard, network television in its heady early days served as an important "conduit for the West's position in the Cold War." Most of the news was "scripted if not produced by the defense establishment" under the belief that the threat from Communism was too serious to allow for independent information. Communists were referred to as "Reds" regardless of their nationality and characterized as "power-drunk atheists" and "blood-thirsty barbarians" with no room for nuance or criticism of U.S. foreign policy.[81]

Media critic Edward S. Herman pointed out that *New York Times* publisher Arthur Hays Sulzberger "regularly [admonished] his editors to focus on the Soviets as 'colonialists,' and to use the phrase 'Iron Curtain.'"[82] This followed a tradition of anti-Communist reporting at the *Times* that began with the U.S. invasion of Soviet Russia in 1918.[83] The first major report on the revolution by Arthur Copping characterized the Bolsheviks as "thieving, murderous, cowardly and cruel," while the Allied invaders were depicted as noble and heroic. Copping admitted that he knew the revolution "only by hearsay as he was reporting from a protected zone." He quoted from an ex-Petrograd professor who alleged his son's playmate had been beaten over the head, stabbed, and thrown in a river by "insensate bolsheviki" who had unleashed the darkest chapter in Russian history. Repeating disinformation promoted by the U.S. Committee on Public Information that had been created to propagandize on behalf of the First World War, Copping concluded that "the sinister figure of the Hun lurks unseen behind the brutish figure of the Bolshevik, his victim and his tool."[84]

Subsequent articles by Copping quoted from opposition leaders who predicted the Bolsheviks' imminent demise, and emphasized the gallantry of U.S. soldiers fighting against the "lawless armed hordes . . . stiffened and organized by the Germans" in an attempt to create a "free and enlightened Russia."[85] The *Times* nationalistic bias was again revealed in the Greek crisis in 1947, when Dana Adams Schmidt characteristically wrote that the leftist guerillas enforced their authority in the countryside "through terror." While acknowledging that elections were held and peasant debts cancelled in guerrilla-controlled regions, and that if there was "anything rotten in Greece it [was] at the top, with the oligarchy that lives in comfort in Athens," Schmidt claimed that Greece would be in "danger if Yugoslavia, Bulgaria and Albania recognized the rebel government" and expressed hope that "extermination of the guerrillas" could be carried out successfully next summer after the army had been better trained.[86]

The *Times* went on to wholeheartedly support the Korean War, blaming the "Soviet puppet regime" in the north for its outbreak. It refused to publish a letter by Arthur Davis of Union College, who suggested that Southeast Asian peasant societies were undergoing social revolutions and that Asian nationalism was dedicated to freeing itself from Western domination; hence the Soviets were not responsible for the war.[87]

Following the 1965 anti-Communist coup in Indonesia, the *Times* ran an article by James Reston titled "A Gleam of Light in Asia" when hundreds of thousands of alleged Communist Party sympathizers were being slaughtered or thrown into concentration camps.[88] U.S. intervention in Vietnam the same year enjoyed near total editorial support from the *Times* and other media that refused to admit the United States had committed aggression. Instead, they blamed Hanoi for invading its own country. During the Gulf of Tonkin crisis, the *Times* published a phony photo on the front page of a North Vietnamese boat that allegedly attacked a U.S. ship, which helped sell the war. When it became clear that the United States could not win, the *Times* followed the elite consensus in portraying the war as a "tragic mistake" motivated by the "loftiest intentions" that was proving too costly for the U.S. side. Only rarely did their reporters make any effort to see the war from the point of view of "the enemy"—the peasants of South Vietnam, Laos, or later Cambodia.[89]

During the 1970s and 80s, the *Times* presented alarmist depictions of Soviet military capabilities derived from a report issued by a Pentagon financed lobby group, the Committee on the Present Danger, and refused to review a book that discredited its claims.[90] This set a precedent for the alarmism surrounding the "New Russian imperialism," which follows reporting patterns dating to the Cold War.

5. Truman, McCarthyism, and Domestic Repression

In an April 19, 2017, *New York Times* article, "Trump Adviser's Visit to Moscow Got the FBI's Attention," Scott Shane, Mark Mazzetti, and Eric Goldman suggest that Carter Page, a Navy veteran and Trump adviser, was disloyal because he was critical of American policy toward Russia in terms that "echoed the position of Vladimir Putin." The Senate Intelligence Committee headed by Mark Warner (D-VA) and Richard Burr (R-NC) subsequently asked Page, an oil industry consultant with extensive business dealings and contacts in Russia, to supply the committee the names and details of almost anyone he contacted who could be a Russian official over an eighteen-month period, and all electronic and other communications.

Journalist Robert Parry has pointed out that this request amounts to a perjury trap because Page is sure to miss someone or something, and is hence liable to be prosecuted for obstructing the investigation or lying to investigators, as had been the case with National Security Adviser Michael Flynn following a conversation with Russian ambassador Serge Kislayek. The government has complete records, as it has surveilled Page's activities since the Obama administration obtained a Foreign Intelligence Surveillance Act (FISA) warrant following a speech he gave at Moscow's New Economic School.[1]

Backed by liberal Democrats aiming to discredit Trump, the tactics of the Senate Intelligence Committee have rekindled some of the old methods of the House Committee on Un-American Activities (HUAC), which first used clandestine surveillance and methods of entrapment during the Cold War to prosecute Americans suspected of treason, including most famously the Hollywood Ten and Alger Hiss. The media during the Cold War also vilified progressive voices like Henry Wallace. Filmmaker Oliver Stone, after airing a series of interviews with Putin on Showtime in June 2017, was denounced in similar terms to Wallace. He was accused in the *New York Times* of being an Islamophobe, Stalin apologist, and "breathless admirer of Putin," which was not at all true.[2]

The history of American politics is rank with hypocrisy; however, not much could top the sorry specter of liberal Democrats, purporting to champion human rights, adopting the methods of McCarthyism in the attempt to discredit Donald Trump—a man mentored by Joe McCarthy's top aide—and uphold a confrontationist policy toward Russia. In December 2016, President Obama signed a military authorization bill that included a $160 million bureaucracy to identify and counter alleged Russian propaganda. Some fear that the new agency could evolve into a Ministry of Truth designed to censor critical voices as occurred in the Cold War.[3]

This chapter continues an examination of the domestic repression spawned by the First Cold War, which today is repeating itself in a guise Marx undoubtedly would have considered farcical. The repression of the First Cold War built upon the legacy of the first Red Scare following the Russian Revolution, which resulted in the imprisonment and deportation of thousands of radicals, and the destruction of the socialist and anarchist movements. The anti-Communist hysteria of the 1940s and 1950s also resulted in the jailing and deportation of radicals, while contributing to the decimation of organized labor and a rightward shift in the political culture. The GOP spearheaded the witch-hunting climate as part of an electoral strategy designed to break the Democratic Party's dominance during the FDR New

Deal–Truman Fair Deal era. Liberal Democrats weakened themselves by acquiescing to McCarthyism and would never reclaim the progressive spirit seen under Roosevelt.[4] One could draw a direct line from the red-baiting days of the Cold War to the Russia-Gate witch hunt, which draws on the worst of U.S. political traditions.

"Many are the Crimes": The Cold War Red Scare

The term *McCarthyism* derives from the anti-Communist crusading of Senator Joseph McCarthy (R-WI), who catapulted himself to national prominence after giving a speech in Wheeling, West Virginia, in February 1950, claiming without any evidence that there were 205 card-carrying members of the Communist Party working in the U.S. State Department. The anti-Communist fervor gripping the United States would transcend the political career of McCarthy, who was personally discredited after extending his accusations to the U.S. Army and appearing as a bully on national television.[5]

Historians have explained McCarthyism as a form of populism gone sour that was associated with the status anxiety of certain ethnic groups—like the Irish, Eastern-European-born Catholics, and Germans—xenophobia, and a kind of anti-intellectualism of the frontier. Other studies have shown, however, that Senator McCarthy was supported by wealthy business interests, who saw in the Red Scare an opportunity to help roll back New Deal reforms benefitting the working class by equating left-wing views with Communism. From 1946 to 1948, the U.S. Chamber of Commerce initiated a propaganda campaign depicting labor militancy as a product of Kremlin machinations, and spread an apocalyptic view of Communism that fueled anti-Soviet hysteria.[6]

Fitting with a "counter-subversive" tradition in U.S. history that demonized the "Other" as a means of reaffirming national identity and superiority, Communists were considered "alien beings" whose destruction was "easy to justify" both at home and abroad. According to political scientist Michael Paul Rogin, "The counter-subversive needs monsters to give shape to his anxieties and to permit him to

indulge his forbidden desires. . . . Demonization allows the counter-subversive, in the name of battling the subversive, to imitate his
enemy."[7]

Much like the overhyped charges today of political interference
and election hacking, the danger of Communism was wildly over-
estimated throughout the original Cold War as party membership
hovered around 32,000 a year after 1950 in a nation of 150 million
people. Nearly a quarter of these were FBI informants. Though a few
Soviet spies were uncovered, most of them engaged in espionage
during the Second World War when the United States and the Soviet
Union were allies. The number did not justify the mass public hysteria and repression. In a 1951 memorandum found in the Moscow
archives, KGB officials acknowledged they no longer had any significant inside sources within the U.S. government. By 1955, the FBI
wrote off the U.S. Communist Party as a serious espionage threat.[8]

The Communists' heyday was in the Great Depression when
they were at the forefront in organizing the unemployed and people
evicted from their homes, as well as coal miners in Harlan County,
Kentucky, farmworkers in California, black sharecroppers in the
South, and even the integration of professional sports.[9] Abraham J.
Muste, a proponent of Gandhian, nonviolent, revolutionary paci-
fism, and Congregationalist minister affiliated with the Fellowship of
Reconciliation, noted:

> When you looked out on the scene of misery and desperation
> during the Depression, you saw it was the radicals, the left-
> wingers, the people who had adopted some form of Marxian
> philosophy, who were doing something about the situation, who
> were banding together for action, who were putting up a fight.
> . . . In many cases these doers and fighters were communists or
> those set in motion by them. Without them, the unions in the
> mass production industries would not have been built.[10]

Dalton Trumbo, a Hollywood scriptwriter blacklisted during
McCarthyism, further noted that while the Communist Party may

have been organized hierarchically, the people who joined it in the 1930s and 1940s

> joined for very good, humane reasons, in my view, most of them. In a time that began with the Depression and the total collapse of the American economy, with fourteen million unemployed, and soon spread throughout the world; in a world that had fascism in Germany and Spain, and Italy, and an era that culminated in the forties in a war that killed fifty or one hundred million people—and saw the fires, not only of Hiroshima and Nagasaki, but the fires of Auschwitz and Treblinka—in such a world and such a time, it was not madness to hope for the possibility of making a better sort of world. And that, I think, is what most of those who joined wanted to do.[11]

In the Cold War climate, this idealistic spirit was crushed. The Communist Party was made illegal and people were ostracized for expressing left-of-center or antiwar views. To maintain "respectability" or their jobs, many held back on offering political critiques or joining political organizations. Hundreds of professors and teachers were fired in universities and schools in an academic witch hunt, militant labor leaders were purged, immigrants were deported, 2,700 employees lost their jobs and 12,000 resigned following the institution of loyalty oaths by the Truman administration.[12] In Houston, Texas, even Jehovah's Witnesses were arrested because they advocated pacifism and opposed nationalism.[13]

Becky Jenkins, a high school student in California whose father had been in the Communist Party, reported: "When I was in my first year of high school the Korean War was going on. In social studies class, I said something about it being a civil war and [that] America should stay out of it. . . . The teacher responded with 'That's the position of the Communists!' And the class started to laugh and scream and hoot at me, yelling, 'Commie!' I ran home from school sobbing, just humiliated."[14]

Both children and adults in this kind of political climate suffered from mental illness. A California psychologist reported in the

summer of 1950: "A great many young men are approaching me pro-
fessionally with questions, in a mood of extreme anxiety. . . . They
feel that the United States has become a police state, in which citizens are no longer free to speak frankly, and where to desire peace is
considered subversive, almost unlawful. Life in the United States has
become a sort of nightmare to them."[15]

In one of many injustices, Communist Party leader Steve Nelson
was sentenced to twenty years in prison under sedition laws in
Pennsylvania by a fascist-leaning judge who regarded the left-wing
newspapers seized from Nelson's office, including one containing a
cartoon pointing to the destructiveness of the Korean War, as "more
dangerous than firearms." A juror who believed in Nelson's innocence
was badly beaten as an act of intimidation and went "missing" the
day of the verdict. Nelson was left to serve his sentence at Blawnox
Workhouse where the "administration followed medieval practices;
prisoners were treated as subhuman, beaten at will by the guards,
thrown in the hole and kept on bread and water for nine days at a
time."[16]

In Charleston, South Carolina, an anti-Communist member of the
National Maritime Union (NMU) named Rudolfo Serreo telephoned
the police to announce that he intended to murder Robert New, the
twenty-eight-year-old port agent for the NMU and chairman of the
local Wallace for President Committee. After following through,
Serreo was convicted only of manslaughter and sentenced to three
years in prison with the victim being known around town as a "nigger
lover." Police elsewhere said they saw no more reason to protect
Wallace supporters than gangsters. As Detroit's police commissioner
put it, they "ought to either be shot, thrown out of the country or put
in jail."[17]

The abuses of McCarthyism were perpetuated with the acquiescence of the Catholic Church, which considered the Cold War a
righteous struggle against an atheistic, collectivist ideology. Harry
Truman had personally denounced Joseph McCarthy's tactics, but
his foreign policy rhetoric and domestic loyalty program raised the
level of public anxiety about Communism and helped outline the

right-wing case. In a strong reflection of his conservative views, Truman told students at Cornell University that Communists were engineering the student sit-downs at lunch counters in the South. Challenged by Martin Luther King Jr. and Roy Wilkins of the NAACP to prove it, Truman replied that he had no proof. "But I know that usually when trouble hits the country the Kremlin is behind it."[18]

Hubert Humphrey, a prominent Democratic senator from Minnesota, who had led a ruthless purge there of leftists in the Democratic Farmer Labor Party (DFL), sponsored the 1954 Communist Control bill that declared the U.S. Communist Party "the agency of a hostile foreign power," an "instrumentality of a conspiracy to overthrow the government of the United States," and a "clear and present danger to the security of the country." The bill provided penalties for membership under the Internal Security Act, fines of up to $10,000 or imprisonment for five years or both.[19] Humphrey stated: "The bill was not perfect and it had its limitations," referring to its ineffectiveness not its threat to civil liberties. His main goal was to take Communist hunting out of the headlines and committee circuses and put it in the courts, a position supported by prominent liberal senators like Lyndon B. Johnson of Texas and Albert Gore Sr. of Tennessee.[20]

The culture of the Cold War overwhelmingly "gave ammunition to opponents of social change and calls to extend the New Deal," in the words of historian Eric Foner. The most influential liberal text was Harvard historian and later Kennedy adviser Arthur Schlesinger Jr.'s *The Vital Center*, written in 1949. It castigated "doughface progressives," the fellow traveler whose "sentimentality has softened [him] up . . . for Communist permeation and conquest," and called for a vigorous foreign policy to combat Soviet totalitarianism.[21] Texas oilmen such as Clint W. Murchison Sr., Hugh R. Cullen, and Howard L. Hunt financed politicians like Martin Dies and Joseph McCarthy who opposed internal subversion, caused according to Murchison by "commies," blacks, liberals, the CIO, "egg-heads and long hairs."[22] Starting with his 1946 campaign for Congress in which he attacked Democratic Party opponent Jerry Voorhis as a tool of the

Communists, Richard Nixon (R-CA) received financial support from big eastern financial interests, the Bank of America, private utilities, and big companies like Standard Oil that stood to benefit from the Red Scare.[23]

Historian Landon Y. Storrs concluded that the Cold War "stunted the development of the American welfare state. Conservatives in and out of government used concerns about Soviet espionage to remove from public service many officials who advocated regulatory and redistributive policies intended to strengthen democracy."[24] Leon Keyserling, Truman's key economic adviser, evolved quite typically from a champion of labor rights and economic planning in the 1930s to a leading proponent of economic growth and militarizing the Cold War after a potentially career-ending investigation interrogated his view of capitalism.[25] In the 1952 election, the Socialist candidate Darlington Hoopes got only 20,189 votes, fewer than any previous Socialist candidate.[26] The spectrum of reputable opinion had narrowed, shriveling the framework within which realistic political choices were entertained.

Bernard Gordon, a reader for Paramount Pictures, fired for left-leaning politics, and author of *Living in Interesting Times, or How I Learned to Love the Blacklist,* told an interviewer in 1997 that most people

> think about the terrible personal effects [of McCarthyism], the ruined careers and lifetimes, even the deaths of people who were affected—all true enough and not to be slighted. . . . Others think of the fear not only engendered in the entertainment industry and schools and universities in the press and the media, all true too. But my own sense goes beyond even that. I feel that the black period laid the groundwork for much that has followed, the Nixon and Reagan regimes which glorified the Cold War as a holy enterprise, which used the slogans of anticommunism to construct monstrous military machines that virtually bankrupted the country and placed the industrial-military complex in such a powerful position that even today, with the "evil

empire" gone, there seems to be no way to stop the expenditures for arms and the export of arms. Eisenhower warned of this in his farewell address. Beyond this even there is a sense that the convenient anticommunism has become anti-government with respect to all social programs that came out of the FDR era. The rich and powerful, who grow more rich and powerful each day, used blacklisting and McCarthyism to dismantle everything liberal, to make liberalism a dirty word, so that today both parties vie to be more reactionary.[27]

These comments refute the nostalgic view of Thomas L. Friedman in his column "Cold War Without the Fun" and confirm Gorbachev's that the Cold War made losers of everybody.[28] The drift toward neo-liberalism, an unregulated capitalism accompanied by cuts to public services, and militarized state capitalism in the United States were key consequences of the destruction of left-wing movements in the Cold War—the sole force capable of constraining corporate power and forging a more decent society.[29]

THE VICTIMS I: THE ROSENBERGS

On July 23, 2017, on a night CNN aired a special on Russian spying and the media were filled with stories of Russia-Gate and Russia's alleged efforts to sway the 2016 election, CBS's *60 Minutes* re-invoked memory of the Rosenberg spy-saga by telling the story of the couple's two sons and their efforts to exonerate their mother. The timing could not have been coincidental.

Julius and Ethel Rosenberg were a young Jewish couple living on the Lower East Side of Manhattan, who like many of their generation gravitated to leftist and Communist ideals because they had experienced the harshness of the capitalist system during the Great Depression and, as Ethel's son Robert Meeropol put it, "wanted to make the world a better place."[30] Described by the *New York Times* as a "little woman with soft and pleasant features," Ethel, Robert said, "saw people being thrown in the streets and evicted, and it was the

Communists helping the people to get their homes back. . . . They were heroic." She became a political activist who organized strikes before her twentieth birthday.

Julius shared his wife's political commitments while working as an Army Signal Corps engineer, testifying at his trial that the Soviet government had improved "the lot of the underdog . . . made a lot of progress in eliminating illiteracy, built up a lot of resources [such as dams] . . . and contributed a major share in destroying the Hitler beast who killed six million of my co-religionists [Jews]." Julius's main reason for collaborating with the Soviets was to help defeat the Nazi army, a fact underplayed in the *60 Minutes* special. He gave Russian agents information on technology used for the development of jet fighters, radars, and detonators, but he provided nothing directly on the atomic bomb, as declassified VENONA transcriptions of KGB files confirm. VENONA was a top-secret U.S. effort to gather and decrypt messages sent to the KGB.

In December 1945, Ethel's brother, David Greenglass, provided the Russians crudely drawn sketches of a cross-section of the bomb related to high-explosive lenses, though these were considered by experts to be "unimpressive," to display "naïve misunderstandings," and to disclose "ludicrously little" about a complex program. (Holding a low-grade security clearance, he had only a high school degree and had failed eight classes at Brooklyn Polytechnic Institute.) David had told prosecutors Ethel had typed up his notes and helped recruit him into the spy ring, but he later admitted he was lying to protect his wife. Ethel was never in reality given a code name, and according to KGB agent Alexander Feklisov, "never worked for us," a fact the U.S. government knew.

In June 1961, FBI Director J. Edgar Hoover declared: "Who, in all good conscience could say that Julius and Ethel Rosenberg, the spies who delivered the secret of the atomic bomb into the hands of the Soviets, should have been spared when their treachery caused the shadow of annihilation to fall upon all of the world's people." The evidence from the case, however, shows these comments to be untrue, on a par with the preposterous claim of Judge Irving Kaufman that the

Rosenbergs caused the "Communist aggression in Korea, with resultant casualties exceeding 50,000" and that of Dwight Eisenhower, who said that by "immeasurably increasing the chances of atomic war, the Rosenbergs may have condemned to death tens of millions of innocent people all over the world."[31]

Robert Meeropol points out that the main reason the Feds went after Julius was because he was the recruiter who got others involved in giving information to the Soviets. Julius was "the idealistic head of a politically generated group who remained true to his beliefs.... He was asked to turn in all his comrades, which he refused to do." And Ethel stood loyal to her husband. The bias of the trial was epitomized by the fact that Roy Cohn, the assistant district attorney and an aide to Joseph McCarthy, discussed the case with Judge Kaufman by phone from the courthouse lobby.[32]

The Victims II: Alger Hiss

Along with the Rosenberg trial, the Alger Hiss spy case helped fan the flames of McCarthyism and drove American political culture to the right. Joan Brady, author of *America's Dreyfus*, writes that the "Red Scare whipped up around the case became for America what anti-Semitism had been to Germany [in the 1930s], a force to unify the people and deflect attention from an economic rearrangement that could not function freely without chipping away at their rights."[33]

Convicted in federal court of perjury in January 1950, Alger Hiss was the embodiment of the liberal New Deal establishment. Educated at Harvard Law School, Hiss clerked for Supreme Court Justices Felix Frankfurter and Oliver Wendell Holmes, and worked for the State Department before moving on to head the Carnegie Endowment for International Peace. Supportive of Roosevelt's policy of accommodation toward the Soviets, Hiss had been present at the 1945 Yalta conference, and had also worked for the Nye Committee in the 1930s, a congressional investigation into war profiteering that exposed high-level corruption and connections between U.S. companies and the growth of the Nazi war machine. Hiss thus had made many powerful enemies. The Republican Party at this time was looking to revive its fortunes through red-baiting tactics that would deflect attention away from their anti-labor program. Journalist Alistair Cooke pointed to the Republicans' eagerness to "show that the Roosevelt administration had been criminally 'soft' toward communists, if it was not actually riddled with them," and that Soviet power was a "waking plot initiated long ago in the reign of the New Deal." As the *New York Times* put it: "A cornerstone of the Republican campaign strategy was the oft-repeated charge that the Roosevelt and Truman administration had been dyed pink by Moscow."[34]

Hiss's alleged treason provided the proof in the pudding. His actual connection to Soviet espionage remains unproven, however, and he never left any traces of being a socialist. The documents he is alleged to have smuggled were mundane and would have done nothing to harm national security. His case furthermore was marred by prosecutorial misconduct and illegalities. He was entrapped by prosecutors who benefited from FBI surveillance of Hiss's witnesses and then shared information with their leading witness, Whittaker Chambers.[35]

Chambers was a *Time* magazine editor who said he had known Hiss in the mid-1930s when he went by the name George Crosley. His testimony gained credibility in the eyes of the second jury that convicted Hiss on perjury charges because of an intimate knowledge of Hiss and his family, which was based on surveillance tapes and information leaked to him by the FBI.[36]

The Hiss trial is most famous for the dramatics involving Richard Nixon, a junior congressman with HUAC, who in a carefully choreographed event was led to a pumpkin patch on Chambers's property holding microfilmed documents allegedly provided by Hiss, and was photographed reviewing them, an image that cemented his reputation as an anti-Communist sleuth. Nixon said the documents were conclusive proof of "the greatest treason conspiracy in this nation's history . . . proof that cannot be denied."

As revealed by grand jury testimony declassified twenty-five years later, Nixon knew all along the documents were unimportant. They included blanks along with synopses about economic conditions in

Manchuria, German trade policy in Brazil, and unclassified manuals for operating naval rafts, parachutes, and fire extinguishers. Many pages came from the open shelves at the Bureau of Standards Library and were available to any member of the public.

Like other defectors from Communism, Chambers's credibility is put into question by contradictory statements that he made and false testimony. William A. Reuben, who spent four decades researching the Hiss case, found that "the first thing to note about Whittaker Chambers's confessions of Communist underground work is that it has never been corroborated, either by documentary evidence or by the word of any other human being."[37]

Hiss's detractors believed they had their smoking gun years after the trial when encrypted Soviet cables released following the opening of the Soviet archives in 1991 exposed a State Department spy code-named Ales whom they believed to be Alger Hiss. However, a 2007 *American Scholar* article by Kai Bird and Svetlana Chervonnaya, argues that a more likely candidate was Hiss's colleague, Wilder Foote, because the information came from someone inside the Lend-Lease Administration, and a KGB operative placed Ales in Mexico City when Hiss was known to be in the United States.[38] Bird and Chervonnaya point out further that the alleged collaboration took place during the Second World War when U.S.-Soviet relations were good, so Ales may not have even thought of himself as a spy. The Soviets showed little interest in the political information he could provide, since the Cambridge Five (famed British spies) leaked the major secret documents related to Yalta. Ales hence does not appear to have violated the Espionage Act, which requires specific injury to U.S. national interests.[39]

As with the Rosenbergs, the Hiss case exemplifies the abuse of the judicial system and manipulation of public opinion by opportunists like Richard Nixon during the Cold War. It was key to discrediting New Deal liberals who stood as a barrier to Wall Street's vision of a new world order and were bent on prosecuting some influential white-collar criminals and business executives who had colluded with the Nazis in the Second World War. The case also extended the life of

HUAC by another twenty-five years after it had failed to catch any spies, before Hiss or after. Decades after the case, Alger Hiss remains a "bogeyman" who, as Joan Brady puts it, continues to serve as the embodiment of what happens when we let our guard down.[40]

The Victims III: Owen Lattimore

During his reign of terror, Senator Joseph McCarthy accused Asia scholar Owen Lattimore of being the boss of a ring of spies of which Alger Hiss was a part, though in the absence of any evidence, later switched to proclaiming Lattimore as the man whose policies in the Far East resulted in the loss of China to communism. This was a reference to the Chinese Revolution of 1949 and triumph of the Maoists, which served as a major blow to U.S. foreign policy interests in Asia. An expert on the history and culture of the Mongol people, Lattimore had been appointed as a State Department adviser to Chiang Kai-shek during the Second World War, and came to embrace the view of General George C. Marshall that the Chiang government was hopelessly corrupt and had lost its mandate to rule.

Lattimore consequently became a prime target of the China lobby, a collection of businessmen, journalists, and politicians who supported Chiang Kai-hek and an aggressive anti-Communist policy in Asia. They helped supply McCarthy and other Congress inquisitors like Senator Pat McCarran of Nevada with often false information, which led to Lattimore losing his job as director of the Walter Page School of International Affairs at Johns Hopkins University.

Part of the attack was directed at the Institute of Pacific Relations, a leading research institution on the Far East headed by Lattimore, which attracted the venom of China lobbyist Alfred C. Kohlberg, who had made a fortune from sweatshop labor in Chiang's China. In his book *Ordeal by Slander*, Lattimore noted that his inquisitors were "unwilling to seek to gain their purpose by the democratic and honorable method of open debate. To gain their ends—whether those ends are sinister, fanatical or ideological—they use the weapons of personal attack and character assassination. They are masters of the dark techniques of villainy. They are artists of conspiracy. They are embittered, ruthless, and unprincipled."[41]

The Lattimore affair was especially tragic because it deprived the U.S. government of a knowledgeable expert on Asia, who understood the strength of the revolutionary movements and opposed an alliance with reactionary regimes like that of Syngman Rhee in South Korea and Bao Dai in Vietnam. The purging of Lattimore and other China hands like John S. Service, John Carter Vincent, John Paton Davies, Oliver Edmund Clubb, and the marginalization of writers like Edgar Snow, Jack Belden, and William Hinton, sympathetic to the aims of the Chinese Revolution, led ultimately to the adoption of a foreign policy based on ignorance, with the result being catastrophic wars in Korea and Vietnam.[42] James Peck's study *Washington's China* points to a virulent and mind-numbing hostility toward Maoist China among even those on the dovish end of the national security establishment like George F. Kennan. They and their counterparts misrepresented China's expansionist proclivities, Soviet ties, and relationship with the rest of Asia, rationalizing in turn a major military commitment to the region Lattimore and the China hands had warned against.[43]

THE VICTIMS IV: FRANK OLSON

Errol Morris's 2017 Netflix documentary *Wormwood* focuses on the efforts of Eric Olson to uncover the truth surrounding the death of his father, Frank, a CIA biochemist who worked at Fort Detrick in November 1953.[44] The Olson family was told that there had been an accident and that Frank jumped or fell to his death from the 13th floor of the Statler Hotel in New York. In 1975, the CIA changed its story, and claimed Frank was unwittingly drugged with LSD. Eric later had Frank's body exhumed by a forensic pathologist, whose findings were inconclusive as to whether Frank had LSD in his system, and that he died from blunt force trauma to the head. The likely scenario is that two CIA hatchet men entered Frank's hotel room from a side door, struck Frank with a baseball bat, smashed the window, and threw Frank out to make his death look like a suicide.[45]

In 2012, U.S. District Judge James Boasberg dismissed a lawsuit by the Olson family on technical grounds, notably that the family had already been awarded compensation by the CIA, but stated that the "public record supports many of [the family's] allegations, far-fetched as they may sound." The CIA appeared to be following the modus operandi of its assassination manual published the year of Olson's death. It recommended drugging someone, hitting the person in the head with a blunt object and then throwing the body from a high place to make it look like a suicide. The manual also emphasized the method of the "contrived accident" which when successfully executed, "causes little excitement and is only casually investigated."[46]

Dr. Olson was involved with secret government experiments in drug testing, chemical and biological warfare, and the behavioral sciences during the early years of the Cold War. These experiments, which entailed collaboration with Nazi scientists under Operation Paperclip, resulted in the mistreatment or poisoning of animals and human guinea pigs, and led to the apparent adoption of germ warfare by the United States in the Korean War, which the U.S. government has long sought to deny.

Prior to his death, Dr. Olson cryptically told his wife, Alice, that he had "made a terrible mistake." Although we don't know exactly what he meant, he may have recognized he had placed himself in danger as a security threat, that his colleagues perceived him as unreliable and capable of exposing government secrets. CIA consultant Stanley Lovell referred to Olson as "having no inhibitions. Baring of inner man," meaning he had wrongly spoken out, violating the CIA's code of *omertà*.[47]

The Olson case exemplifies the intolerance for the slightest possibility of leakage and dissent during the early Cold War. After the New York District Attorney decided to reopen the Olson case in 1996, he was astounded to discover a number of odd deaths of people connected to the case, including former CIA director William Colby who died in a suspicious boating accident four days before he was scheduled for an interview. Eric Olson told the media that his father's coffin had "turned out to be a Pandora's box. It's no surprise that the

CIA's unethical human experiments would turn out to be linked to assassination. Once the value of human life has been cheapened, then murder lurks just around the corner."[48] These statements provide a powerful commentary on the corrupting influence of the Cold War.

The Victims V: The Hollywood Ten

Victor Navasky, publisher of *The Nation*, wrote: "If you want to scare a country, scare its royalty, and Hollywood is America's royalty."[49] The persecution of the Hollywood Ten—prominent screenwriters and directors convicted of perjury after being accused of membership in the Communist Party—and subsequent blacklisting of many film workers can best be understood in this context as an effort to strike fear in American royalty and reverse Hollywood's turn to the left in the 1930s and early 1940s. One scholar noted, "Virtually overnight the atmosphere in Hollywood became one of terror. Lives were wrecked, careers destroyed, marriages and families shattered as friend betrayed friend, sometimes after swearing devotion the night before."[50] According to journalist I. F. Stone, "The striking aspect of the Hollywood inquiry was the complete absence of any evidence that even one of the many films written and directed by the men under investigation contained anything which could reasonably be described as Communist propaganda."[51]

The October 1947 HUAC inquest of the Hollywood Ten (the eleventh victim, Bertolt Brecht, went back to Germany to avoid being jailed) followed extensive FBI investigation of alleged Communist infiltration in Hollywood, assisted by the anti-Communist Motion Pictures Alliance, headed by such figures as Walt Disney and Ayn Rand. The dean of the Hollywood Ten, John Howard Lawson, had produced films valorizing the defenders of the fledgling Spanish Republic in their fight against fascism, and the exploits of the Communist-led National Maritime Union in its efforts to deliver supplies to the Soviet ally in Murmansk during the Second World War.[52]

Dalton Trumbo, author of the antiwar novel *Johnny Got His Gun* (1938), participated in a radio series to educate people about the dangers of atomic warfare and condemned the Truman administration for acting in a warlike manner. He thought the USSR did "not represent a threat to the national security of the United States; there were no Russian troops in most of the places where U.S. troops were stationed; no Russian fleets in the world's great waterways, no Russian air bases, no Russian troops anywhere in the world engaged in putting down the movement of colonial peoples toward freedom."[53]

After his appeal was denied, Trumbo penned a political pamphlet, "The Time of the Toad: A Study of Inquisition in America," which denounced HUAC for flouting the Constitution and ushering in an epoch where the nation "turns upon itself in a kind of compulsive madness." HUAC, he said, had "accepted hearsay and perjury as evidence, served as a rostrum for American fascism ... acted as an agent for employer groups against labor, and set itself up as a censor over science, education and the cinema and as arbiter of political thought [while] institut[ing] a reign of terror over all who rely in any degree upon public favor for the full employment of their talents."[54]

Trumbo considered Americans for Democratic Action (ADA) liberals of the Schlesinger-type complicit with the inquisition as their collective "zeal was expended predominantly against the Communists. . . . When the battle is joined on a specific issue involving the lives and rights of existing men—as in the recent case of the Trenton Six [African Americans falsely accused of murdering a white shopkeeper]—these [liberals] abandon such earthy matters to organizations designated 'subversive' by the attorney general, engaging their own energies in spirited manifestos in support of the status quo antebellum."[55]

Following his blacklisting, Trumbo continued to write provocative screenplays under a pseudonym, winning the Academy Award for *The Brave One* (1956; written under the name Robert Rich) and other classics such as *Exodus* and *Spartacus*. Ring Lardner Jr., another Hollywood Ten defendant who ironically shared a jail cell with his inquisitor J. Parnell Thomas, who had been indicted on corruption charges, went on to earn an Oscar as screenwriter for the film *M*A*S*H*.

The disruption of the 1954 filming of *Salt of the Earth*, a movie directed by Hollywood Ten defendant Herbert Biberman, which was based on a real-life strike by Mexican-American mine and smelter workers in New Mexico who faced a Taft-Hartley injunction that prompted their wives to take over the picket line, showed the difficulty of producing socially conscious films in the McCarthy era. Congressman Donald Jackson (R-CA) called the film a "new weapon for Russia" in depicting the United States as an enemy of all colored people (a term often used at the time to refer to African Americans). Vigilante mobs attacked some of the actors and burned one of their homes; the lab company, Pathé, refused to process daily film prints; and the female lead, Rosaura Revueltas, was deported to Mexico. Once finished, *Salt of the Earth* was shown in only a few theaters nationwide. Reviews were quite positive except for that written by a young Pauline Kael, who was to become the longtime *New Yorker* film critic; she wrote that the film was "as clear a piece of propaganda as we have had in many years."[56]

RED SCARE IN POPULAR CULTURE

Historian Michael Denning points out that the anti-Communist purge in Hollywood helped "eradicate much of the radical culture of the Popular Front." By this he was referring to plebeian artists and intellectuals who had formed proletarian literary clubs, workers' theaters, film and photo leagues, Red dance troupes and revolutionary choruses, and published proletarian stories, poems, songs, and plays supporting social justice causes like that of the Scottsboro Boys (nine black teenagers falsely accused of raping two white women in Arkansas) and a miners' strike in Harlan, Kentucky.[57]

Popular culture in the late 1940s and the 1950s, by contrast, promoted consumerist values and anti-Communist themes, which Trumbo said were "calculated to provoke hatred, incite war" and "prepare the minds of its audiences for the violence and brutality and perverted morality which is fascism."[58] Fitting Trumbo's warning, Mickey Spillane's novel *One Lonely Night* (1951) depicted vigilante detective Mike Hammer rescuing a millionaire's granddaughter by torching the headquarters of Communists who had taken her hostage, boasting that he had "shot them in cold blood and enjoyed every minute of it. . . . They were Commies. . . . They were red sons-of-bitches who should have died long ago."[59]

Look magazine, which had a subscription base of close to three million, published an iconic piece by Leo Cherne in March 1947, "How to Spot a Communist," which noted that "because the whole Communist apparatus is geared to secrecy, it is not always easy to determine just who is a Communist. . . . To [him] everything—his country, his job, his family—takes second place to his Party duty. Even his sex life is synchronized with the obligations of the cause." The Communist, Cherne continued, was prepared to "use a dictator's tactics or lies and violence to realize his ambitions of a Soviet America." Communists "thought differently from other kinds of Americans. . . . They are men of weak personality . . . forceful, aggressive and ruthless."[60]

Cherne's remarks epitomize the stereotyping of Communists as a manipulative and alien force in American life poised to subvert society from within. That conservative Americans could be "forceful, aggressive and ruthless" was overlooked. Arthur Schlesinger Jr. suggested in *Life* that the Communist Party looked to the "lowest echelons of American society to harvest subversives" filling the "lives of lonely and frustrated people" who were provided with "social, intellectual and even sexual fulfillment" they could "not obtain in existing society."[61] Here we see Communism depicted as a form of social pathology, preying on the vulnerable, which could only be defeated through a complete societal mobilization against it.

Hollywood had begun making anti-Bolshevik films immediately following the Russian Revolution and in many cases received direct support from the Pentagon and FBI. The Soviet Union was stereotypically portrayed as "monstrously gray and pockmarked by labor camps" long after the Stalinist repression, and Soviet officials as wily, and lascivious while ordinary Russians were down-trodden, clinically depressed or drunkards, and even deprived love partners.[62]

The "Russians are coming" theme was well represented in films like *The Manchurian Candidate* (1962), in which U.S. POWs in the

Korean War are brainwashed and programmed as assassins, and Soviet agents plot the takeover of the U.S. government. In *Red Dawn* (1988), history is turned on its face as Soviet soldiers invade a small Colorado town and erect red banners and pictures of Lenin. They are confronted by a group of young men led by a former high school quarterback (played by Patrick Swayze) who wage guerrilla war in the model of frontier-fighters. *Red Dawn* became a cult hit in the military, which named the mission to kill Saddam Hussein after Swayze's team (the Wolverines). A teacher in New Jersey interviewed about the film found, however, that it reinforced his students' association of Soviets with "Reds," "stubborn," "oppression," "emotionless," and "vodka."[63]

One particular genre that flourished during the Cold War was the spy film. Dozens of Hollywood films depicted evil Soviet agents trying to steal military or scientific secrets, sabotage U.S. military installations, or plot against the government. Many others featured heroic CIA agents outmaneuvering their brutal KGB counterparts, who were depicted as the worst of all villains. Is it any wonder, then, that media pundits and politicians who grew up in the culture of the Cold War have gone crazy in the face of an ex-KGB man leading the Russian government and cannot help but refer to him as a thug?

RISE OF THE RADICAL RIGHT

The Cold War helped empower the radical right, creating the genesis of the modern-day Tea Party. Fred Koch, the father of right-wing billionaires Charles and David Koch, was an early member and intellectual of the John Birch Society, an extreme anti-Communist group founded by a Boston candy manufacturer, Robert Welch, in honor of an OSS agent and missionary allegedly killed by the Communists during the Chinese civil war. Modeled ironically after the Communist Party in its organizational structure, members of the society promoted conspiratorial views, considering even President Dwight Eisenhower a Communist agent.

In a 1960 political pamphlet, Koch claimed that "the Communists have infiltrated both the Democrat [*sic*] and Republican parties."

Protestant churches, public schools, universities, labor unions, the armed services, the State Department, the World Bank, the United Nations, and modern art, in his view, were all Communist tools. Koch wrote admiringly of Benito Mussolini's suppression of Communists in Italy and disparagingly of the American civil rights movement, promoting the impeachment of Chief Justice Earl Warren after the Supreme Court voted to desegregate the public schools in Topeka, Kansas, Koch's home state. "The colored man looms large in the Communist plan to take over America," Koch claimed. Welfare in his view was a secret plot to attract rural blacks to cities, where he predicted that they would "foment a vicious race war."[64]

The Cold War political climate was conducive to right-wing demagogues such as Billy James Hargis, a Tulsa, Oklahoma, preacher whose Christian Crusade organization promoted anti-Communist, anti-union, and pro-segregation policies. During the late 1950s, Hargis teamed up with Major General Edwin Walker, who had supplied right-wing literature to U.S. Army forces in Germany, to speak about the twin threats of Communism and racial war, reaching a wide audience because of financial backing from oil tycoons like H. L. Hunt. During one Hargis speech railing against President John F. Kennedy, Lee Harvey Oswald was apparently in the audience. In the 1960s, Hargis would change his message to focus on the evils of drug use and the sexual revolution. The many political and religious figures who associated with Hargis continue to shape America's conservative landscape today, including conservative talk radio hosts like Rush Limbaugh who borrow from Hargis's speaking style.[65]

WEAKENING THE WOMEN'S MOVEMENT

The Cold War had a negative effect on the women's rights movement as it promoted a rigid conformity with conservative gender norms and resulted in the persecution and silencing of radical women. Women were over-represented among defendants in federal loyalty cases.[66] Many stalwarts of the labor movement and Communist Party, which emphasized the interconnection between class, racial, and gender oppression, were further red-baited, blacklisted and jailed. Among them was Claudia Jones, a Trinidadian-born intellectual and the communist movement's chief spokesman for black women who was deported, and "the rebel girl," Elizabeth Gurley Flynn, who was purged from the American Civil Liberties Union (ACLU), which she had helped found, and spent two years in prison after having been prosecuted under the Smith Act.[67]

Some feminists who had been active in the Communist Party and labor movement later covered up or renounced their radical past in order to fit in better with the mainstream. The feminist movement in this way further lost its radical edge and connection with working-class women. A prime example is feminist icon Betty Friedan, the founder of the National Organization of Women and author of *The Feminine Mystique*, a bible for the 1960s feminist movement. As historian Daniel Horowitz has documented, Friedan suppressed her background as a labor organizer and radical journalist in the 1940s because she did not want to be stigmatized as a "Red." Her book *The Feminine Mystique* spoke to the interests of white middle-class women seeking career fulfillment, rather than addressing the plight of working-class women who had to work outside the home in demeaning and poorly paid jobs.[68] The feminist movement today, as represented by Hillary Clinton, Facebook's Sheryl Sandberg, and Lady Gaga, follows from this tradition, promoting women's rights absent any attempt to forge a broader political movement to challenge the power structure of society and empower all marginalized groups.

The Cold War and Black Americans—and Two Prominent Victims

McCarthyism also had terrible consequences for African Americans, slowing the growth of the civil rights movement by crushing a strong and vibrant progressive left in the black community. During the 1930s, black political activists such as W. E. B Du Bois, a pioneering scholar of Reconstruction and the slave trade, developed a radical political economic analysis of capitalism and imperialism as lying at the heart of racial inequality, and cultivated solidarity with anti-colonial activists and Pan-Africanists such as Kwame Nkrumah of Ghana.[69] Blacks were much more likely to be skeptical of programs like the Marshall Plan and Truman Doctrine: *The Crisis,* the NAACP's official publication, criticized the idea that the U.S. would liberate "enslaved peoples" in Eastern Europe, while "Washington, the capital of the Free World, for instance, is the most thoroughly Jim-Crow capital in the world." The Cold War and McCarthyism, however, placed pressure on black activists that led many to move away from a more radical critique and embrace the credo of anti-Communism and "American exceptionalism." For example, NAACP Secretary Walter White abandoned solidarity with anti-colonial activists, championed NATO and the Korean War, attacked peace movements as communist-inspired, and stifled criticism of American race relations at the United Nations.[70]

Historian Manning Marable pointed to a divide between working-class blacks who identified with Communists as the most dedicated proponents of racial equality and aspiring middle-class blacks who embraced the dominant anti-Communist ideology of the Cold War and began to distance themselves from leftist activists like Du Bois. As an independent socialist, he had expressed belief that the Soviets' "anti-imperialist positions promoting the necessity of African political independence from European colonial rule were genuinely progressive." The black liberation movement in turn "had to incorporate a socialist perspective," with blacks at the forefront in promoting peaceful coexistence with the Soviet bloc.[71]

Du Bois was to pay dearly for these views. In February 1951, after he ran for the Senate in New York State on the American Labor Party ticket, and "denounced the anti-Communist policies of both major parties," he was indicted as an "agent of a foreign principal" because of his antiwar work with the Peace Information Center in New York City. In November 1951, a federal judge dismissed all charges when the government "failed to introduce a single piece of evidence that implied that he was a Communist agent." Despite his acquittal, Du Bois's extraordinary scholarship was "removed from thousands of libraries and universities," and the U.S. State Department "illegally withheld his passport for seven years." As black public opinion moved to the right, NAACP Legal Defense Fund lawyers refused to assist Du Bois, with the central office contacting NAACP local chapters "with strongly worded advice about 'not touching' Du Bois's case."[72]

Du Bois's contemporary Paul Robeson was also deprived of his passport, subjected to extensive FBI surveillance, and called before HUAC on June 12, 1956, when he challenged his inquisitors. Asked about Stalin, Robeson said he wasn't there to talk about Stalin; that was a matter for the Soviet people. He then said he would "not argue with a representative of the people who in building America wasted 60 to 100 million lives of my people, black people drawn from Africa on the plantations. You are responsible, and your forebears, for 60 to 100 million black people dying in the slave ships and on the plantations, and don't you ask me about anybody please." When subsequently asked about Benjamin Davis, one of his closest friends who had been convicted of violating the Smith Act (against Communist Party membership), Robeson turned on his inquisitors further, exclaiming, "You gentlemen belong with the Alien and Sedition Acts, and you are the non-patriots, and you are the un-Americans and you ought to be ashamed of yourselves."[73]

These comments epitomize the defiant spirit that makes Robeson such a compelling historical figure. The son of an escaped slave, he had a remarkable career as a professional football player, actor, and singer (his signature songs "Ol' Man River" and "Swing Low Sweet Chariot" remain classics) while devoting his life "to fight for my people [so] that they shall walk this earth as free as any man."[74] He "recognized earlier than Du Bois that the rise in domestic anti-Communism would become a force to stifle progressive change and the civil rights of blacks." He was bitterly attacked for such views, resulting in the destruction of his career. To undermine Robeson's powerful impact among blacks, HUAC even solicited baseball legend Jackie Robinson to denounce him, something that Robinson came to regret.[75]

The leftist dissent in the 1940s and '50s that aroused such vicious attacks was played out again in the late 1960s with Dr. Martin Luther

King Jr.'s courageous dissent against the war in Vietnam. In his historic New York's Riverside Church oration on April 4, 1967—one year before his assassination—King eloquently proclaimed that he "could not be silent in the face of such cruel manipulation of the poor. . . . I knew that I could never again raise my voice against the violence of the oppressed in the ghettos without having first spoken clearly to the greatest purveyor of violence in the world today—my own government." The war was "a symptom of a far deeper malady within the American spirit, and if we ignore this sobering reality we will find ourselves organizing" committees to oppose other wars "for the next generation [and] attending rallies without end unless there is a significant and profound change in American life and policy."[76]

Vice President Hubert Humphrey; the *New York Times, Time, Newsweek,* the *Washington Post* and *Life;* Ralph Bunche, Nobel Laureate and United Nations diplomat; and Roy Wilkins, NAACP director, were among those to attack King for his stand. *Life* stated: "Much of his speech was a demagogic slander that sounded like a script for Radio Hanoi." In the view of scholar Edward P. Morgan, these media responses to King "echoed their unquestioned support for the war's ideological justification."[77] The *Times* called King's effort to link civil rights and opposition to the war a "disservice to both," and in *Reader's Digest*, black journalist Carl Rowan accused King "of being an egomaniac who was under the sway of Communists."[78] A year later, King was shot and killed under suspicious circumstances. The attacks on him had helped to weaken and divide the civil rights movement, exemplifying the negative consequences yet again of the Cold War.

WOODY GUTHRIE: COLD WAR DISSENTER

Folksinger Woody Guthrie (1912–1967) is another compelling figure who defied the repressive culture of the Cold War. A supporter of Henry Wallace, Guthrie's worldview was forged by the poverty he experienced growing up in rural Oklahoma during the 1910s and by the Sooner Socialist Party, the second largest in the country outside of New York City. His music consistently voiced opposition to the injustices bred by U.S. foreign policy and warned about the threat of nuclear annihilation.[79]

Woody thought little of President Truman, of whom he sang, "Don't like my trade unions; don't like organized labor, don't like the Communist Party, don't like the human race."[80] In Woody's view, the Republicans and Democrats are "all out for one thing, which is to rake in big stacks of profits for the gambler that owns the House and the Senate Chamber too."[81]

In "Henry Wallace Man," Woody sang that he had "felt bad when Truman drove Henry from his seat, the Senate bunch and the Congress gang, they call you silly names, because you worked your fields of peace, and not in their gambling games"—gambling with the fate of all of humanity, that is, by threatening nuclear war. "You wanted peace with the Russians, and you wanted all colors free."[82]

In July 1946, Woody wrote a song to protest the U.S. backing of Chiang Kai-shek in terms similar to some of the China specialists purged by Senator McCarthy. Woody asked Mr. Chiang if he remembered "the exact number of common workers that you murdered, is there a record, is there a paper, is there a number of dead and wounded. . . . Count all the peasants, count all the unionists, count all the students, count all the radicals. . . . Shyang Shgagy Shye, Runnerdog Chyange Kai Shek, ya kild too many millions, cowerd dog shiang Kaie Shek."[83]

Six years later, Guthrie depicted South Korea's anti-Communist leader Syngman Rhee in similar terms in "Mr. Sickyman Ree."[84] This song went along with other anti-Korean War ballads such as "Talking Korean Blues" and "Hey General Mackymacker" (1952), where Woody wrote: "Ho, ho Mister Lovvitt [reference to Defense Secretary Robert Lovett], that blizzard sure did bite [reference to cold winter]; I don't see you packin' a pack, where you marched us here to die? Man are you walking or are you running? Hey Diggedy Mackymaker, sez Christmas I'll walk home, but you did not say which Christmas. Boy I'd just like to know will I be walking or will I be running? If we atom bomb these communists [as MacArthur had advocated], and then they atom bomb us, nobody will be running."[85]

This antiwar song conveyed Woody's deep anxiety about the prospects of nuclear annihilation and his concern for U.S. soldiers who had been sent on suicide missions by hubristic leaders who didn't assume any risk to themselves and misled the public in proclaiming imminent victory. Woody's songs more broadly convey the triumph of independent thinking and humanity in the face of Cold War barbarism and hysteria. His was a principled dissent that deserves to be remembered at a time when the political culture of the Cold War threatens to reemerge.

CHAPTER 6

A War on the Global South: The Cold War in the Third World

In 1993, the U.S. Congress passed legislation signed by President Bill Clinton authorizing a $100 million Victims of Communism Museum, which was supposed to commemorate the estimated 100 million who died in the "unprecedented imperial Communist holocaust" called the Cold War. Backed by liberal senators Joseph Lieberman and Joe Biden, the plans called for the re-creation of the Soviet Gulag, a hall of infamy featuring Communist dictators, a torture room from the Hanoi Hilton, a cell from Castro's infamous Isle of Pines, and hall of heroes featuring statues of anti-Communist heroes like Ronald Reagan and Margaret Thatcher. As historian Jon Wiener points out, the Victims of Communism Museum was never built because many in the public saw through its distorted view of history, which inflated the number of deaths bred by Communist regimes—including the killing of Nazi collaborators and victims of famines which also occurred in capitalist nations—while ignoring the reasons many supported Communism and extensive crimes of anti-Communist regimes and U.S. imperialism.[1]

In his Bancroft Prize–winning *The Global Cold War: Third World Intervention and the Making of Our Time*, historian Odd Arne Westad argues that rather than representing an epic struggle of good versus evil, or era of "long peace" as one triumphalist historian depicted it, the Cold War actually was an extension of the age of colonialism. The United States "empire of liberty" now vied for power and control of the Third World with the Soviet "empire of justice," propping up proxy regimes and establishing a network of military bases that helped secure access to strategic resources. Superpower competition and neocolonial interference in turn warped democratic development and intensified or sparked new ethnic conflict, resulting in failed states that would provide a hub for terrorism in the twenty-first century.[2]

Echoing the new "Great Game" thesis, depicting the two superpowers vying for world supremacy by trampling on state sovereignty and human rights, Noam Chomsky has emphasized that for the Soviets the Cold War was primarily a war against the people of Eastern Europe and for the United States it was a war on the Third World justified under the pretext of fighting Communism. Chomsky writes that the policies pursued within the Cold War framework served to entrench a "particular system of domestic privilege and coercion" on both sides and were "unattractive to the general population," which could only accept them through propaganda designed to instill the fear of an evil enemy "dedicated to its destruction." While supporting "miserable tyrants and gangsters" such as Mengistu in Ethiopia and the neo-Nazi Argentine generals, Soviet foreign policy did at least offer support to targets of U.S. subversion and attack, thus impeding the designs of the one truly global power, and engaged in some heroic actions, such as supporting anti-apartheid activists in South Africa.[3]

Historian William Blum estimates that in the name of fighting a moral crusade against Communism, the United States carried out "extremely serious interventions" in over seventy nations during the Cold War. U.S. methods included subsidizing political candidates and manipulating elections, financing literary journals and spreading propaganda, sponsoring private armies sometimes financed through the drug trade, coups d'état and assassination, copious arms shipments, military and police training, wide-scale surveillance, sponsoring black-flag terrorist attacks blamed on left-wing groups to discredit them, and chemical and biological warfare and economic sabotage, along with conventional military interventions and bombing. The CIA was adept at using proxies to ensure plausible deniability, many of whom were discarded or died later under mysterious circumstances.[4]

When Gorbachev said "The Cold War made losers of us all," surely the biggest losers were countries in the Third World in which millions of civilians were killed, thousands more subjected to unjust imprisonment and torture, and the prospects for independent development eroded. Eqbal Ahmad sums this up well in his essay "The Cold War from the Standpoint of Its Victims," which should be required reading for citizens who seek a just U.S. foreign policy. Ahmad estimates that some "21 million people died, uncounted millions were wounded, and more than a hundred million were rendered refugees by . . . the limited, invisible, forgotten, and covert wars of the 1945–1990 period" as the United States took the lead in an "arms race [that] had no parallel in history. One superpower became so concentrated on inventing and producing weapons that it lost to junior partners, like Japan and Germany, the art of peacetime production. Another superpower—or so it was designated—literally went broke trying to play catch-up." The addiction to armaments "spread to poverty-stricken Third World countries and the indulgently rich petroleum producers of the Middle East, raising the costs of multiple wars . . . to astronomical proportions" as endemic poverty and underdevelopment persisted.[5]

Barbarism Unleashed 1: The Korean War

The Cold War first became hot in Greece and then Korea. One of the most barbarous wars in history, it resulted in the death of 36,574 Americans and three to four million Koreans, including one out of every nine North Koreans, according to a UN estimate.[6] Pablo Picasso's painting *Massacre in Korea* (1951) captured much about the war's horrors in depicting a group of robot-like soldiers descending on a village—thought to be Sinchon in South Hwangae Province, North Korea—and preparing to execute women and children suspected of sheltering guerrilla combatants.

The roots of the Korean War lay in the arbitrary division of Korea at the 38th Parallel after the Second World War. The Soviets occupied the North and the United States the South. Each side wanted to reunify the country under its own control. When fighting broke out in June 1950, *Time* claimed that "Russia's latest aggression had united the U.S.—and the U.N.—as nothing else could," quoting a thirty-seven-year-old resident of Sycamore, Illinois, who supported the war on the grounds that "we had to take some kind of action against the Russians."[7] Senator Lyndon B. Johnson threatened nuclear attack on the Soviet Union because, he said, "We are tired of fighting your stooges." Soviet leaders, however, reluctantly sanctioned the North Korean invasion, which had resulted from South Korea's provocation, and Stalin made the former pay for military hardware.[8]

Charles K. Armstrong's scholarship shows that North Korea experienced a genuine social revolution in the years 1945–50, which was driven from the top down as well as the bottom up. Though the liberating aspects of this revolution were compromised by the establishment of a repressive police state and personality cult around Kim Il-Sung, North Korea was not the puppet of the Soviet Union or China as the U.S. public was told, and had progressive features such as a land reform program that benefitted over 700,000 households.[9]

South Korea under Syngman Rhee by contrast stifled social reform and relied heavily on Japanese collaborators, in part because Rhee had been out of the country for over forty years when Kim had led the anti-colonial resistance in Manchuria. When strikes and demonstrations erupted, Rhee deployed his U.S.-trained police and constabulary forces to brutal effect, jailing and killing tens of thousands of people before the Korean War officially broke out.[10] Pak Wan-so, a South Korean writer who faced imprisonment and torture by police, commented, "They called me a red bitch. Any red was not considered human. . . . They looked at me as if I was a beast or a bug. . . .Because we weren't human, we had no rights."[11]

The scale of repression in South Korea at this time far surpassed that of North Korea. In Mokpo seaport, the bodies of prisoners who had been shot were left on people's doorsteps as a warning in what became known as a "human flesh distribution case." A government official defended the practice saying they were the most "vile of Communists."[12] After a rebellion erupted on the southern island of Cheju-do in 1948, U.S.-backed units aided by aerial reinforcements and spy planes swept over the mountains, waging "an all-out guerrilla extermination campaign," as Everett Drumwright of the U.S. embassy characterized it, resulting in the death or displacement of a third of the population.[13]

When North Korea invaded the South in June 1950 (after ample South provocation), it looked like the Korean People's Army (KPA) would prevail, but the U.S.-UN forces managed to reverse the KPA blitzkrieg at the Battle of Pusan Perimeter. In mid-September, General MacArthur engineered an amphibious landing behind enemy lines at Inchon. After retaking Seoul, a town "literally shot to hell," the U.S.-U.N. forces occupied North Korea where they perpetrated what one contemporary termed a "nauseating reign of terror." They hanged captured North Korean soldiers on ground-posts and tied up POWs and threw them off a bridge to drown in the Sok Dang River, partly in retaliation for North Korean atrocities such as the execution of U.S. POWs. Francis Hill, an Army colonel in the civil assistance office, reported in November 1950 that South Korean soldiers would periodically go "commie hunting" and "drag former Communists (or suspects) and their families from their villages," an example of the dehumanizing rhetoric of the Cold War that rationalized the commission of large-scale atrocities.[14]

After MacArthur took the offensive toward the Yalu, the People's Republic of China (PRC) sent troops to assist the DPRK for supporting its revolution, and to ensure a strategic buffer to its south. Chinese soldiers endured nearly one million casualties, including Mao Zedong's son, Anying. From air bases in Okinawa and naval aircraft carriers, the U.S. Air Force launched over 698,000 tons of bombs (compared to 500,000 in the entire Pacific theater in the Second World War) over North Korea, which was left, in Maj. Gen. Emmett O'Donnell Jr.'s words, a "terrible mess." Eighteen out of twenty-two cities were obliterated, including 75 percent of Pyongyang and 100 percent of Sinuiju.[15] Gen. Curtis LeMay, head of the Strategic Air Command during the Korean War, later told an interviewer:

> We slipped a note kind of under the door into the Pentagon and said, "Look, let us go up there . . . and burn down five of the biggest towns in North Korea—and they're not very big—and that ought to stop it." Well, the answer to that was four or five screams—"You'll kill a lot of non-combatants," and "It's too horrible." Yet over a period of three years or so . . . we burned down *every* town in North Korea and South Korea, too. . . . Now, over a period of three years this is palatable, but to kill a few people to stop this from happening—a lot of people can't stomach it.[16]

These comments epitomize the barbarism of the Korean War, whose history has been suppressed in popular memory. The Koje-do POW camp, twenty miles southwest of Pusan, was the site of atrocities reminiscent of Abu Ghraib prison during the U.S. occupation of Iraq. According to a letter written to the Red Cross by two North Korean army colonels, the prisoners lived "day after day under unbearable fear and horror" and were subjected to sexual abuse.[17] To win a propaganda victory in the Cold War, many were forced into defection and tattooed with anti-Communist slogans like "Oppose Communism and Resist Russia" and sent on dangerous clandestine missions where they would usually be killed. When inmates seized a U.S. camp commandant in May 1952, Gen. James Van Fleet approved the use of tear gas, mounted machine guns, Patton tanks, and flamethrowers to quell the riot, leaving forty killed and dozens wounded.[18] Two other prison massacres occurred that year including in Pongam-do island prison camp, where U.S. troops killed eighty-seven North Korean POWs and injured 262 after they had refused to stop singing revolutionary songs and allegedly threw some stones.[19]

Another dark secret of the Cold War was the adoption of unethical medical testing on North Korean POWs, and the United States apparently experimented with bacteriological weapons by unleashing parasitic flies, anthrax, and diseases in North Korea and over

Northeast China. Scientists at Fort Detrick had developed a capacity for producing and delivering bacteriological weapons through expertise acquired secretly from Japanese scientists such as Gen. Shiro Ishii, commander of the Kwantung Army's Unit 731, whose human experiments in the Second World War had killed an estimated 585,000 Chinese. According to geneticist Masataka Mori, there were striking similarities between the diseases and weapons used by the Japanese military in China in the Second World War and those allegedly deployed by the United States against targets in North Korea. "The bombs found on the Korean Peninsula were made of metal, while those used in China were ceramic," Mori stated, "but the symptoms reported in North Korea are very similar to those witnessed in China."[20]

In April 1951, President Truman recalled and fired General Douglas MacArthur for insubordination, fearing that MacArthur's aggressive policies would ignite a world war involving China and the Soviet Union. MacArthur, with support from leading Republicans, wanted to take the war into China and use every means, including nuclear weapons, to win the conflict.[21]

After MacArthur's farewell speech, irate Americans phoned their newspapers denouncing the "traitorous State Department," which planned to "sell us down the river to . . . the Communists." The Republican Party policy committee accused the "Truman-Acheson-Marshall triumvirate" of planning a "super-Munich" in Asia and abandoning "China to the Communists." California's freshman Republican senator Richard M. Nixon gave stump speeches asserting that the "happiest group in the country will be the Communists and their stooges…. The president has given them what they always wanted, MacArthur's scalp." MacArthur, said Nixon, had been fired simply because "he had the good sense and patriotism to ask that the hands of our fighting men in Korea be untied." This right-wing theme was later applied to scapegoat peace activists and liberal politicians for America's defeat in Vietnam. After sponsoring a Senate resolution condemning Truman's action, Nixon received six hundred telegrams in less than twenty-four hours. All commended him, the largest spontaneous reaction he'd ever seen, which in turn helped catapult him toward the White House.[22] The whole episode provides a revealing window into the political culture of the Cold War that resulted in the violent destruction in Korea and subsequently Vietnam.

"Crushing the Left": CIA Regime Change Operations

Many articles in the mainstream media denouncing Vladimir Putin have noted his KGB background in order to highlight his allegedly brutal and thuggish tendencies. However, the same columnists never stigmatize ex-CIA agents in this way, even though the CIA undertook lawless actions during the Cold War that put the KGB to shame.

Former CIA officer John Stockwell has estimated that the CIA oversaw 3,000 major and 10,000 minor covert operations from 1961 to 1975 before some of its activities were reined in as a result of the Church Committee hearings.[23] Its exploits included hiring the Mafia to kill foreign leaders and stir up unrest, producing assassination manuals, and testing drugs on "expendables" who were later killed to ensure deniability. Historian Vijay Prashad notes that under the pretext of the Cold War, "the CIA and the old social classes crushed the left in many parts of the darker nations, enlivened the old social classes, and later, much later—found that they had created a monster they could not control," referring to the rise of Islamic fundamentalism.[24]

The ideological imperative underlying U.S. rollback policies was provided by conservative philosopher—and former leader of the U.S. Trotskyist movement—James Burnham, who called for the consolidation of a worldwide imperium by the United States to thwart the growth of Soviet totalitarianism and liberate "enslaved peoples."[25] Revolutions were said to be caused by the "fiendish ploy of subversives," the "superhuman fanaticism of guerrillas," and "outside aggression," though never, as Michael Parenti points out, "the moral and political bankruptcy of the social order under attack."[26] The 1953 coup in Iran was directed against the democratically elected Mohammed Mossadegh who was reviled for promoting the nationalization of Iran's oil industry. The CIA spread propaganda linking

Mossadegh to international Communism and paid conservative cler-
ics and disaffected minorities along with criminal gangs to foment
unrest. The consequence was the twenty-five-year dictatorship of the
Shah, whose internal security forces were built up by the CIA.[27]

In Guatemala, the Eisenhower administration similarly used the
climate of the Red Scare to orchestrate a regime change that benefitted crass economic interests, in this case the United Fruit Company,
whose executives had worked closely with CIA director Allen Dulles
and Deputy Director Robert Amory Jr. when they were corporate lawyers.[28] The hypocrisy underlying U.S. policy was vividly captured in
one of the most compelling pieces of Cold War political art, *Glorious
Victory* by Diego Rivera, which depicted Secretary of State John Foster
Dulles shaking hands over a pile of dead corpses with Castillo Armas,
who deposed Guatemala's left-leaning president Jacobo Arbenz. CIA
director Allen Dulles stands next to the pair, his satchel full of cash,
while Dwight Eisenhower's face is pictured in a bomb.[29]

Edward Lansdale, the prototype for the *Quiet American* in Graham
Greene's novel of the same name, was valued by the agency for adopting macabre tactics like the "vampire trick," in which "secret teams"
would snatch and kill a captured guerrilla, drain their body of blood
and place it on a jungle trail for intimidation. Lansdale had been sent
to the Philippines to suppress the leftist Hukbalahap, who were working to complete the anti-colonial revolution begun over fifty years
earlier. In 1952, the CIA provided $3 million to ensure the election
of Ramon Magsaysay, whom William Pomeroy, a Second World War
veteran who took up arms in support of the Huk, characterized as
one of the "most perfect puppets who ever danced on a U.S. string."
He eagerly backed U.S. policy in Vietnam and adopted economic
policies that catered to U.S. business interests that also donated to his
campaign.[30]

CIA subversion in Chile resulted in the overthrow of democratically elected socialist Salvador Allende in 1973. After Allende won
the 1970 election, President Richard Nixon had issued instructions
to CIA director Richard Helms to create a "coup climate," sponsoring propaganda and economic sabotage efforts designed to "make

the economy scream."[31] The International Telephone and Telegraph Company (ITT) supported the subversion, no surprise, as it had holdings of $153 million threatened under Allende's nationalization program.[32]

In December 1972, Allende gave an eloquent speech before the UN in which he discussed how his government had been undermined by U.S. policies designed to "strangle our economy and to paralyze trade in our principal export, copper, and to deprive us of access to sources of international financing." Allende said that huge transnational corporations, empowered by the Cold War, were waging war against sovereign states and that they were "not accountable to or regulated by any parliament or institution representing the collective interest." "In a word," Dr. Allende said, "the entire political structure of the world is being undermined."[33]

Less than a year later, a coup led by fascist General Augusto Pinochet was consummated. Facing execution at Pinochet's hands, Allende committed suicide, with thousands of his supporters killed or tortured at the Villa Grimaldi prison. Chile in turn became a "laboratory" for laissez-faire economics. University of Chicago professors descended on the country to promote deregulation, privatization, reduced taxes, reduction of trade barriers, and cuts to public services. These neoliberal policies resulted in record inflation levels within a year, rising cost of living, declining service in health and education, economic contraction, and the loss of 177,000 industrial jobs between 1973 and 1983. The main beneficiaries in this new capitalist utopia were foreign corporations and a small number of Chileans, with the country's debt exploding in 1982 when unemployment rates hit 30 percent—ten times higher than under Allende.[34]

The bloodiest episode in the CIA's history during the Cold War occurred in Indonesia; another laboratory for neoliberal economics, where the agency played a crucial role in the 1965 coup that brought to power anti-Communist General Haji Mohammad Suharto. He presided over the slaughter of anywhere from half a million to over a million suspected Communists and progressive activists as well as ethnic Chinese. The Communists were accused of plotting a coup, which Suharto used as a pretext to seize political power. The ground-work for the coup was laid with the CIA's secret 1290(d) program, predecessor to the Public Safety Program, inaugurated in June 1951 under Colonel Gordon L. Beach. It provided weapons and communications equipment to the police, and built up a paramilitary mobile brigade as a counterweight to the military, which was loyal to Achmed Sukarno, Indonesia's first post-independence leader who threatened to expropriate U.S.-owned businesses and plantations.[35]

In 1957, the CIA began funneling arms including bazookas to regional separatists and Muslim extremists—dubbed the "sons of Eisenhower"—in oil and rubber-rich Sumatra. The CIA station chief, Val Goodell, was a rubber industry magnate, and future CIA director John McCone, a driving force behind the campaign, owned $1 million in stock of Caltex's parent company, Standard Oil of California, which helped finance the rebellion to secure its own interests. The operation was exposed after a CIA contract pilot was shot down and taken prisoner after shelling an Indonesian village and bombing a church.[36]

Though documentation remains scarce, the CIA advised General Suharto in the apparent false-flag operation that brought him to power and contracted with mobs to burn down the Communist Party (PKI) headquarters in Jakarta. The CIA and the Pentagon also equipped army and police intelligence operatives that helped to orchestrate the anti-PKI pogrom with high-tech weaponries, and provided radio communications equipment and small arms packaged as medicines, developing computerized databanks of "subversives" targeted for liquidation.[37]

American Cold War policies in sub-Saharan Africa helped engender the overthrow of Pan-Africanist heroes such as Patrice Lumumba of Congo, and Kwame Nkrumah of Ghana, who in 1999 was voted Africa's Man of the Millennium. According to the State Department, Nkrumah's "overpowering desire to export his brand of nationalism" made Ghana one of the "foremost practitioners of subversion in Africa." Nkrumah was even "furnishing money and sabotage training to 'extremists' [Nelson Mandela's African National Congress] bent on overthrowing the white supremacist regime in South Africa," which provided missile and space tracking facilities and a naval base to the United States, and sold it uranium.[38]

Cold War pretexts further rationalized American backing of conservative autocrats like Haile Selassie (Ethiopia), William Tubman (Liberia), Ahmadou Ahidjo (Cameroon), and Joseph Mobutu of Congo who received money from diamond exporter Maurice Tempelsman in exchange for lucrative concessions in Katangan copper and diamonds (former CIA station chief Lawrence Devlin, who was implicated in Lumumba's assassination, became one of Tempelsman's employees).[39] The CIA station in Congo coordinated the suppression of the Simba rebellion led by Lumumba supporters and backed by "Che" Guevara, financing right-wing Cuban, South African, and Rhodesian mercenaries that Kwame Nkrumah likened to "thugs employed by the Ku Klux Klan." Scores of civilians were massacred, including those in the November 1964 "rape of Stanleyville," where journalists reported hungry dogs fighting over the corpses of the dead.[40] To ensure access to airfields necessary for counterinsurgency operations, the CIA trained the internal security forces of the Hutu-dominated regime in Rwanda, while allegedly paying off agents in Burundi to assassinate prime minister Pierre Ngendandumwe who was sympathetic to Lumumba and the Simba nationalists.[41] The killing set off years of ethnic conflict, culminating in a 1972 genocide.

The Cold War generally provided justification for heightened U.S. military and CIA intervention and deadly meddling in the affairs of Third World nations. It amounted to a war on the Global South as independent nationalist regimes were targeted for regime-change operations that benefited U.S. corporate investors, and local ethnic conflicts were often exacerbated.

COLD WAR AND COUNTERREVOLUTION: JFK AND CUBA AND THE KILLING OF CHÉ

U.S. Cold War policies resulted in the Cuban Missile Crisis of October 1962 that brought the world to the edge of a nuclear holocaust. The U.S. business community was incensed by Cuba's 1959 Revolution because the new Castro regime nationalized foreign-owned business and instituted land reform that undercut the United Fruit Company. President John F. Kennedy hated Communism, declaring in 1960 that "the enemy is the Communist system itself, implacable, insatiable, unceasing in its drive for world domination." His administration intensified CIA plans to mold an exile army to invade Cuba out of Miami, Guatemala, and Nicaragua, even though the CIA "had no intelligent evidence that Cubans in significant numbers could or would join the invaders or that there was any kind of cohesive resistance movement under anybody's control."[42]

Backed by citizen militias and defense committees, Castro's army ambushed the invading brigades, sank gunboats, and downed four B-26 bombers through anti-aircraft missiles. The Kennedy administration responded by trying to assassinate Castro, hiring the Mafia and using toxic poisons developed by CIA scientists, and by launching a $50 million per year paramilitary operation, Operation Mongoose, headed by Edward Lansdale, who was also deeply involved in Vietnam. Mongoose was designed to bring the "terrors of the earth" to bear against Castro, though it was acknowledged that "Castro and the revolution retain positive support of a substantial portion of the Cuban people. There are substantial number of Cubans . . . under the spell of Fidel Castro's magnetic personal leadership who feel a surge of nationalist pride in revolutionary Cuba."[43]

A Cuban official cited over 5,000 acts of terrorism, sabotage, and murder linked to Operation Mongoose, including an attack on an oil refinery and strangling a guard with rope.[44] To deter American aggression, Soviet missiles were placed on Cuban territory, partly also to counter the U.S. stationing of missiles aimed at the Soviet Union in Turkey. The result was the thirteen-day Missile Crisis in which cooler heads fortunately prevailed. Though the Kennedys are often credited for urging restraint upon the military, the entire crisis could have been averted if the CIA's Office of National Intelligence Estimates prediction had been heeded: Castro's response to sabotage would be an "increase of internal security controls, political moves against the U.S. and requests to the Soviets for assistance in defense."[45]

Afterward, Senator Barry Goldwater (R-AZ) declared that he was "appalled the president had made any sort of concession to the Soviets ... and angry that we had forfeited our right to invade Cuba."[46] Kennedy is most lauded in liberal circles for promoting the Alliance for Progress, a large-scale aid program in Latin America modeled after the Marshall Plan, whose underlying goal was to prevent the growth of worker-peasant socialism. Advancing a top-down vision of social change centered on the growth of the middle class, the Alliance promoted harsh labor reforms breeding inevitable resistance, which the Kennedy administration helped suppress through generous financing of internal security forces. Historian Stephen Rabe notes that there were military coups against six elected presidents in Latin America during Kennedy's presidency resulting in the installation of regimes that carried out vicious campaigns against civilians.[47]

In one of the lesser known cases, Alliance for Progress aid helped empower the Bolivian military and regime of Victor Paz Estenssoro. CIA station chief Larry Sternfield characterized him as pro-Nazi, and his secret police chief, Claudio San Román, ran torture chambers with "skin, blood, arms, legs and blood on the wall." Estenssoro's staunchest supporters were liberals like Arthur Schlesinger Jr., the Harvard historian and Kennedy adviser; Teodoro Moscoso, chief Alliance administrator; and U.S. ambassador Ben Stephansky. All were strong advocates of economic austerity measures that led to large-scale job loss and the deterioration of already poor working conditions in the tin mines. Rather than considering these reforms anti-labor, they were seen to restore "balance against excessive and anarchical influence" in the unions and helping to "get rid of the commies." Historian Thomas Field, quoting a Bolivian expert, notes that Stephansky "liked to fancy himself as an unbiased liberal, and perhaps deep down he was. Between smiles and handshakes, he did more damage than all his boorish predecessors: Texans who smelled like cattle, screwballs who collected lighters and unimaginative bureaucrats."[48]

Ernesto "Ché" Guevara, the Argentine doctor who played a key role in the Cuban Revolution, considered the Alliance a policy to bring Latin American economies in line with the interests of the monopolies. The aid allowed for the cheaper extraction of raw materials through the building of road infrastructure and the keeping of labor costs down, while "lessening internal discontent in each Latin American country by making minor concessions to the people . . . on condition that these countries surrender their interests completely and renounce their own development."[49] While trying to export revolution to Bolivia, Ché was hunted down and assassinated by CIA-backed military forces that had been empowered under Kennedy's policies. This marked a major turning point in the Cold War since Ché represented the hopes of radical, anti-capitalist movements worldwide.[50]

Cold War Barbarism II: The Indochina Wars

As one of the two major wars fought by the United States during the Cold War, the war in Vietnam left a legacy of death and devastation. Some 3.8 Vietnamese were killed, and more than 14 million people became refugees. About 15.5 million tons of bombs, ground and naval munitions landed on Vietnam, more than double the air and ground munitions the United States used in all of the Second World War, and more than 18 million gallons of poisonous herbicides including Agent Orange were sprayed over South Vietnam.[51]

The conflict is often seen through the lens of the Cold War, and blamed on the aggressive and expansionist policies of the Soviet Union—and later China. Although this official story is repeated ad nauseam, it is untrue. The Vietnamese struggle against France was underway decades before any material aid was sent by the Soviet Union or China, and the Vietnamese had a long history of conflict with an aggressive China before the Communist Revolution triumphed in 1949, and later in 1979 when the regime there invaded northern Vietnam, having been given a green light by the Carter administration.

The war in Vietnam was really an example of U.S. imperialism, which adopted the veneer of a moral crusade during the Cold War reminiscent of the civilizing mission of empires past. The primary drivers of the war were the dominant social classes whose underlying aim was "to make the world safe" for multinational corporations, as historian Michael Parenti notes, and to "prevent alternative, independent, self-defining nations from emerging . . . that might threaten" U.S. control and provide a model for other nations to follow.[52] As in South Korea, American policy-planners had hoped to convert South Vietnam into a base for regional military operations, a market for U.S. investments, and supplier of rice, lumber, rubber, and other vital goods to Japan, America's junior partner in the Cold War.[53]

Following its epic defeat of the French, which had been buttressed by over $2 billion in U.S. military aid, Vietnam was partitioned along the 17th Parallel under the terms of the 1954 Geneva Accords. Communist leader Ho Chi Minh was allowed to rule in the North and free elections were to take place in the South after two years. Recognizing that Ho would receive 80 percent of the vote, the Eisenhower administration never signed the Accords and instead established the Southeast Asia Treaty Organization (SEATO) to protect the so-called free territory in the South, which would be treated as a sovereign nation.[54] The United States in turn set about building a client regime under Ngo Dinh Diem, a Catholic anti-Communist, who immediately began repressing all opposition, including remnants of the pro-Communist Vietminh that had resettled in the South following victory over France.

In 1959 Diem passed legislation allowing for the execution of regime opponents after military trial; a year later the National Liberation Front (NLF) was officially established, which sought to overthrow the Diem regime and reunify Vietnam under Ho Chi Minh's leadership. Following Buddhist immolations in protest against the injustice of the regime, the Kennedy administration sanctioned the overthrow of Diem in 1963, an action that backfired and furthered political instability. The United States came to support Nguyen Cao Ky, a man described by Ambassador Maxwell Taylor as having all the qualities of a successful juvenile gang leader, and Nguyen Van Thieu, whose top power broker, General Dang Van Quang, was heavily involved in the narcotics trade.[55]

Under the 1964 Gulf of Tonkin resolution, Congress sanctioned the sending of U.S. ground troops, who committed many atrocities owing to their inability to distinguish enemy from friend, the dehumanization of the Vietnamese "commie gooks," and the pressure placed upon them to obtain high body count totals as part of a perverse policy designed by Robert S. McNamara. Torture in interrogation became systematic under the CIA's Phoenix Program, which was designed to eradicate the NLF leadership but resulted in the killing of thousands of civilians, as CIA director William Colby acknowledged.[56]

The worst atrocities resulted from the massive air attacks over North and South Vietnam designed to intimidate the population into submission. They caused huge bomb craters, environmental wreckage and displacement, and destroyed treasured historical monuments. Military analyst Bernard Fall warned that South Vietnam, which was bombed four times more than the North, was "threatened with extinction" as "the countryside literally dies under the blows of the largest military machine ever unleashed on an area of this size."[57]

Government lying was an essential part of the war in Vietnam, which reflected the corrupting genesis of the Cold War national security state. One huge lie that had a profound impact was the official story of the Tonkin Gulf crisis of August 1964. President Johnson and Robert McNamara told the public that the North Vietnamese had attacked U.S. warships on "routine patrol in international waters"; that this was clearly a "deliberate" pattern of "naked aggression"; that the evidence for the attack was "unequivocal"; that the attack had been "unprovoked"; and that the United States, by responding in order to deter any repetition, intended no wider war. These assertions were all untrue.[58]

At the Winter Soldier hearings in Detroit in early 1971, sponsored by Vietnam Veterans Against the War, Eric Herter, the grandson of Christian Herter, Eisenhower's secretary of state, spoke of the devastating consequences of American style techno-war, where an "entire culture" was being decimated by "an automated electronic and mechanical death machine." This killing was "one-sided, unseen and universal. . . . Those of us who testify . . . have seen the mechanical monster, the mindless devastation, the agony of simple people caught in the firestorm of our technological rampage."[59]

The military man at the helm of the "death machine" from June 1964 to June 1968, General William C. Westmoreland, was callous in his attitude toward Vietnamese civilian deaths and saw technical advances in Vietnam as inaugurating a new way of war. He told an army lobbying group in October 1969 that "on the battlefield of the future, enemy forces will be located, tracked and targeted almost instantaneously through the use of data links, computer-assisted intelligence evaluation and automated fire control. With first-round kill probabilities approaching certainty, and with surveillance devices that can continually track the enemy, the need for large forces to fix the opposition will be less important."

These comments convey the enthusiasm among military leaders for the kind of machine-driven war pioneered in the Cold War and later adopted in the Global War on Terror, both deeply rooted in U.S. cultural fantasies that all-powerful machines are being used for beneficial purposes. The results in Vietnam reminded the historian Larry Berman of Tacitus's famous saying, "They make a desert and call it peace."[60]

The horrifying consequences of the war in Vietnam extended to Laos and Cambodia, which were subjected to massive bombing campaigns that resulted in the deaths of hundreds of thousands of civilians, and displacement of countless more. Many of the facts about the secret war in Laos came to light in Fred Branfman's 1972 *Voices from the Plain of Jars: Life Under an Air War*, one of the few books written from the viewpoint of Indochinese peasants. Branfman was a twenty-seven-year old International Voluntary Service (IVS) worker who taught agricultural principles in a southern Laos village. After coming into contact with refugees from U.S. bombing operations in the north, he was shocked to hear their stories of seeing relatives burned and buried alive, their livestock killed, and their homes and pagodas demolished. One woman proclaimed her life had become like that of a "hunted animal desperately trying to escape their hunters. . . . . Human beings, whose parents carefully brought them into the world and carefully raised them with overflowing love, these human beings would die from a single blast." Another refugee lamented, "What terrible sadness, so many loved ones killed, because of the huge bombs the airplanes rained down upon us, so many loved ones forced to leave their native villages, leaving behind spacious rice-fields and gardens now turned to dust."

Seeking to find out where the bombing was coming from, Branfman infiltrated the top-secret Nakhon Phanom Royal Thai base, which housed giant super-computers in a heavily fortified underground bunker that received signals from electronic sensors and radar devices in order to select the targets for bombing. The atmosphere inside, Branfman said, resembled a stock-market exchange, where self-confident military officers ordered attacks on Laotian rice farmers without much second thought, never hearing the victims' anguish. Branfman later found out that the extensive bombing of Laos began in 1968 after a bombing lull over North Vietnam. Monteagle Stearns, deputy chief of mission in Laos from 1969 to 1972, told Congress, "We had all those planes sitting around and couldn't just let them stay there with nothing to do."

This rationalization sums up the evil of a Cold War military-industrial complex that forced U.S. national security managers to employ the death machinery somewhere, anywhere, based on bureaucratic imperative. The Laotian people and other Cold War victims were little thought about.[61]

"Metastasized Like an Undetected Cancer": Police Training and Torture

In April 2004, the American public was stunned when CBS Television broadcast photos from Abu Ghraib prison in Iraq showing Iraqis naked, hooded, and contorting in humiliating positions while U.S. soldiers stood over them smiling. The Bush administration, in damage-control mode, linked the atrocities to a "few bad apples," in a refrain echoed by media commentators like New York Times columnist William Safire who branded the perpetrators as "creeps." Historian Alfred W. McCoy details in *A Question of Torture: CIA Interrogation from the Cold War to the War on Terror,* how the torture methods at Abu Ghraib had been developed and perfected by the CIA and other military agencies during the Cold War, having "metastasized like an undetected cancer inside the U.S. intelligence community over the past half-century."[62]

During the Korean War, government officials became convinced the North Koreans and Chinese had brainwashed American POWs, including twenty-one who had defected and others who confessed to dropping pest-laden bombs. The CIA in turn began financing research into human consciousness that reached an annual cost of a billion dollars between 1950 and 1962, a veritable Manhattan Project of the mind. The research included unethical experiments with hallucinogenic drugs, electric shock, and sensory deprivation, yielding, as McCoy points out, a "new approach to torture that was psychological, not physical, perhaps best described as no touch torture." Engaged in and "under the pressure of actual field operations after 1963, psychological methods gave way to unimaginable cruelties, physical and sexual, by individual perpetrators whose improvisations, plumbing the human capacity for brutality, are often horrifying."[63]

Many of the new torture techniques were disseminated through police advisers working under the United States Agency for International Development's (USAID) Office of Public Safety (OPS), established by the Kennedy administration in 1962 for the purpose of "identifying early the symptoms of an incipient subversive situation," and maintaining "law and order without unnecessary bloodshed and an obtrusive display of the bayonet." Hundreds of foreign police were brought each year for training at the International Police Academy (IPA) in Washington, D.C., whose trademark was a two-story pistol range with cardboard targets dressed as "subversives." The culmination was a mock counterinsurgency operation in which students had to suppress a Communist disturbance and protect the ruling government from being swept from power. Most controversial was a secret bomb-making course in Los Fresnos, Texas, in which police were taught not only how to defuse but also how to make bombs.[64]

The police program was exposed in 1971 after Dan Mitrione, head of the OPS in Uruguay, was kidnapped and killed by the left-wing Tupamaro guerrillas. Eulogized in the press as a family man and a victim of Communist terror, Mitrione led riot control units in Brazil and Dominican Republic and was responsible for heinous human rights violations. The director of the Uruguay police stated that he had snatched beggars off the streets for Mitrione to use as subjects for teaching interrogation methods. He brutalized them before his students, torturing four to death. One of the attendees commented that the special horror of the course was "its academic, almost clinical atmosphere. His motto was the 'right pain in the right place at the right time.'" [65]

In 1973, after being met by a delegation of Brazilians who had been victimized by Mitrione's methods, Senator James Abourezk (D-SD) lobbied for the abolition of the OPS. However, many of its agents found undercover work for the Drug Enforcement Agency (DEA). Abourezk stated in an interview that OPS was a "program to teach the dictators how to torture," with the goal of fortifying U.S. client governments in the Cold War. [66] Sensory and sleep deprivation, bright lighting, extreme temperatures, and other torture techniques refined by the CIA were also used to break political prisoners in the United States, including former psychology professor and controversial advocate for psychedelic drugs Timothy Leary, and others in the 1960s who promoted free love, consciousness raising through drugs and peace, and challenged the Cold War national security state. [67]

A counterpart to the OPS was the U.S. Army School of the Americas, whose purpose was to cultivate top military leaders and enhance U.S. influence in Latin America. Nicknamed "the School of the Assassins," its graduates include dictators Manuel Noriega (Panama 1981 to 1989), Hugo Banzer of Bolivia (1970 to 1978), General Romeo Lucas Garcia of Guatemala (1978 to 1982), Policarpo Paz Garcia of Honduras (1978 to 1982), and Leopoldo Galtieri, who headed the Argentine military junta during a period when 30,000 people were "disappeared." Thousands of military officers serving the Pinochet (Chile) and Somoza (Nicaragua) dictatorships were also trained at the SOA, including infamous human rights abusers such as Hector Gramajo, a key architect of Guatemala's counterinsurgency war convicted in civil court of overseeing the torture of a U.S. nun, and Luis Alonso Discua, founder of death battalion 316 in Honduras. Representative Martin Meehan noted that if "the SOA held an alumni meeting, it would bring together some of the most unsavory thugs in the hemisphere."[68]

Originally based in Panama, the core of the SOA's curriculum centered on counter-insurgency, with courses in commando operations, sniper training, laying mines, psychological operations, and interrogation. Several SOA graduates stated that torture methods were promoted, including denial of sleep, isolation, and the administration of pain. A U.S. Army doctor dressed in green fatigues allegedly taught the students about nerve endings in the body. José Valle, a member of Honduras's Death Squad Battalion 316 during the 1980s, told Father Roy Bourgeois, a Vietnam veteran who has coordinated a yearly protest, that he "saw a lot of videos which showed the type of interrogation and torture they used in Vietnam. . . . Although many people refuse to accept it, all this was organized by the U.S. government."[69]

Valle's revelations directly counter the assertion of Robert S. McNamara, secretary of defense from 1961 to 1967, that the SOA served to "acquaint military officers with democratic philosophies and ways of thinking which they in turn take back to their nations."[70] They in turn exemplify the Washington connection to major human rights violations in the Cold War as synonymous with the growth of the capitalist empire. As Soviet repression eased following Stalin's death, studies have shown that unjust imprisonment, torture, and other human rights abuses were far more extensive in so-called free world nations than behind the Iron Curtain,[71] though no congressional representative has proposed any museums to commemorate these victims.

REVIVING THE COUNTER-SUBVERSIVE TRADITION: RAMBO REAGAN'S COLD WAR

After a brief period of détente in the 1970s, President Ronald Reagan revived rhetoric about an "evil empire" and aggressive anti-Communist foreign policy, feeding off conservative lobbying groups that helped revive the Red Scare paranoia of the 1950s.[72] Inspired by

Whittaker Chambers's testimony in the Hiss trial, Reagan had been a Cold Warrior during the anti-Communist crusade in Hollywood while head of the Screen Actors Guild from 1947 to 1952. As a former actor, Reagan lived most of his life in fantasy. He internalized Hollywood's depiction of Communism as a mirror image of fascism while extolling the possibility that super-weapons could save the United States from alien evil. Reagan in turn was the perfect embodiment of the counter-subversive tradition in U.S. politics underlying McCarthyite repression, which, as Michael Rogin put it, "needs monsters to give shape to his anxieties and to permit him to indulge his forbidden desires," including a lust for violence.[73]

Reagan's speeches brought together themes long prevalent in counter-subversive discourse, including the invocation of the threat of alien contamination and a secret diabolical plot by the Kremlin to sponsor subversion around the world, which denied the agency of local revolutionaries. Reagan further conjured up a titanic struggle between the forces of good and evil, which justified the reinvigoration of U.S. military power following the war in Vietnam.[74]

The Carter administration set the groundwork for the Reagan years by focusing its concern about human rights on abuses behind the Iron Curtain, and through a large-scale military buildup in its last two years that included production of the mobile nuclear M-X (Missile-Experimental), which required the construction of 4,600 hardened shelters for a warhead that had a 300-kiloton yield, twenty times stronger than that of the atomic bomb used to destroy Hiroshima.[75] Reagan increased military research and development by 31 percent from $13.6 billion in 1980 to $33.6 billion in 1986, initiated a major Navy buildup, doubled the budget for overseas military base construction to over $2 billion, and expedited development of new weapons like M-1 Abrams and M-2 Bradley tanks; Blackhawk, Cobra, and Apache helicopters equipped with side-firing missiles; and Stinger, Patriot, and Tomahawk cruise missiles.[76] To help bring the public in line, CIA director William Casey and his pliant deputy Robert Gates oversaw the creation of inflammatory assessments on Soviet intentions and Moscow's alleged role in international terrorism, including the attempted assassination of Pope John Paul II.[77]

In 1983, Reagan launched the Strategic Defense Initiative—SDI dubbed "Star Wars"—that aimed to create space battle stations from which laser weapons were to be refracted through large mirrors and deployed against incoming Soviet ballistic missiles and nuclear warheads.[78] Frances FitzGerald in her book *Way Out There in the Blue* highlights how the SDI helped Reagan lay claim to the role of a prophet. He was calling on the same scientists who developed the atomic bomb to achieve redemption by developing a defensive system that would protect the United States and enable it to resume its divinely ordained mission of expanding the frontiers of liberty. Reagan, however, was misled by Edward Teller, creator of the hydrogen bomb, who told Reagan in a September 1982 meeting that he could produce an X-ray laser in five years, when in fact it was many years away. Reagan shared with the "science hero of the Republican right" the tendency to slip into fantasy, and the SDI proved to be a billion-dollar boondoggle exemplifying the wasteful military expenditure of the Cold War years.[79]

Reagan's followers, with God's kingdom on earth now protected from the danger of nuclear war, took up a righteous crusade against Communism in Central America, where multinationals dealing in electronics, textiles, chemicals, agribusiness, and machinery viewed the region as important for moving manufacturing plants to enhance competitiveness against rivals from Western Europe, Southeast Asia, and Japan.[80]

Historian Greg Grandin in *Empire's Workshop* details the horrendous human costs of Reagan's Central American wars, and how they provided a testing ground for counterinsurgency and population control methods later adopted in Iraq.[81] A symbol of the devastation was the killing of 923 unarmed civilians by the U.S.-trained Atlacatl battalion in the village of El Mozote, El Salvador, the worst massacre in modern Latin American history. A U.S. adviser said that because "El Mozote was controlled by the guerrillas . . . you're not going to be able to work with the population up there, you're never going to get a permanent base there. So you just decide to kill everybody. That'll scare everyone else out of the zone."[82]

These comments epitomize the quasi-genocidal nature of the U.S. Cold War ideology in which one was better off dead than red.

In Nicaragua, where Reagan warned about the creation of a Soviet beachhead mere miles from Texas, the CIA organized remnants from ousted dictator Anastasio Somoza's National Guard to sabotage the socialist Sandinista government, which came to power in a 1979 revolution. The Sandinistas had a strong popular base, distributing land to more than 40,000 landless farmers, increasing production of basic food crops, giving universal access to health care and education, and cutting infant mortality by a third.[83] Supported by right-wing lobby groups and labor-intensive industries like mining, lumber, and agribusiness that were threatened by a rise in wages and nationalization measures, the Reagan administration supplied over $100 million in weapons to counterrevolutionaries, dubbed "Contras," who were also financed by right-wing Cubans, Argentines, Saudis, and the Israeli Mossad. A strategy of sabotage and terror was adopted to intimidate the population into repudiating the Sandinistas. In January 1984, CIA agent Duane Clarridge inaugurated a program to mine Nicaragua's harbors from vessels confiscated in drug busts. Two Nicaraguans were killed and fifteen sailors were injured and shipping during harvest season for key export crops was disrupted. The Sandinistas denounced the "escalation of acts of military aggression" before the UN Security Council, receiving majority support, and took their case to the World Court and won. The U.S. Congress passed the 1984 Boland Amendment prohibiting military support to the Contras for the purpose of overthrowing the government, though it allowed "humanitarian aid."[84]

Driven by Reagan's hyper-masculine Rambo complex, National Security Council staff led by Colonel Oliver North and Admiral John Poindexter continued to arm the Contras clandestinely through illegal sale of Hughes TOW and Hawk missiles to Iran, brokered through Israeli and CIA middlemen such as Richard Secord in exchange for American hostages, and through other criminal ventures. Once exposed, the Iran-Contra affair cast light on the existence of a secret government dominated by veterans of the Castro assassination plots and Indochina shadow wars that carried out illicit operations involving shipments of high-tech weaponry and drugs in the name of the Cold War.[85] As part of the blowback, U.S. cities such as Los Angeles were flooded with cocaine and weapons from the Contra supply network, fueling a growth in gang violence. Thirty thousand civilians died in the Contra war, thousands were wounded, and development was set back for decades with $9 billion in damage.[86]

Besides his exploits in Central America, the major highlights from Reagan's presidency included an invasion of the Caribbean island of Grenada on the false pretext that U.S. medical students were endangered following a left-wing coup, the bombing of Libya targeting the "mad dog" Muammar Qaddafi, the arming of right-wing guerrillas in Angola led by a man characterized by the State Department as a "monster" (Jonas Savimbi), and the backing of apartheid in South Africa under the benign sounding policy of "constructive engagement." Most foolhardy was a $2.6 billion CIA program to arm anti-Soviet Islamic rebels fighting the Soviets in Afghanistan through the Pakistani intelligence services (ISI), which helped create what historian Mahmood Mamdani referred to as an "armed jihad of which the Muslim world had not seen for nearly a century."[87]

The Carter administration, as we now know from an interview given by National Security Council adviser Zbigniew Brzezinski, actually worked to induce a Soviet invasion by arming the mujahidin beginning in the summer of 1979, five months before Moscow's intervention there, hoping to give the Soviets their Vietnam.[88] During the mid-1980s, lobbying by Representative Charlie Wilson (D-TX) and Senator Paul Tsongas (D-MA) resulted in the provision of over a thousand Stinger missiles to the mujahidin that were used to down an estimated 275 Soviet helicopter gunships.[89] Popular books and films have celebrated the Stinger as key to the defeat of the "evil" Soviet empire, underplaying local agency and the fact that most CIA assistance went to violent fundamentalist warlords, including Jalaluddin Haqqani and Gulbuddin Hekmatyar, a heroin trafficker known for pouring acid in the faces of women who did not wear the veil.[90]

Afghans overwhelmingly opposed the Soviet occupation with all its brutality, yet mujahidin fighters were strange liberators as they waged assassination campaigns against professors and civil servants, bombed movie theaters, kidnapped humanitarian workers, and even razed schools and clinics.[91] According to Chalmers Johnson, the CIA

> unapologetically moved to equip and train cadres of high holy tech warriors in the art of waging a war of urban terror against a modern superpower. . . . Before it was over, the CIA and USSR between them turned Afghanistan, which had been a functioning state with a healthy middle class, into a warring collection of tribes, Islamic sects and heroin-producing warlords. In human terms, the effort cost 1.8 million Afghan casualties and sent 2.6 million fleeing as refugees, while ten million unexploded land mines were left strewn around the country.[92]

This episode of U.S. foreign policy epitomizes the shortsightedness of the U.S. cold warriors who would support any rogue thought capable of inflicting harm to the USSR without thought to the human cost or long-term implications. When some of the jihadists turned against the United States because it stationed military bases on Muslim holy ground in Saudi Arabia, few Americans recognized the attacks as a form of blowback. Contrary to Reagan's Hollywood-inspired fantasies, the United States was not always on the opposing side of evil and military intervention could actually make the world more dangerous.

IN JUNE 2007, UNVEILING A Cold War memorial in Washington, President George W. Bush spoke about "the victims of imperial Communism," an ideology he said that took the lives of an estimated 100 million innocent men, women, and children, adding that "evil was real and must be confronted."[93] The 100 million number was drawn from *The Black Book of Communism* edited by Stéphane Courtois, whose publishers were subjected to a lawsuit by two of the contributors who said the 100 million number was inflated.[94]

The implications of Bush's remarks were clear in justifying U.S. foreign policies in the Cold War, war in Iraq, and confrontational policies toward other "rogue" states including Russia. Failing to offer

any reflection on the social conditions that bred the Communist revolutions of the twentieth century or social gains that resulted, Bush
helped advance the conventionally myopic view of the Cold War as
a righteous struggle against evil, which obscures the many victims of
U.S. imperialism and true history of the conflict.

The last four chapters have documented the repressive practices
and abuses bred by U.S. policies in the Cold War along with some
of its victims and iconoclasts. Rather than invoking nostalgia or
pride, this history should better be remembered as one of political
repression in the United States and reckless foreign policy intervention under the pretext of a moral crusade. Though the victims of
Communist government atrocities are certainly worthy of commemoration and the failings of Communist systems exposed, it is even
more important for the United States to look critically at its own fail-
ures and crimes. Otherwise we are doomed to repeat the past, which
we are in the process of doing. Some of the political elites driving
anti-Putin and Russia hysteria are old cold warriors and veterans of
groups like the Committee on the Present Danger and counterparts
that lobbied against détente then and now. They include neoconser-
vative and liberal hawks bent on securing control over Eurasian oil
and gas resources, as well as Eastern European emigrés.[95] Much of the
public remains susceptible to the Russophobic discourse and propaganda because they grew up amid the intense anti-Communist and
anti-Soviet culture of the Cold War that has warped their thinking.
The prospects for wide-scale resistance thus remain dim, though hope
appears to reside in a younger generation that looks to alternative
news sources for information, and is more sympathetic to socialist
principles because of the downward mobility they have experienced.

Avoiding a Third World War

In his political broadside *The Causes of World War III*, published in 1958, sociologist C. Wright Mills pointed out that economic prosperity in the United States was underpinned by a war economy. When unemployment rates rose or other problems emerged, the kneejerk response of political leaders, whether Democrat or Republican, was to increase military contracts, which could then be justified by exaggerating threats to national security or precipitating conflicts abroad.[1]

During the first Cold War, the Soviet Union was a perfect foil for the United States because the absence of political freedom could be played up for propaganda purposes. The true danger, however, was that Communism represented an alternative to capitalist industrialization, structured around a command economy, attractive to Third World nations that equated capitalism with colonialism.

Putin's Russia fulfills a similar function in U.S. demonology, just as the Soviet Union did—an object of derision and ridicule alongside North Korea and Islamic terrorism. Russia helps to reaffirm U.S. national identity and visions of exceptionalism and righteousness at a time of escalating domestic crises, and helps rationalize the expansion of NATO and maintenance of huge military budgets. The result is that we are again threatened with the outbreak of a Third World War, with the United States again bearing considerable responsibility.

Political scientist Andrei Tsyganov has pointed out that a Russophobic discourse in American media has resulted in part from the absence of an organized pro-Russia lobby capable of promoting Russian interests and narratives.[2] It has also flourished because of historical amnesia surrounding the Cold War and its pernicious effects. Popular mythology depicts the First Cold War as a heroic episode in U.S. history, with a few excesses such as Vietnam, but generally it was a sound strategy in confronting the "evil" totalitarian empire whose values were completely antithetical to those of the United States.

Commenting on CNN's twenty-four-part 1998 Cold War history series, considered the "most important production in CNN's eighteen-year history," historian John L. Gaddis said that in showing such Soviet atrocities as "the Red Army rapes in Germany in 1945, the crushing of the Hungarian uprising in 1956, the suppression of the Prague Spring in 1968, the invasion of Afghanistan in 1979 and the persecution of dissidents in the Soviet Union and Eastern Europe throughout the Cold War," most students would not only reject the accusation of moral equivalence but find it "laughable."[3]

Horrible as these Soviet actions may have been, Gaddis's assessment fails to take into account the horrific atrocities that the United States helped perpetrate in invading and attacking Vietnam; leaving North and South Korea in smoking ruins from an unprecedented bombing campaign; running secret covert interventions in Laos, Indonesia, Philippines, and Cambodia; and overthrowing elected leftist democratic governments in Iran, Guatemala, Brazil, the Dominican Republic, Chile, and elsewhere. Nor does Gaddis consider the U.S. role in using the Mafia to assassinate foreign leaders or CIA sponsorship of death squads and torture. The accusation of moral equivalence is not actually "laughable" if we take all this into account, along with the corrupting effects of the military-industrial complex on U.S. democracy and the U.S. role in fueling a near suicidal nuclear arms race.

Our assessment is more in line with Mikhail Gorbachev's—that the Cold War "made losers of us all." The first blow in the Cold War came under the liberal Democrat Woodrow Wilson when, in violation of its own Constitution and international law, the United States invaded the newly established Soviet Russia in 1918, a fact that remains virtually unknown to this day.

This intervention was followed by a policy in which the United States encircled the Soviet Union by setting up a network of military bases, reneged on the spirit of the Yalta agreement, and sent secret ex-Nazi and neo-Nazi teams into Eastern Europe to undermine pro-Soviet governments taking shape there. The United States at the same time spread anti-Soviet propaganda through Radio Free Europe, manipulated elections in Italy and across the Third World, and aimed missiles at them while the U.S. public was kept in fear that the "Russians are coming."

On the homefront, democratic standards were eroded with the establishment of a vast centralized national security bureaucracy, while scientific and academic talent was corrupted, and anti-Communist paranoia resulted in the spread of political repression. Dissenters who were red-baited, vilified, harassed, fired from jobs, and arrested for their political views were tragically among those most supportive of economic and racial justice.

Building off the repression following the Russian Revolution and the First World War, the Red Scare in the United States resumed in earnest right after the Second World War under the Democratic presidency of Harry S. Truman, five years before Senator Joseph McCarthy burst onto the scene. Attacks on Communists, leftists, and radicals were aided and abetted by liberals who made up what the eminent historian and Kennedy adviser Arthur Schlesinger Jr. called "The Vital Center" in U.S. politics. The anti-Communist attacks strengthened right-wing attacks on political dissent during the Cold War and destroyed prospects for social democracy in the country.

Much like today with Putin, the corporate media were at the forefront in drumming up public fears, resulting in a war psychosis. Since the Russian Revolution in 1917, the most prestigious and influential U.S. news source, the *New York Times*, has been consistently and relentlessly anti-Soviet and anti-Russian. What journalists

Walter Lippmann and Charles Merz wrote about the *Times* in their special study of the paper's reporting on that regime and country in the early years, 1917–1920, remains true today. It presented a profoundly biased picture of events that kept the public misinformed on every important question during the early Cold War, something that has continued for a century. Since the Russian Revolution, the corporate media, including the *Times*, have been faithful and uncritical stenographers for a powerful government elite that has enacted policies detrimental to large sectors of humanity, including a huge number of U.S. citizens.

One clear lesson we can draw from history is that the Russians have more reason to fear us than we have to fear them. We should not be fooled by alarmist claims about Putin and a new Russian imperialism, a form of projecting our own behavior onto someone else, something familiar to the history of American imperialism.

As this book has detailed, it was the United States that invaded the Soviet Union—not vice versa. It was the United States that encircled the Soviet Union with military bases during the Cold War and initiated many other provocative policies while intervening aggressively in third world nations under the pretext of fighting Communism. A study by Ruth Leger Sivard that analyzed 125 military conflicts from 1946 to 1981, 95 percent in the Global South, found "Western powers accounting for 79 percent of the interventions, Communists for 6 percent." Most of the latter were enacted around their borders with the exception of Cuba, which supported multiple African liberation wars against European colonial powers.[4]

After the Cold War ended, it was the United States that expanded NATO toward the Russian border in violation of a promise not to, and meddled in the affairs of nations on Russia's border, including Ukraine and Georgia, while overthrowing defiant leaders like Qaddafi in Libya—all of which alarmed the Russians. Today, it is the U.S. government that spends nearly $700 billion on defense, at least ten times more than Russia. And it is the United States that interfered in their politics and elections, as in 1996 when it enabled the election of Boris Yeltsin, whereas there is scant concrete evidence the

Russians affected the outcome of the U.S. election of 2016, despite much hysteria about it.

Russia has a checkered past as a nation as do we. However, it has never intervened militarily in Mexico or Canada, funneled expansive military aid to them, tried to manipulate their politics, or engaged in military exercises "across from El Paso and Brownsville, Texas," as conservative commentator Patrick J. Buchanan points out.[5] And Russia has often been open to diplomatic engagement with the United States. This is true of Putin, who cooperated with George W. Bush for a period in the "War on Terror"; Stalin at Yalta; Khrushchev, who supported an arms reduction agreement in 1955; and Lenin, who was willing to exempt specific U.S. companies from the Bolshevik nationalization decree in return for a diplomatic alliance (a policy advocated by State Department envoy William Bullitt but rejected by liberal icon Woodrow Wilson).

Keeping this history in mind, peace is possible if we change our approach. We are among those who believe—along with many others, including conservatives like Buchanan, Reagan's former ambassador to the Soviet Union Jack Matlock Jr., and former Assistant Treasury Secretary Paul Craig Roberts—that cooperation is in our mutual interest.[6] We can work with Russia to help solve global problems such as climate change, terrorism, and the threat of nuclear proliferation, and can cooperate economically, as with China, to our mutual benefit.

A related lesson we can learn from the Cold War is to be wary of media and political manipulation. Even Douglas MacArthur acknowledged that during the early phases of the Cold War, the Russians were decimated by the Second World War and not bent on reckless expansion. The U.S. public, however, was kept in a state of panic and fear owing to alarmist media depictions and political rhetoric that eerily echoed some of the anti-Russian propaganda promoted by imperialists in Britain and France going back to the age of Napoleon and even Charlemagne.[7] Alongside reactionary sectors in the Catholic Church, the main interests pressing for a Cold War confrontation were the arms manufacturers and aerospace industry, which feared a loss of production following the war. The CIA, however, found no threat of a Russian invasion of Western Europe. To sustain heightened military spending, it became necessary to scare and manipulate the public, while demonizing progressive politicians like Henry Wallace who followed in the footsteps of Abraham Lincoln in recognizing the benefits of cooperation with Russia.[8]

In the absence of an accurate historical consciousness, we are seeing history repeat itself, this time as farce. The United States had good relations with Putin when he first came to power; however, as he became more assertive, he was seen as a threat by elite interests bent on perpetuating predatory financial practices and controlling the Eurasian region with its oil and gas resources. The arms merchants were also looking for a new enemy after the end of the Cold War to supplant the threat of Islamic terrorism, particularly after the killing of Osama bin Laden. The media followed politicians in promoting alarmist stories about Russian imperialism, and played up Putin's human rights abuses (including his attacks on gays) while ignoring those of U.S. government allies. A false impression was created of a new tsar who threatened world security, whereas many of his policies are sensible in lieu of Russia's recent history and American provocations, and more popular than those of his predecessor.

By understanding the agenda underlying the demonization of Putin, and how the media help manufacture consent with the imperial designs and interests of the elite class to create false moral panic, we can avoid falling prey to the dominant stories and in turn repudiate recklessly dangerous policies. Alternatively, we can learn to thoroughly investigate issues, think more independently and critically, and then work across the political spectrum to build a movement for peace.

As the Bernie Sanders campaign, Occupy Wall Street, and spinoffs like the Democracy Spring movement have reminded us, the priorities of U.S. government elites in both the Republican and Democratic parties are not the same as those of the public at large. Greedy, ideologically driven plutocrats want open markets, control of world resources, and access to military bases that could enable the extension of corporate interests, power, and U.S. hegemony. The public at large wants peace, security, a healthy environment, and access to good jobs, which plutocratic interests threaten at every turn.

The vilification campaign against Russia today as during the Cold War fits very much within the elite agenda. It is designed to deflect public attention from our domestic ills by scapegoating a foreign nation, creating the perception of a military and security threat that can be used to mobilize public support for heightened military budgets and intervention. Imperial strategists like the late Zbigniew Brzezinski long held that control of Eurasia and its rich oil and gas resources is key to world domination, which a strong Russia could challenge.[9]

The history of the Cold War shows us the dangerous consequences of trying to rule the world through force, and arrogance underlying the assumption that "we own the world." We believe it is now imperative to learn from the history we have described in this book, and resist the propaganda leading us into a new dangerous confrontation that threatens world security and peace. We must educate ourselves and engage our fellow citizens, especially youth, and develop alternative programs that can help safeguard the latter's future, as the United States is beginning to come apart at the seams from years of imperial pursuits.

In 1795, James Madison warned:

Of all the enemies to public liberty war is, perhaps, the most to be dreaded, because it comprises and develops the germ of every other. . . . In war, too, the discretionary power of the Executive is extended; its influence in dealing out offices, honors, and emoluments is multiplied; and all the means of seducing the minds, are added to those of subduing the force, of the people. . . . No nation could preserve its freedom in the midst of continual warfare.[10]

These words sound prophetic in light of the corrupting effects on U.S. politics and society bred by years of Cold War and the War on Terror. Amid all the diversionary hysteria about Putin and alleged election-hacking, we believe that our only hope remains the development of a citizens' campaign for peace and justice along the lines of the anti-Vietnam War movement, one capable of restoring some sanity to our foreign policy. We must do everything in our power to try to stop the new Cold War, which threatens even more damage to humanity than the first one, started by Woodrow Wilson following the Russian Revolution and extended by Harry S. Truman & Co.

.

Notes

1. David Sanger, Eric Schmitt, and Michael R. Gordon, "Trump Gets an Opening from Russia, but the Path Is Risky," *New York Times,* December 30, 2016.

2. Joshua R. Itzkowitz Shifrinson, "Russia's Got a Point: The U.S. Broke a NATO Promise," *Los Angeles Times*, May 30, 2016; Chris Kaspar de Ploeg, *Ukraine in the Crossroads* (Atlanta, GA: Clarity Press, 2017).

3. Andrei P. Tsygankov, *Russophobia: Anti-Russian Lobby and American Foreign Policy* (New York: Palgrave Macmillan, 2009), 153; Alexander Dugin, *Putin vs Putin: Vladimir Putin Viewed from the Right* (London: Arktos Media, 2014); Eric Schmitt, "U.S. Troops Train in Eastern Europe to Echoes of the Cold War," *New York Times*, August 6, 2017; Wayne Madsen, "Washington's Civil Society: CIA Financing of Chechen and Caucuses Regional Terrorists," *Global Research*, May 6, 2013, http://www.globalresearch.com.

4. See Stephen Lendman, *Flashpoint in Ukraine: How the U.S. Drive for Hegemony Risks World War III* (Atlanta, GA: Clarity Press, 2014); Richard Sakwa, *Frontline Ukraine: Crisis in the Borderland* (London: I. B. Tauris, 2016).

5. Jerry Brown, "A Stark Nuclear Warning," *New York Review of Books*, July 14, 2016, http://www.nybooks.

6. William J. Broad and David E. Sanger, "Race for Latest Class of Nuclear Arms Threatens to Revive Cold War," *New York Times*, April 16, 2016; William J. Broad and David E. Sanger, "As U.S. Modernizes Nuclear Weapons, Smaller Leaves Some Uneasy," *New York Times*, January 11, 2016; Sally Denton, *The Profiteers: Bechtel and the Men Who Built the World* (New York: Simon & Schuster, 2016).

7.   John F. Harris and Bryan Bender, "Bill Perry Is Terrified. Why Aren't You? How an 89-Year-Old Cold Warrior Became America's Nuclear Conscience," *Politico*, January 6, 2017,   http://www.politico.com; William J. Perry, *My Journey at the Nuclear Brink* (Palo Alto, CA: Stanford Security Studies, 2015); Defense Intelligence Agency, *Russian Military Power: Building a Military to Support Great Power Aspirations* (Washington, D.C.: 2017).

8.   Lee Fang, "U.S. Defense Contractors Tell Investors Russian Threat is Great for Business," *The Intercept*, August 21, 2016, https://theintercept.com.

9.   See Dan Kovalik, with foreword by David Talbot, *The Plot to Scapegoat Russia: How the CIA and the Deep State Have Conspired to Vilify Putin* (New York: Skyhorse, 2017).

10. Karl Marx, *The Eighteenth Brumaire of Louis Bonaparte*, trans. Daniel De Leon, 3rd ed. (Chicago: Charles H. Kerr & Co., 1963).

11. Veteran Intelligence Professionals for Sanity, "Was the Russian Hack an Inside Job," *Counterpunch*, July 25, 2017, https://www.counterpunch.org; Patrick Lawrence, "A New Report Raises Big Questions About Last Year's DNC Hack," *The Nation*, August 9, 2017.

12. See William Browder, *Red Notice: A True Story of High-Finance, Murder and One Man's Fight for Justice* (New York: Simon & Schuster, 2015); Alex Krainer, *The Killing of Bill Browder: Deconstructing William Browder's Dangerous Deception* (Monaco: Equilibrium, 2017); Andrei Nekrasov and Torstein Grude, directors, *The Magnitsky Act: Behind the Scenes,* Piraya Films, 2016; Robert Parry, "How Russia-Gate Met the Magnitsky Myth," *Consortium News*, July 13, 2017, https://consortiumnews.com.

13. See Robert Parry, "The McCarthyism of Russia-Gate," *Consortium News*, May 7, 2017, https://consortiumnews.com; Robert Parry, "The Did-You Talk to the Russians Witch-Hunt," *Consortium News*, February 18, 2017, https://consortiumnews.com.

14. Dugin, *Putin vs Putin*; Krainer, *The Killing of Bill Browder*; Marshall I. Goldman, *Petro-State: Putin, Power and the New Russia* (New York: Oxford University Press, 2010).

15. See Guy Mettan, *Creating Russophobia: From the Great Religious Schism to Anti-Putin Hysteria* (Atlanta, GA: Clarity Press, 2017); Martin Malia, *Russia Under Western Eyes: From the Bronze Horseman to the Lenin Mausoleum* (Cambridge, MA: Harvard University Press, 2000).

16. Browder, *Red Notice*; Krainer, *The Killing of Bill Browder*.

17. Mettan, *Creating Russophobia,* 139.

18. David C. Engerman, *Modernization from the Other Shore: American Intellectuals and the Romance of Russian Development* (Cambridge, MA: Harvard University Press, 2003), 263–65.

19. See Frank Kofsky, *Harry S. Truman and the War Scare of 1948: A Successful Campaign to Deceive the Nation* (New York: St. Martin's Press, 1993), 293.

20. William Blum, *Killing Hope: CIA and US Military Interventions Since World War II* (Monroe, ME: Common Courage Press, 1998), 8; Frederick

L. Schuman, *American Policy Toward Russia Since 1917* (New York: International Publishers, 1928), 125.

21. Carl J. Richard, *When the United States Invaded Russia: Woodrow Wilson's Siberian Disaster* (New York: Rowman and Littlefield, 2012), 155.

22. See Olive Sutton, *Murder Inc. in Greece* (New York: Prism Key Press, 2013); Noam Chomsky, *Year 501: The Conquest Continues* (Boston: South End Press, 1993). For a sympathetic portrait of a key Cold War ally, Chinese secret police chief Dai Li, considered the "Asian Himmler," see Lt. Cmdr. Charles G. Dobbins, "China's Mystery Man" *Collier's*, February 16, 1946, 19.

23. Arthur Koestler, "Freedom—At Long Last," *Collier's*, October 27, 1951, 55.

24. Noam Chomsky, "Vietnam and U.S. Global Strategy" (1973) in *The Chomsky Reader*, ed. James Peck (New York: Pantheon, 1987), 250–51; also quoted in Noam Chomsky, *Deterring Democracy* (New York: Hill & Wang, 1992), 27.

25. Quoted in Fred Cook, *The Warfare State,* foreword by Bertrand Russell (New York: Macmillan, 1962), 175.

26. Sidney Lens, *The Military-Industrial Complex* (Philadelphia: Pilgrim Press, 1970), 1–2; Cook, *The Warfare State*; Gabriel Kolko, *Main Currents in Modern American History* (New York: Harper & Row, 1976), 327.

27. See Ellen Schrecker, *Many Are the Crimes: McCarthyism in America* (Princeton: Princeton University Press, 1998).

28. See http://victimsofcommunism.org/mission/history/.

29. Tsygankov, *Russophobia,* 55.

1. Anti-Russian Hysteria in Propaganda and Fact

1.   David Talbot, foreword to Daniel Kovalik, *The Plot to Scapegoat Russia: How the CIA and the Deep State Have Conspired to Vilify Russia* (New York: Skyhorse Publishing, 2017), ix.

2.   Maureen Dowd, "Bobby Sticks It to Trump," *New York Times*, August 5, 2017; Guy Mettan, *Creating Russophobia: From the Great Religious Schism to Anti-Putin Hysteria* (Atlanta, GA: Clarity Press, 2017).

3.   See Noam Chomsky and Edward S. Herman*, Manufacturing Consent: The Political Economy of the Mass Media* (New York: Pantheon, 1989); Edward S. Herman, "All The News that's Fit to Print (Part I): Structure and Background of the New York Times," *Z Magazine*, April 1998, http://www.greanvillepost.com.

4.   "The Putin Puzzle," *New York Times*, March 26, 2000. In June 2017, Masha Gessen in the *Times* accused Putin and filmmaker Oliver Stone of being Stalin apologists, which is not true. See Masha Gessen, "How Putin Seduced Oliver Stone—and Trump," *New York Times*, June 25, 2017.

5.   "Keeping Vladimir Putin on Track," *New York Times*, June 26, 2003.

6.   Philip Taubman, "The Risks and Rewards of Ranch Diplomacy," *New York Times*, July 20, 2001; Robert McFarlane, "What's Good for Russia is Good for America," *New York Times*, September 26, 2003.

7.   William Safire, "The Russian Reversion," *New York Times*, December 10, 2003; Mettan, *Creating* Russophobia, 271.

8.   "Putin's Old-Style K.G.B. Tactics," *New York Times*, October 29, 2003, A24.

9.   Nicholas D. Kristof, "The Poison Puzzle," *New York Times*, December 14, 2004. Kristof rehashes the right-wing theory of Jeane J. Kirkpatrick, Reagan's ambassador to the UN, that right-wing authoritarian regimes could be reformed but not left-wing ones. His claim that Pinochet ushered in economic success is false, as is the claim that he and Franco paved the way for democracy. In Chile, for example, the 1973 coup that brought Pinochet to power destroyed democracy.

10.   Steven Lee Myers, "No Cold War, Perhaps, but Surely a Lukewarm Peace," *New York Times*, February 18, 2007.

11.   Thomas L. Friedman, "What Did We Expect?" *New York Times*, August 19, 2008. For a better analysis, see Gerard Toal, *Near Abroad: Putin, the West, and the Contest Over Ukraine and the Caucuses* (New York: Oxford University Press, 2017); George Friedman, "The Russo-Georgian War and the Balance of Power," Stratfor.com, April 12, 2008, https://worldview.stratfor.com; Max Seddon, "The Rise and Fall of Mikheil Saakashvili," *BuzzFeed News*, October 28, 2013, https://www.buzzfeed.com. The passport of an American, Michael Lee White of Houston, was found on the battlefield, indicating to Russia direct American support for the Georgian cause.

12.   *Times* articles, for example, focused attention on Yanukovych's building of "pharaonic seaside resort" which was depicted as a "gargantuan folly of excess" justifying his overthrow. Andrew Higgins, "An Unfinished Ukraine Palace and a Fugitive Leaders Folly," *New York Times*, February 25, 2014.

13.   C. J. Chivers and Patrick Reveel, "Russia Moves Swiftly to Stifle Dissent Ahead of Secession Vote," *New York Times*, March 14, 2014.

14.   Mettan, *Creating Russophobia,* 288–90. In 1991, 94 percent of Crimeans had also voted to rejoin Russia in a vote that was annulled.

15.   Michael R. Gordon and Andrew E. Kramer, "Scrutiny Over Photos Said to Tie Russia Units to Ukraine," *New York Times*, April 22, 2014; "Ukraine's War and Europe's Passivity," *New York Times*, July 21, 2014; Editorial, "Russia and the Group of 8," *New York Times*, March 19, 2014; Steven Lee Myers, "Violence in Ukraine Creates Deepening Clash between East and West," *New York Times*, February 19, 2014; David M. Herszenhorn and Peter Baker, "Russia Steps Up Help for Rebels in Ukraine War," *New York Times*, July 25, 2014.

16.   Neil Macfarquhar, "Early Memo Urged Moscow to Annex Crimea, Report Says," *New York Times*, February 25, 2015; Oliver Boyd-Barrett, *Western Mainstream Media and the Ukraine Crisis: A Study in Conflict Propaganda* (New York: Routeledge, 2017), 63–65. A year after the Crimean referendum, 4 percent of residents said annexation with Russia was the absolutely right decision.

17.   Barry Grey, "New York Times Covers Up Fascist Atrocity in Odessa," World Socialist Website, May 5, 2014, https://www.wsws.org. The *Times*

reported that dozens died in a fire related to clashes between pro- and anti-Russian forces whereas the *Washington Post* acknowledged the fire was set by pro-Kiev forces. The *Wall Street Journal* accused Russia of committing the arson.

18. Roger Cohen, "The Suns of August: Flight 17: Ukraine's War and Europe's Passivity," *New York Times*, July 21, 2014. Sen. Saxby Chambliss, quoted in Boyd-Barrett, *Western Mainstream Media and the Ukraine Crisis*, 104.

19. Andrew Higgins and Michael Gordon, "Russians Open Fire in Ukraine, NATO Reports," *New York Times*, August 22, 2015. Left out was that the United States established a back-door arms pipeline through the United Arab Emirates (UAE) to Ukraine to help get around any bad publicity, something the *Times* and mainstream media failed to report, along with the use of Blackwater mercenaries.

20. Boyd-Barrett, *Western Mainstream Media and the Ukraine Crisis*, 71, 96, 130; Chris Kaspar de Ploeg, *Ukraine in the Crossfire* (Atlanta, GA: Clarity Press, 2017). An exposé of the East Ukraine rebels by C. J. Chivers and Noah Sneider, "Behind the Masks in Ukraine, Many Faces of Rebellion" (*New York Times*, May 3, 2014) spotlighted the background of a former Soviet commander in Afghanistan, whom the authors suggested could make for a "capable Kremlin proxy" though no similar exposés unmasked the neo-Nazi background of pro-government fighters.

21. Michael D. Shear, Alison Smale, and David M. Herszenhorn, "Obama and Allies Seek Firm, United Response as Russia Grips Crimea," *New York Times*, March 23, 2014. Not to be outdone, conservative columnist Ross Douthat referenced the "Crimean Anschluss" in "Our Russia Problem," *New York Times*, September 10, 2016.

22. Amy Chozick and Ian Lovett, "Clinton Ratchets Up Criticism of Putin and Backs Obama," *New York Times*, March 6, 2014.

23. See Orlando Figes, *The Crimean War: A History* (New York: Picador, 2010), 20, 491.

24. Editorial, "Russia's Fury over Montenegro and NATO," *New York Times*, December 4, 2015; Kathryn Stoner, "The U.S. Was Wrong to Think Russia Was No Longer a Player," *New York Times*, December 22, 2016; Figes, *The Crimean War*, 48, 49.

25. Editorial, "Sharing the NATO Burden," *New York Times*, February 17, 2017.

26. Ellen Nakashima, "U.S. Government Officially Accuses Russia of Hacking Campaign to Interfere with Elections," *Washington Post*, October 7, 2016; David E. Sanger and Shane Scott, "Russian Hackers Acted to Aid Trump in Election, U.S. Says," *New York Times*, December 9, 2016.

27. See Charles M. Blow, "Donald Trump and the Tainted American Presidency," *New York Times*, January 9, 2017; Charles M. Blow, "Putin Meets His Progeny," *New York Times*, July 10, 2017.

28. Thomas L. Friedman, "Donald Trump's Putin Crush," *New York Times*, September 14, 2016; Friedman, "Two Ex-Spies and Donald Trump," *New York Times*, September 21, 2016; Ian Schwartz, "Friedman: Flynn

Resignation Shows Russia Hacking Was on Scale with 9/11, Pearl Harbor," *RealClear Politics*, February 14, 2017, http://www.realclear.com.

29. Nicholas Kristof, "Did Putin Try to Steal an American Election?" *New York Times*, July 28, 2016.

30. Timothy Snyder, "How a Russian fascist is meddling in America's election," *New York Times*, September 21, 2016. Russian scholars more properly characterize Putin as predominantly non-ideological and a pragmatic realist in foreign policy with ambitions of reviving a multipolar world order. There is no large-scale repression or violence with the exception of the Chechen war.

31. Paul Krugman, "Useful Idiots Galore," *New York Times*, December 16, 2016.

32. "Russians Remain Confident in Putin's Global Leadership," Pew Research Center, June 20, 2017, http://assets.pewresearch.org. See Sara Joffe, "Many Young Russians See a Hero in Putin," *National Geographic*, December 2016, http://www.nationalgeographic.com.

33. Steven Lee Myers, *The New Tsar: The Rise and Reign of Vladimir Putin* (New York: Alfred A. Knopf, 2015). On historical perceptions, see David Foglesong, *The American Mission and the "Evil Empire"* (New York: Cambridge University Press, 2007).

34. Gail Collins, "Trump and Putin, in the Barn," *New York Times*, December 16, 2016. Collins went on to write: "But Donald Trump adores him and you can't get into the Trump Cabinet unless you think Putin is a great guy."

35. *Wall Street Journal* editorialist Holman W. Jenkins, Jr., in fact compared Putin to Saddam. Holman W. Jenkins, Jr., "The Putin Puzzle," *Wall Street Journal*, January 5, 2005.

36. Roger Cohen, "Trump and the End of Truth," *New York Times*, July 26, 2016; Paul Krugman, "Conquest Is for Losers," *New York Times*, December 21, 2014; and Krugman, "Thugs and Kisses," *New York Times*, September 12, 2016.

37. Michael McFaul, "Confronting Putin's Russia," *New York Times*, March 24, 2014.

38. Mettan, *Creating Russophobia*, 21.

39. See Natylie Baldwin and Kermit Heartstrong, *Ukraine: Zbig's Grand Chessboard & How the West Was Checkmated* (San Francisco: Next Revelation Press, 2015), 130–32, 305, 332; Alexander Dugin, *Putin vs Putin: Vladimir Putin Viewed from the Right* (London: Arktos Media, 2014), 31, 168, 188, 189; Alex Krainer, *The Killing of William Browder: Deconstructing Bill Browder's Dangerous Deception* (Monaco: Equilibrium, 2017), 98–102. For a critical analysis of Putin's regime, see Karen Dawisha, *Putin's Kleptocracy: Who Owns Russia?* (New York: Simon & Schuster, 2014); Anna Politkovskaya, *Putin's Russia: Life in a Failing Democracy* (New York: Metropolitan Books, 2004).

40. Katrina Vanden Heuvel, "Yeltsin—Father of Democracy?" *The Nation* blog, April 27, 2007, https://www.thenation.com; Baldwin and Heartstrong,

Ukraine. 120–23; Foglesong, *The American Mission and the "Evil Empire,"* 208–9.

41. Quoted in Kovalik, *The Plot to Scapegoat Russia,* 73.

42. William J. Broad and David Sanger, "Race for Latest Class of Nuclear Arms Threatens to Revive Cold War," *New York Times,* April 16, 2016.

43. Stephen Cohen, interview with David Barsamian, *Alternative Radio,* New York, NY, December 3, 2016. https://www.alternativeradio.org/

44. Jeremy Kuzmarov, email interview with filmmaker Andrei Nekrasov, September 21, 2017.

45. Robert Parry, "Escalating the Risky Fight with Russia," *Consortium News,* December 28, 2016. https://consortiumnews.com;and Parry, "MH-17's Unnecessary Mystery," *Consortium News,* January 15, 2016. https://consortiumnews.com; "The Ever Curiouser MH-17 Case," *Consortium News,* March 16, 2016, https://consortiumnews.com.

46. See "MH17 Ukraine Plane Crash: What We Know," BBC News, September 28, 2016, www.bbc.com; Boyd-Barrett, *Western Mainstream Media and the Ukraine Crisis,* 107; Robert Parry, "MH-17 Probe Trusts Torture Implicated Ukraine," *Consortium News,* June 13, 2016, https://consortiumnews.com; Parry, "Troubling Gaps in the New MH-17 Report," September 28, 2016, *Consortium News,* https://consortiumnews.com. The Russian military countered the Dutch report with radar releases that show that pro-Kiev forces had at least three anti-aircraft batteries in the area on the day of the crash, and that a Ukrainian war plane armed with air-to-air missiles had flown within striking distance of the Malaysian airliner shortly before the crash.

47. Neil Macfarquhar, "A Powerful Russian Weapon: The Spread of False Stories," *New York Times,* August 28, 2016; Peter Baker, "Sanctions Revive Search for Secret Putin Fortune," *New York Times,* April 27, 2014; Andrew E. Kramer, "More of Putin's Opponents End up Dead," *New York Times,* August 20, 2016; Jonathan Marshall, "Alleged Russia Taliban Arms Link Disputed," *Consortium News,* May 29, 2017, https://consortiumnews. com. Frederik Wesslau concludes in a report for the pro-NATO European Council on Foreign Relations that there is some "circumstantial evidence" to go with "rumors of covert support for radical parties [in Europe] but little solid evidence." The latter is true of all the charges highlighted above. Wesslau, "Putin's Friends in Europe," October 19, 2016, European Council on Foreign Relations, http://www.ecfr.eu.

48. Seymour Hersh, "Trump's Red Line," *Welt, N-24,* June 25, 2017, https://www.welt.de; Seymour Hersh, "We Got a Fuckin' Problem," *Welt, N-24,* June 25, 2017. Collateral damage was caused by the strike that killed between 80 and 92 civilians. Critics say that Hersh's reporting is unreliable because it is based on sources who refuse to disclose their identity. Trump subsequently initiated a Tomahawk missile strike without confirmed intelligence of a chemical weapons attack.

49. Edward S. Herman, "Fake News on Russia and Other Official Enemies: *New*

York Times, 1917–2017," *Monthly Review* (July–August 2017). An exception to the norm was the excellent piece on civilian casualties in the war against ISIS by Anand Gopal and Azmat Khan, "The Uncounted," *New York Times Magazine*, November 16, 2017, https://www.nytimes.com/interactive/2017/11/16/magazine/uncounted-civilian-casualties-iraq-airstrikes.html.

50. Edward S. Herman and David Peterson, "The Ukrainian Crisis and the Propaganda System in Overdrive," in *Flashpoint in Ukraine: How the US Drive for Hegemony Risks World War III*, ed. Stephen Lendman (Atlanta, GA: Clarity Press, 2014); de Ploeg, *Ukraine in the Crossfire*. 40, 49.

51. Kovalik, *The Plot to Scapegoat Russia*, 126, 127; Boyd-Barrett, *Western Mainstream Media and the Ukraine Crisis*. The Ukraine government used cluster and other incendiary munitions and committed serious war crimes, including torture in secret prisons.

52. James Carden, "A Reprise of the Iraq-WMD Fiasco?" *Consortium News*, February 3, 2017, https://consortiumnews.com.

53. Ibid.

54. Robert Parry, "US Report Still Lacks Proof on Russia 'Hack,'" *Consortium News*, January 7, 2017, https://consortiumnews.com. See also Jeremy Scahill, "Seymour Hersh Blasts Media for Uncritically Promoting Russian Hacking Story," *The Intercept*, January 25, 2017, https://theintercept.com.

55. Gareth Porter, "How the New Cold Warriors Cornered Trump," February 27, 2017, *Antiwar.com*, http://original.antiwar.com.

56. Ibid.; de Ploeg, *Ukraine in the Crossfire*, 299.

57. "U.S. Intel Vets Dispute Russia Hacking Claims," *Consortium News*, December 12, 2016, https://consortiumnews.com.

58. Ibid.

59. Veteran Intelligence Professionals for Sanity, "Was the Russian Hack an Inside Job?" *Counterpunch*, July 25, 2017, https://www.counterpunch.org; Patrick Lawrence, "A New Report Raises Big Questions about Last Year's DNC Hack," *The Nation*, August 9, 2017; Mike Whitney, "The Russian Hacking Story Continues to Unravel," *Counterpunch*, September 14, 2017, https://www.counterpunch.org/2017/09/14/the-russian-hacking-story-continues-to-unravel/.

60. Scott Shane, "The Fake Americans Russia Created to Influence the Election," *New York Times*, September 7, 2017; Scott Shane and Vindu Goel, "Fake Russian Facebook Accounts Bought $100,000 in Political Ads," *New York Times*, September 6, 2017; Andrew E. Kramer and Andrew Higgins, "In Ukraine, a Malware Expert Who Could Blow the Whistle on Russian Hacking," *New York Times*, August 16, 2017.

61. "Against Neo-McCarthyism," *The Nation*, July 27, 2016; Max Boot, "Donald Trump: A Modern Manchurian Candidate?" *New York Times*, January 11, 2017; Paul Krugman, "Donald Trump, the Siberian Candidate," *New York Times*, July 22, 2016; Maureen Dowd, "White House Red Scare," *New York Times*, January 7, 2017; Dowd, "Bobby Sticks It to Trump," *New York Times*, August 5, 2017.

62. See Jasmin C. Lee and Alicia Parlapiano, "How Key Trump Associates Have Been Linked to Russia," *New York Times*, June 7, 2017.

63. De Ploeg, *Ukraine in the Crossfire,* 314–17. Daniel Hoffman, a thirty--year CIA veteran, commenting on a meeting between Donald Trump Jr., Paul Manafort, Jared Kushner, and a Russian lawyer who allegedly had information on Clinton, writes in a piece highly critical of Putin that "there is no conclusive proof the Kremlin arranged the meeting." Daniel Hoffman, "It Wasn't about Collusion," *New York Times*, July 29, 2017. An investigation by journalist Craig Unger found that Trump's fortune was salvaged in the late 1990s with the help of Russian oligarchs and mafia figures who rented luxury condominiums in Trump's high-rises; however, Unger claims, any sinister connection between Trump and the Kremlin or to Trump's political success is purely hypothetical. See Craig Unger, "Trump's Russia Laundromat," *The New Republic*, July 13, 2017.

64. De Ploeg, *Ukraine in the Crossfire,* 314–17. The abuse of civil liberties stems from the wide subpoena powers of the investigating committee and their efforts to entrap witnesses into committing perjury through use of surveillance records.

65. Dugin, *Putin vs Putin,* 268.

66. Marie Elise Sarrotte, "A Broken Promise?" *Foreign Affairs* 93/5: 90–97; de Ploeg, *Ukraine in the Crossfire,* 290.

67. Stephen Cohen, interview with David Barsamian, "Reheating the Cold War," December 3, 2016, https://www.alternativeradio.org/products/cohs001#. See also Robert Parry, "Dangers of Democratic Putin-Bashing," *Consortium News*, February 1, 2017, https://consortiumnews.com. For an intelligent assessment of Putin, also see Dugin, *Putin vs Putin.*

68. See Naomi Klein, *The Shock Doctrine: The Rise of Disaster Capitalism* (New York: Metropolitan Books, 2007), 216–244; Stephen Cohen, *Failed Crusade: America and the Tragedy of Post-Soviet Russia* (New York: W. W. Norton, 2001), 16.

69. Matt Taibbi, "Something about the Russia Story Stinks," *Rolling Stone*, December 30, 2016; Jeremy Kuzmarov, "Spirit of McCarthyism Seen in Attacks on Oliver Stone's 'Putin Interviews,'" *Huffington Post*, June 26, 2017, https://www.huffingtonpost.com/entry/spirit-of-mccarthyism-seen-in-attacks-on-oliver-stones_us_5951ce7ce4b0f078efd9846c.

70. Dana Rohrabacher, Chairman, Subcommittee on Europe, Eurasia and Emerging Threats, to Ed Royce, Chairman, House Committee on Foreign Affairs, September 6, 2017, https://rohrabacher.house.gov.

71. Boyd-Barrett, *Western Mainstream Media and the Ukraine Crisis*, 47; Andrea Shalal, "U.S. Navy Eyes Greater Presence in Arctic," Reuters, March 1, 2014, https://www.reuters.com/article/us-usa-arctic-navy/u-s-navy-eyes-greater-presence-in-arctic-idUSBREA1Q2DU20140301.

72. Dina Smeltz, "American Opinion on U.S.-Russia Relations: From Bad to Worse," The Chicago Council on Global Affairs, August 2, 2017, https://www.thechicagocouncil.org/publication/american-opinion-us   -russia-relations-bad-worse; Margaret Vice, "Publics Worldwide Unfavorable

Towards Putin, Russia," Pew Research Center, August 16, 2017, http://www.pewglobal.org/2017/08/16/publics-worldwide-unfavorable-toward-putin-russia/; "Polls Show Sudden Improvement in U.S. Public Opinion of Putin," *Russia Beyond the Headlines*, February 23, 2017, https://www.rbth.com. 35 percent of Republicans viewed Russia positively in another poll, compared to only 16 percent of Democrats, and only 10 percent of Democrats had a positive view about Putin.

2. "The Time You Sent Troops to Quell the Revolution"

1. Epigraphs: Poem by a Michigan man, in Godfrey J. Anderson, *A Michigan Polar Bear Confronts the Bolsheviks: A War Memoir*, ed. and with an introduction by Gordon L. Olson (Grand Rapids, MI: William B. Eerdman Publishing, 2010), 180–81; speech delivered at major battle site, in Harry J. Costello, *Why Did We Go to Russia?* (Detroit, MI: Harry J. Costello Publishing, 1920), 39.

2. Barack Obama Jr., *The Audacity of Hope: Thoughts on Reclaiming the American Dream* (New York: Crown Publishers, 2006), 285, 289.

3. This mythical view is promoted by the supposed dean of Cold War historians, John L. Gaddis, in *The Cold War: A New History* (New York: Penguin, 2013), a book that was endorsed by Henry Kissinger, and Walter Isaacson in *The Wise Men: Six Friends and the World They Made*, rev. ed. (New York: Simon & Schuster, 2013).

4. William S. Graves, *America's Siberian Adventure 1918–1920* (New York: Peter Smith, 1941), 348. Haiti is another good example of the strong trampling the weak under the rubric of Wilsonian idealism. See Hans Schmidt, *The United States Occupation of Haiti* (New Brunswick, NJ: Rutgers University Press, 1971).

5. D. F. Fleming, "The Western Intervention in the Soviet Union, 1918–1920," *New World Review* (Fall 1967); D. F. Fleming, *The Cold War and Its Origins, 1917–1960*, vol. 1 (New York: Doubleday, 1960); William Blum, *Killing Hope: U.S. Military and CIA Interventions since World War II* (Monroe, ME: Common Courage Press, 1998), 8.

6. Orlando Figes, *The Crimean War: A History* (London: Picador, 2012), 314; Thomas A. Bailey, *America Faces Russia: Russian-American Relations from Early Times to Today* (Ithaca, NY: Cornell University Press, 1950), 84. Albert A. Woldman, *Lincoln and the Russians* (New York: Collier Books, 1952), 166. Abraham Lincoln's secretary of state, William Seward, wrote to Cassius Clay, a U.S. envoy to St. Petersburg, that the friendship between the United States and Russia could be explained by the fact that Russia and the United States were both "improving and expanding empires: one toward the East and one toward the West, each conveying civilization to new regions and each resisted at times by nations jealous of its prosperity or alarmed by its aggrandizement."

7. Walter LaFeber, *America, Russia and the Cold War, 1945–1990*, 9th ed. (New York: McGraw Hill, 2002), 3.

8.   William A. Williams, *American-Russian Relations 1781–1947* (New York: Rinehart, 1952), 52, 83, 84, 85.

9.   See John Reed, *Ten Days That Shook the World*, with an introduction by Granville Hicks (New York: New American Library, 1967); *New York Times*, quoted in Christopher Lasch, *The American Liberals and the Russian Revolution* (New York: Columbia University Press, 1962), 54.

10. Lasch, *The American Liberals and the Russian Revolution*, 28, 29.

11. Williams, *American-Russian Relations 1781–1947*, 85; Richard Goldhurst, *The Midnight War: The American Intervention in Russia, 1918–1920* (New York: McGraw Hill, 1978), 114. For Kennan's views on Russia, see David C. Engerman, *Modernization from the Other Shore: American Intellectuals and the Romance of Russian Development* (Cambridge, MA: Harvard University Press, 2003), 74; Donald Davis and Eugene P. Trani, *Distorted Mirrors: Americans and Their Relations with Russia and China in the 20th Century* (Columbia: University of Missouri Press, 2009).

12. Lasch, *The American Liberals and the Russian Revolution,* 130; Williams, *American-Russian Relations 1781–1947*, 93. Lansing was staunchly pro-imperialist, believing it was "utterly untenable to hold that either Ireland or India should break away from the British Empire."

13. Lasch, *The American Liberals and the Russian Revolution,* 131.

14. Williams, *American-Russian Relations 1781–1947,* 85, 150; Evans Clark, *Facts and Fabrications About Soviet Russia* (New York: Rand School of Social Sciences, 1920), 21, 22, quoting Gompers and a letter from notables supporting military intervention.

15. Williams, *American-Russian Relations 1781–1947,* 98, 122, 144, 146–47; Raymond Robins, quoted in Carl J. Richard, *When the United States Invaded Russia: Woodrow Wilson's Siberian Disaster* (New York: Rowman & Littlefield, 2012); Beatrice Farnsworth, *William C. Bullitt and the Soviet Union* (Bloomington: Indiana University Press, 1967), 42–45. Bullitt reported that the "soviet government seemed to have done more for the education of the Russian people in a year and a half than czardom had in fifty years."

16. Richard, *When the United States Invaded Russia*, 67.

17. Jim Aiken, "The Intervention of Woodrow Wilson in the Russian Civil War, 1917–1920," Master's thesis, University of Tulsa, 2012, 5; Arthur S. Link, ed., *The Papers of Woodrow Wilson* (Princeton: Princeton University Press, 1983), vol. 1, 572; Charles A. Beard, *An Economic Interpretation of the Constitution of the United States* (New York: Macmillan, 1963), 199.

18. Williams, *American-Russian Relations 1781–1947,* 116.

19. Walter Lippmann and Charles Merz, "A Test of the News," *The New Republic*, August 4, 1920, 19, 20; Williams, *American-Russian Relations 1781–1947,* 116; Lasch, *The American Liberals and the Russian Revolution,* 160; George Stewart, *The White Armies of Russia: A Chronicle of Counter-Revolution and Allied Intervention* (New York: Macmillan Company, 1933), 241–42.

20. "The Report of General Wilds P. Richardson," in *Detroit's Polar Bears: The*

American-Russian Expeditionary Forces, 1918–1919 (Frankenmuth, MI: Polar Bear Publishing, 1985), 12–13. Richardson compared the Russian mind to the "Oriental mind," which explained "why Russians are discontented with the democracy they find in the United States."

21. Williams, *American-Russian Relations 1781–1947,* 171; Clifford Kinvig, *Churchill's Crusade: The British Invasion of Russia, 1918–1920* (London: Hambledon Continuum, 2006).

22. John Cudahy, *Archangel: The American War with Russia* (Chicago: A.C. McClurg & Co., 1924), 64; Graves, *America's Siberian Adventure 1918–1920,* xxi. Arthur Bullard of the State Department advised Colonel House that Kolchak was "surrounded and dependent on the support of reactionary elements" whose principle of government was the "reconquest of former grafts." One of his generals was alleged to be a descendent of Attila the Hun.

23. Goldhurst, *The Midnight War,* 153; Graves, *America's Siberian Adventure 1918–1920,* 227, 236, 265-266; Stewart, *The White Armies of Russia* 180; Col. John Hall, *With the Die-Hards in Siberia* (London: 1920). Exemplifying his anti-Semitism, Kolchak claimed that sixty liaison officers and translators with the American embassy were Jews and had influenced American policy.

24. Goldhurst, *The Midnight War,* 192–95; Robert J. Maddox, *The Unknown War with Russia: Wilson's Siberian Intervention* (San Rafel, CA: Presidio Press, 1977), 83. The "little" war board was an informal committee set up by Wilson to expedite the procurement and shipping of goods destined for Russia. It was headed by Bernard Baruch of the War Industries Board, Vance C. McCormack, head of the War Trade Board, and Edward N. Hurley, chairman of the U.S. Shipping board.

25. David Foglesong, *America's Secret War Against Bolshevism* (Chapel Hill: University of North Carolina Press, 1991), 108, 114, 231–32.

26. Ibid., 127. Capt. John A. Gade, a naval intelligence officer who proposed the blueprint for the OSS, went on a secret mission to organize anti-Bolshevik governments in Estonia, Latvia, and Lithuania.

27. Gibson Bell-Smith, "Guarding the Railroad, Taming the Cossacks: The U.S. Army in Russia, 1918–1920," *Prologue Magazine* 34/4 (Winter 2002), in National Archives, https://www.archives.gov.

28. Graves, *America's Siberian Adventure 1918–1920,* 241, 246; Richard, *When the United States Invaded Russia,* 8994; Goldhurst, *The Midnight War,* 80; Jamie Bisher, *White Terror: Cossack Warlords of the Trans-Siberian* (New York: Routledge, 2006). After the war, Semonoff took refuge in Manchuria where he became a kingpin in one of the century's most diabolical criminal enterprises, the extortion, prostitution, and narcotics syndicate run by Japanese intelligence and the Kwantung army, which paved the way for the Japanese invasion and enslavement of Manchuria.

29. Richard, *When the United States Invaded Russia,* 91; Bisher, *White Terror,* 100, 101; Stewart, *The White Armies of Russia,* 314. At one point, Kalmykoff, who earned the nickname "Ataboy kill 'em off," bombed a schoolhouse, leaving a member of the U.S. 27th Regiment to carry what was left of the

schoolchildren away in a coffee sack to bury them. Historian D. W. Fleming referred to the white reign of terror as among the worst mass killings the world had ever seen, eclipsed only later by the Nazi holocaust.

30. Graves, *America's Siberian Adventure 1918–1920*, 90.

31. Ibid., 214–15; Goldhurst, *The Midnight War*, 237.

32. Frederick L. Schuman, *American Policy towards Russia since 1917* (New York: International Publishers, 1928), 125. Graves, *America's Siberian Adventure 1918–1920*, 108; Clark, *Facts and Fabrications about Soviet Russia*, 16; Blum, *Killing Hope*, 8. Some of the headlines included: "Red Agitators from the City Potent in Russia—Atrocities to Young Girls"; "Describe Horrors Under Red Rule—R.E. Simmons and W.W. Welsh Tell Senators of Brutalities of Bolsheviki—Strip Women in the Streets"; "People of Every Class Except the Scum Subject to Violence by Mob"; "Senators Hear Breshkovskaya 'Grandmother of the Revolution' [state that] . . . Lenin and Trotsky Are German Agents—Sees Russia in Utter Ruin—Moscow Looted by Reds."

33. Graves, *America's Siberian Adventure 1918–1920*, xiii, 101.

34. Robert L. Willett, *Russian Sideshow: America's Undeclared War, 1918–1920* (Washington, D.C.: Potomac Books, 2003), 268; Benson Bobrick, *East of the Sun: The Conquest and Settlement of Siberia* (London: Heinemann, 1992), 398.

35. Guy Murchie Jr. "AEF's Strange Adventure," *Chicago Tribune*, April 2, 1939, in World War I Museum Archive, Kansas City, MO, Russia Collection. After the war, Kolchak tried to escape with $300 million of the imperial treasury and Gold, but was captured by the Bolsheviks and executed.

36. Ralph Albertson, *Fighting Without a War: An Account of Military Intervention in North Russia* (New York: Harcourt, Brace and Howe, 1920), 71.

37. E. M Halliday, *The Ignorant Armies*, foreword by S. L. A. Marshall (New York: Award Books, 1964), 159. The book was reprinted as *When Hell Froze Over* (New York: I Books, 2000).

38. Albertson, *Fighting Without a War*, 85–88; Goldhurst, *Midnight War*, 94, 225. The term *bolos* foreshadowed the use of the term *gooks* in the Korean and Vietnam wars.

39. Capt. Joel H. Moore, Lieut. Harry H. Mead, Lieut. Lewis E. Jahns, *The History of the American Expedition Fighting the Bolsheviki: Campaigning in North Russia 1918–1919* (1920, repr.: Nashville, TN: Battery Press, 2003), 109; Cudahy, *Archangel*, 142, 153. Silver Parrish wrote that he took sixteen enemy prisoners and killed two, then his men "burned the village [Toulgas] and my heart ached to have the women fall down at my feet and grab my legs to kiss my hand and beg me not to do it. But orders are orders—and I was in command of the fifteen men who went across that field so I done my duties." Willett, *Russian Sideshow*, 86; Goldhurst, *The Midnight War*, 94, 225.

40. The term "atrocity-producing environment" is used by Robert Jay Lifton

in *Home from the War: Vietnam Veterans Neither Victims nor Executioners* (Boston: Beacon Press, 1973).

41. Moore, Mead, Jahns, *The History of the American Expedition Fighting the Bolsheviki*, 40, 58, 108, 128; Dennis Gordon, *Quartered in Hell: The Story of the American North Russia Expeditionary Force 1918-1919* (Missoula, MT: Doughboy Historical Society, 1982), 67–68; Sylvian G. Kindall, *American Soldiers in Siberia* (New York: Richard R. Smith, 1945), 11.

42. Cudahy, *Archangel*, 52; Albertson, *Fighting Without a War*, 85–88.

43. Halliday, *The Ignorant Armies*, 203.

44. Albertson, *Fighting Without a War*, 85–88.

45. Perry Moore, *Stamping out the Virus: Allied Intervention in the Russian Civil War 1918-1920* (Altgen, PA: Schiffer Military History, 2002), 101; Kinvig, *Churchill's Crusade*, 226, 232; Halliday, *The Ignorant Armies*, 284.

46. John T. Smith, *Gone to Russia to Fight: The RAF in South Russia 1918-1920* (Gloucestershire, UK: Amberley, 2010), 51, 97, 107; Miles Hudson, *Intervention in Russia, 1918-1920: A Cautionary Tale* (South Yorkshire, UK: Pen & Sword Press, 2004), 143.

47. "The Creation of Russia," in Gordon, *Quartered in Hell*, 302.

48. "Recalls Massacre in Siberia," *Kansas City Star*, n.d., World War I Museum Archive, Kansas City, MO, George Jensen Papers.

49. *Detroit's Own Polar Bears*, 78.

50. Willett, *Russian Sideshow*, 212; Norman Saul, *War and Revolution: The United States and Russia, 1917-1921* (University Press of Kansas, 2001), 315; Halliday, *The Ignorant Armies*, 13, 43.

51. Goldhurst, *The Midnight War*, 213.

52. *Detroit's Own Polar Bears*, 78.

53. Maddox, *The Unknown War with Russia*, 102–3.

54. Moore, Mead. Jahns, *The History of the American Expedition Fighting the Bolsheviki*, 298; Gordon, *Quartered in Hell*, 304.

55. Willett, *Russian Sideshow*, 203.

56. Albertson, *Fighting Without a War*, 45; Willett, *Russian Sideshow*, 122.

57. Cudahy, *Archangel*, 29, 30. Graduate of Harvard and the University of Wisconsin Law School, Cudahy was the scion of a wealthy meat-packing family and a Democrat disillusioned with the war. Later he served as ambassador to Poland, Ireland, Belgium, and Luxemburg where he continued to express antiwar views.

58. Willett, *Russian Sideshow*, 45, 46; Costello, *Why Did We Go to Russia?*, 76–79; Gordon, *Quartered in Hell*, 178, 216.

59. Kropotkin quoted in Moore, Mead, Jahns, *The History of the American Expedition Fighting the Bolsheviki*, 247–48. Kropotkin further worried about the development of a "bitter sentiment [in Russia] with respect to the Western nations . . . that will be utilized some day in future conflicts."

60. Richard Polenberg, *Fighting Faiths: The Abrams Case, the Supreme Court, and Free Speech* (New York: Viking Press, 1987); Zosa Szajkowski, "Double Jeopardy—The Abrams Case of 1919," *American Jewish Archives*, April

1971. Jacob Schwartz died from an ailment exacerbated by his treatment by police, which he likened "to the Spanish Inquisition and the blackest page of man's brutality to man." Schwartz in a letter claimed the police stopped at nothing, "from tearing hair to pulling the tongue; from blackjacks to the leg of a chair was used on us because we would not speak." Justice Oliver Wendell Holmes offered an eloquent dissent against the Supreme Court ruling, supported by Louis Brandeis, on grounds of the right to free speech. He would not weigh in on whether military intervention was actually legal, and dissent against it hence justified.

61.   Neil Carey, ed., *Fighting the Bolsheviks: The Russian War Memoir of Private 1st Class Donald E. Carey, U.S. Army, 1918–1919* (Novato, CA: Presidio Press, 1997), x; Foglesong, *America's Secret War Against Bolshevism*, 7.

62.   James Loewen, *Lies My Teacher Told Me: Everything Your American History Textbook Got Wrong* (New York: Touchstone Books, 2007), 16; National World War I Museum, Kansas City, MO.

63.   Maddox, *The Unknown War with Russia*, 138.

64.   George F. Kennan, *Russia and the West Under Lenin and Stalin* (Boston: Little, Brown, 1960), 117; Linda Killen, *The Russia Bureau: A Case Study in Wilsonian Diplomacy* (Lexington: University Press of Kentucky, 1983), 130; Richard, *When the United States Invaded Russia*, 174.

3. Provoking Confrontation

1.   Thomas L. Friedman, "Cold War Without the Fun," *New York Times*, June 24, 2015. For a critical analysis of Friedman's career, see Belen Fernandez, *The Imperial Messenger: Thomas Friedman at Work* (London: Verso, 2011).

2.   Carl Marzani, *We Can Be Friends* (New York: Tropical Books Publishers, 1952), 21–22.

3.   John Culver and John Hyde, *American Dreamer: A Life of Henry A. Wallace* (New York: W. W. Norton, 2000), 456–57; Oliver Stone and Peter Kuznick, *An Untold History of the United States* (New York: Gallery Books, 2012), 221.

4.   See William Appleman Williams, *American-Russian Relations, 1781–1947* (New York: Rinehart, 1952), 193; Joseph E. Davies, "What We Didn't Know About Russia," *Reader's Digest*, March 1942, repr. in *American Views of Soviet Russia 1917–1965*, ed. Peter Filene (Homewood, IL: Dorsey Press, 1968), 142. The Ribbentrop-Molotov Pact was a neutrality pact between Nazi Germany and the Soviet Union signed in Moscow on August 23, 1939, by foreign ministers Joachim von Ribbentrop and Vyacheslav Molotov in a deal the Soviets felt was necessary after the British and French had refused their overtures in forming an anti-Nazi alliance.

5.   See David Schmitz, *The United States Support for Right-Wing Dictatorship, 1921–1965* (Chapel Hill: University of North Carolina Press, 1999).

6.   D. F. Fleming, *The Cold War and Its Origins 1917–1960,* vol 1: *1917–1950* (New York: Doubleday & Company, 1961), 136.

7.   Stone and Kuznick, *An Untold History of the United States* 111.

8. Fleming, *The Cold War and Its Origins 1917–1960*, 148.

9. Richard Overy, *Why the Allies Won* (New York: W.W. Norton, 1995), 75–84, 96, 98.

10. Ibid., 99; Fleming, *The Cold War and Its Origins 1917–1960*, 140–41. Overy's conclusion is based on the views of State Department officials like Edward R. Stettinius Jr.

11. Fleming, *The Cold War and Its Origins 1917–1960*, 146–47; Jacques R. Pauwels, *The Myth of the Good War: America in the Second World War* (Toronto: James Lorimer & Co., 2002), 45.

12. Fleming, *The Cold War and Its Origins 1917–1960*, 155.

13. Quoted in David Kennedy, *The American People in World War II: Freedom from Fear, Part II* (New York: Oxford University Press, 1999), 140.

14. Pauwels, *The Myth of the Good War*, 101, 102, 147; Gabriel Kolko, *The Politics of War: The World and United States Foreign Policy, 1943–1945* (New York: Random House, 1968). The United States supported the pro-Mussolini Marshal Badoglio in Italy.

15. Fleming, *The Cold War and Its Origins 1917–1960*, 253–54; S. M. Plokhy, *Yalta: The Price of Peace* (New York: Viking, 2010), 64.

16. Fleming, *The Cold War and Its Origins 1917–1960*, 256.

17. Diane Shaver Clemens, *Yalta* (New York: Oxford University Press, 1971). See also Walter LaFeber, *America, Russia and the Cold War, 1945–1990* (New York: McGraw Hill, 2002), 15–18; Plokhy, *Yalta*; Michael Parenti, *The Anti-Communist Impulse* (New York: Random House, 1969), 139.

18. Henry Wallace, *Toward World Peace* (New York: Reynal & Hitchcock, 1948), 48, 56; Culver and Hyde, *American Dreamer*.

19. Culver and Hyde, *American Dreamer*, 277.

20. Ibid., 363, 364; Robert Ferrell, *Choosing Truman: The Democratic Convention of 1944* (Columbia: University of Missouri Press, 1994), 80.

21. Stone and Kuznick, *An Untold History of the United States*, 201, 202.

22. See Frank Kofsky, *Harry S. Truman and the War Scare of 1948: A Successful Campaign to Deceive the Nation* (New York: St. Martin's Press, 1998); Stone and Kuznick, *An Untold History of the United States*, 221; Culver and Hyde, *American Dreamer*, 456–57; Athan Theoharis, "The Politics of Scholarship: Liberals, Anti-Communism, and McCarthyism," in *The Specter: Original Essays on the Cold War and the Origins of McCarthyism*, ed. Robert Griffith and Athan Theoharis (New York: Franklin Watts, 1974), 278.

23. Ickes and Roosevelt quoted in Fleming, *The Cold War and Its Origins 1917–1960*, 353.

24. In David Mayers, *Dissenting Voices in America's Rise to Power* (New York: Cambridge University Press, 2007), 312.

25. See Allan Bullock, *Hitler and Stalin: Parallel Lives* (New York: Vintage, 1992); Stephen Cohen, *Soviet Fates and Lost Alternatives: From Stalinism to the New Cold War* (New York: Columbia University Press, 2011). John Foster Dulles stated in 1947 that "war is one thing which the Soviet leadership does not want and would not consciously risk. The economy of the

nation is still weak [and] for the time being the Soviet military establishment is completely outmatched by the mechanized weapons ... available to the United States." Quoted in Gabriel Kolko and Joyce Kolko, *The Limits of Power: The World and United States Foreign Policy* (New York: Harper & Row, 1972), 33.

26.   Edgar Snow, *Stalin Must Have Peace* (New York: Random House, 1968), 132–33; See also John L. Strohm, *Just Tell the Truth: The Uncensored Story of How the Common People Live behind the Russian Iron Curtain* (New York: Charles Scribner, 1947). A detailed assessment of Stalin's foreign policy aims is provided in William Taubman, *Stalin's American Policy: From Entente to Détente to Cold War* (New York: W.W. Norton, 1982).

27.   Marzani, *We Can Be Friends*, 26–27. Historian Richard J. Barnet determined that in 1947, Russia had 2.8 million men under arms, "not a number that suggested aggressive intentions given the immensity of Soviet territory, history of invasion and Russian tradition of maintaining enormous standing armies." Barnet, *The Giants: Russia and America* (New York: Simon & Schuster, 1977), 107. The number increased later in response to the exigencies of the arms race and Cold War.

28.   William H. Neblett, *Pentagon Politics* (New York: Pageant Press, 1953), 6; Harry Rositzke, *The CIA's Secret Operations: Espionage, Counter-Espionage and Covert Action* (New York: Reader's Digest, 1977), 14. Rositzke further stated that "the image underlying the Cold War mentality was that of a powerful and aggressive Soviet Union. As it turned out the image was an illusion."

29.   Gabriel Kolko and Joyce Kolko, *The Limits of Power: The World and United States Foreign Policy* (New York: Harper & Row, 1972).; Sidney Lens, The *Military-Industrial Complex* (Philadelphia: Pilgrim Press, 1971), 20.. See also Parenti, *The Anti-Communist Impulse*, 135.

30.   Fleming, *The Cold War and Its Origins*, vol. 2, 1060; Lens, *The Military-Industrial Complex*, 19.

31.   Noam Chomsky, *Deterring Democracy* (New York: Pantheon, 1989); James Peck, *Washington's China: The National Security World, the Cold War, and the Origins of Globalism* (Amherst, MA: University of Massachusetts Press, 2006). For insights on the revolutions in Eastern Europe from the perspective of the time, see Doreen Warriner, *Revolution in Eastern Europe* (London: Warriner Press, 1950) and Wilfred G. Burchett, *People's Democracies* (Melbourne: World Unity Publishing, 1951). Shell Oil's parent company, Astra, which owned 11 percent of the Romanian oil industry, was forced to dissolve following George Gheorgiu-Dej's nationalization decree. The Anglo-Dutch company had owned 51 percent of the industry. Hugh Seton-Watson, *The East European Revolution* (New York: Praeger, 1962), 240.

32.   Ronald Steel, *Walter Lippmann and the American Century*, rev. ed. (New York: Transaction, 1999), 511.

33.   Marzani, *We Can Be Friends*, 9–10; Mike Lofgren, *Deep State: The Fall of*

the Constitution and the Rise of a Shadow Government (New York: Penguin Books, 2016), 44.

34. See Perry Anderson, *American Foreign Policy and Its Thinkers* (London: Verso, 2015), 44; and *Strategies of Containment* summarized, 45–46. Gaddis's conclusions from his *The United States and the Origins of the Cold War, 1941–1947,* rev ed. (New York: Columbia University Press, 2000); and "The Emerging Post-Revisionist Synthesis and the Origins of the Cold War," *Diplomatic History* (July 1983).

35. Quoted phrases from George Kennan, "Sources of Soviet Conduct," *Foreign Affairs* 25 (July 1947): 566–82; Kennan to the Secretary of State, 22, February, 1946, FRUS, 1946 6: 696–709; and Arthur Krock, *Memoirs: Sixty Years on the Firing Line* (New York: Funk & Wagnalls, 1968), 17, 461–82, appear in Michael Hogan, *Cross of Iron: Harry S. Truman and the Origins of the National Security State, 1945–1954* (Cambridge: Cambridge University Press, 1998), 17. See also Donald E. Davis and Eugene P. Trani, *Distorted Mirrors: Americans and Their Relationship with Russia and China in the 20th Century* (Columbia: University of Missouri Press, 2009).

36. Martin Sommers, introduction in Snow, *Stalin Must Have Peace*, 29.

37. Walter L. Hixson, "What Was the Cold War and How Did We Win It?" *Reviews in American History* 22/3 (1994); 507–11; Thomas Etzold and John Lewis Gaddis, "United States Objectives and Programs for National Security, NSC 68, April 14, 1950," *Containment: Documents on American Politics and Strategy, 1945–1950* (New York: Columbia University Press, 1978), quoted in Robert Bellah, Richard A. Madsen, William M. Sullivan, Ann Swidler, and Stephen Tipton, *The Good Society* (New York: Random House, 1992), 223, 227.

38. NSC-68 quoted in Noam Chomsky, *Deterring Democracy*, 26–27.

39. See Melvyn Leffler, *A Preponderance of Power: National Security, the Truman Administration, and the Cold War* (Stanford, CA: Stanford University Press, 1992); Chomsky, *Deterring Democracy*, 28–29; Statement of Robert S. McNamara, Secretary of Defense, before the Democratic Party Platform Committee, August 17, 1964, RG 200, Records of Robert S. McNamara, Defense Programs and Operations, Box 2, National Archives, College Park. MD.

40. David Vine, *Base Nation: How U.S. Military Bases Abroad Harm America and the World* (New York: Metropolitan Books, 2015), 36–37; George A. Lundberg, "American Foreign Policy in the Light of National Interest at the Mid-Century," in *Perpetual War for Perpetual Peace: A Critical Examination of the Foreign Policy of Franklin Delano Roosevelt and Its Aftermath*, ed. Harry Elmer Barnes (Ostara Publications, 1953, 2013), 616.

41. Aaron B. O'Connell, "An Accidental Empire? President Harry S. Truman and the Origins of America's Global Military Presence," in *Origins of the National Security State and the Legacy of Harry S. Truman*, ed. Mary Ann Heiss and Michael J. Hogan (Kirksville, MO: Truman State University Press, 2013), 196.

42. Wallace, *Toward World Peace*, 60–61.

43. Gar Alperovitz, *Atomic Diplomacy: The Decision to Use the Atomic Bomb* (New York: Vintage, 1996); Marzani, *We Can Be Friends*, 88; Pauwels, *The Myth of the Good War*, 129. General Leslie Grove testified before the Oppenheimer loyalty hearings in 1954 that "there was never—from about two weeks from the time I took charge of the project—any illusion on my part but that Russia was the enemy and that the project was conducted on that basis." Parenti, *The Anti-Communist Impulse*, 126.

44. See Jeremy Kuzmarov, *Modernizing Repression: Police Training and Nation Building in the American Century* (Amherst, MA: University of Massachusetts Press, 2012), 190; Olive Sutton, *Murder Inc. in Greece* (New York: Prism Key Press, 2013); Lawrence Wittner, *American Intervention in Greece, 1943–1949: A Study in Counter-Revolution* (New York: Columbia University Press, 1982).

45. Michael Hogan, *The Marshall Plan: America, Britain and the Reconstruction of Western Europe, 1947–1952* (New York: Cambridge University Press, 1987); Anne Applebaum, *Iron Curtain: The Crushing of Eastern Europe, 1945–1956* (New York: Doubleday, 2012), 219, 220.

46. See Herbert Aptheker, *The Truth about Hungary* (New York: Mainstream Publishers, 1957), 47; Rudy Abramson, *Spanning the Century: The Life of W. Averell Harriman, 1891–1986* (New York: William Morrow, 1992).

47. William Blum, "The Anti-Empire Report," May 21, 2007, https://williamblum.org; William Blum, *America's Deadliest Export-Democracy* (London: Zed Books, 2015); David Painter, "Oil and the Marshall Plan," *Business History Review* 58/3 (Autumn 1984): 362.

48. Peter Dale Scott, "The Dulles Brothers, Harry Dexter White, Alger Hiss, and the Fate of the Private Pre-War International Banking System," *Asia Pacific Journal*, April 20, 2014, http://apjjf.org; Peter Dale Scott, *The American Deep State: Wall Street, Big Oil and the Attack on U.S. Democracy* (New York: Rowman & Littlefield, 2014); Pauwels, *The Myth of the Good War*, 223, 233, 234; Carolyn Eisenberg, *Drawing the Line: The American Decision to Divide Germany, 1944–1949* (New York: Cambridge University Press, 1998).

49. See Jeremy Kuzmarov, "American Military Assistance Programs since 1945," Oxford Research Encyclopedia, March 2017, http://americanhistory. oxfordre.com/.

50. While working for Dillon Read, whose client list included Grumman Aircraft and other defense contractors, Forrestal helped arrange the merger of Texaco and Standard Oil into Caltex. Townsend Hoopes and Douglas Brinkley, *Driven Patriot: The Life and Times of James Forrestal* (New York: Random House, 1992), 399. Johnson's corporate ties, including to the Shroeder Bank which financed German heavy industry development before the Second World War, are discussed in Wilfred G. Burchett, *Warmongers Unmasked: History of Cold War in Germany* (Melbourne, Australia: World Unity Publications, 1950), https://www.marxists.org/archive/burchett/. Robert Lovett, who served as Undersecretary of State and Defense Secretary

after Johnson, was a Wall Street banker who worked for Brown Brothers Harriman, a firm founded by another of Truman's hawkish advisers, W. Averell Harriman, who developed a vendetta against the Soviet government after losing out on a manganese concession in the 1920s.

51. Poll numbers found in "U.S. opinion of Russia," *Fortune* 32 (September 1945): 233–38

52. Kofsky, *Harry S. Truman and the War Scare of 1948*, 241, 242; Kolko and Kolko, *The Limits of Power*; Parenti, *The Anti-Communist Impulse*, 148, 154, 159; William Stivers, "The Incomplete Blockade: Soviet Zone Supply of West Berlin, 1948-1949," *Diplomatic History* 21/4 (Fall 1997): 569. So much food was actually trucked into West Berlin in July and August 1948 during the blockade, at such low prices, that Berlin-grown products were crowded out of the market.

53. Christopher Simpson, *Blowback: The First Full Account of America's Recruitment of Nazis, and Its Disastrous Effect on Our Domestic and Foreign Policy* (New York: Weidenfeld & Nicolson, 1988), 56–58, 65; William Corson, *The Armies of Ignorance* (New York: Dial Press, 1977).

54. Kofsky, *Harry S. Truman and the War Scare of 1948*; Marzani, *We Can Be Friends*, 23.

55. Stone quoted in Lens, *The Military-Industrial Complex*, 11.

56. Daniele Ganser, *NATO's Secret Armies: Operation Gladio and Terrorism in Western Europe* (London: Frank Cass, 2005), 1, 2, 37; Robert Wallace and H. Keith Melton, *Spycraft: The Secret History of the CIAs Spytechs: From Communism to Al Qaeda* (London: Dutton, 2008). For other failed operations behind the Iron Curtain see Gregory Mitrovich, *Undermining the Kremlin: America's Strategy to Subvert the Soviet Bloc, 1947–1956* (Ithaca, NY: Cornell University Press, 2000).

57. Kolko and Kolko, *The Limits of Power*, 147–151, 438–39.

58. Ganser, *NATO's Secret Armies*, 217, 218; Peter Murtagh, *The Rape of Greece: The King, the Colonels and the Resistance* (London: Simon & Schuster, 1994).

59. Peter Grose, *Operation Rollback: America's Secret War behind the Iron Curtain* (Boston: Houghton Mifflin, 2000); Simpson, *Blowback*, 149; Warriner, *Revolution in Eastern Europe*, ix, x. Nazi agents also executed alleged Soviet spies in the American-occupied zone of Germany as part of the CIA policy of plausible deniability.

60. Hoopes and Brinkley, *Driven Patriot*, 313; Simpson, *Blowback*, 159.

61. Grose, *Operation Rollback*, 46.

62. John Prados, *Safe for Democracy: The Secret Wars of the CIA* (Chicago: Ivan R. Dee, 2006), 64.

63. Simpson, *Blowback*, 174.

64. Applebaum, *Iron Curtain*, 459. The Soviet view of the events in Hungary, that they were saving the country from counterrevolution, is presented in Aptheker, *The Truth about Hungary*. The best book on the topic remains Peter Fryer, *Hungarian Tragedy* (1956), available at https://www.marxists.

org. which emphasizes that the uprising was neither organized or controlled by fascists or reactionaries, though reactionaries did try and gain control of it. The goal of the uprising was to build socialism with a human face in opposition to the bureaucratic and oppressive system that had taken hold under Mátyás Rakosi and Erno Gero who had "promised the people an earthly paradise" but instead "gave them a police state as regressive and reprehensible as the prewar fascist dictatorship of Admiral Horthy."

65. Thatcher quoted in Jon Wiener, *How We Forgot the Cold War: A Historical Journey Across America* (Berkeley: University of California Press, 2012), 46.

66. Joseph Stalin, *History of the Communist Party of the Soviet Union/ Bolsheviks: Short Course* (Moscow: Foreign Language Publishers, 1939). This text rewrote history to elevate Stalin's role in the Russian Revolution, among other distortions. On the politicization of history and concept of a usable past, see Peter Novick, *That Noble Dream: The "Objectivity" Question and the American Historical Profession* (New York: Cambridge University Press, 1998).

67. See, for example, Marzani, *We Can Be Friends*, 10, 19–20, 22. Admiral William Standley, the U.S. ambassador to Moscow from 1942 to 1943, described the possibility of war with Russia at this time as "perfectly absurd," saying he did not think the Russians "wanted to establish their rule over the world" and that he saw no difference between "Russia's preoccupation with the internal setup in Bulgaria than our own concern with what was happening in Argentina." In Frank Gervasi, "What's Russia Up To?" *Collier's*, June 22, 1946, 52.

68. Donald M. Nelson, *Arsenal of Democracy: The Story of American War Production* (New York: Harcourt, Brace & Co., 1946), 418.

69. Stone and Kuznick, *An Untold History of the United States*, 29.

70. Ibid., 225. Forrestal was eventually committed to an insane asylum and jumped to his death, although some suspect foul play.

4. The Cold War and the Attack on the U.S. Democracy

1. Robert E. Sherwood, "The Third World War," *Collier's*, October 27, 1951, 19–31, 68–70, 78; Hanson Baldwin, "How the War was Fought," 22–23. The issue was titled "Preview of the War We Do Not Want: Russia's Defeat and Occupation 1952–1960." Walter Winchell wrote that "Stalin's idea of peace was to avoid full-scale war while grabbing off one nation after another in a mad orgy of communist imperialism." ("Walter Winchell in Moscow," *Collier's*, October 27, 1951, 39).

2. Sherwood, "The Third World War,", 29, 70.

3. Scott Nearing, *World Events* 3 (Winter 1950), *World Events* 4 (Winter 1951), Box 2, folder pamphlets, James B. Moullette Papers, Harry S. Truman Library, Independence, MO.

4. See Lance Selfa, *The Democrats: A Critical History* (Chicago: Haymarket Books, 2008).

5. Quoted in Fred Cook, *The Warfare State*, foreword by Bertrand Russell

(New York: Macmillan Co., 1962), 11–13; Colonel James Donovan, *Militarism U.S.A.*, foreword by General David M. Shoup (New York: Charles Scribner's Sons, 1970), 49.

6. Ibid., 119; Donald Nelson, *Arsenal of Democracy: The Story of American War Production* (New York: Harcourt, Brace & Co., 1946); William H. Neblett, *Pentagon Politics* (New York: Pageant Press, 1953), 46.

7. Cook, *The Warfare State*, 188, 195-208; C. Wright Mills, *The Power Elite* (New York: Oxford University Press, 1956); Donovan, *Militarism U.S.A.*, 49.

8. Cook, *The Warfare State*, 205.

9. Michael J. Hogan, "The National Security Discourse of the Early Cold War and the Legacy of Harry S. Truman," in *Origins of the National Security State*, ed. Michael Hogan and Mary Ann Heiss (Kirksville, MO: Truman State University Press, 2015), 1; Michael J. Hogan, *Cross of Iron: Harry S. Truman and the Origins of the National Security State, 1945–1954* (New York: Cambridge University Press, 1998); Richard Barnet, *Roots of War* (New York: Penguin Books, 1973); Cook, *The Warfare State*; Neblett, *Pentagon Politics*, 46.

10. Arthur Schlesinger Jr., *The Imperial Presidency* (Boston: Houghton Mifflin, 1973); Peter Dale Scott, *The War Conspiracy: JFK, 9/11, and the Deep Politics of War*, rev. ed., with foreword by Rex Bradford (New York: Skyhorse Publishing, 2008); Hal P. Albarelli Jr., *A Terrible Mistake: The Murder of Frank Olson and the CIAs Secret Cold War* (Walterville, OR: Trine Day, 2009).

11. Chalmers Johnson, *Sorrows of Empire: Militarism, Secrecy, and the End of the Republic* (New York: Henry Holt, 2005). The NSA budget averaged around $10 billion per year from 2011 to 2017.

12. Ellen Schrecker, "Introduction: Cold War Triumphalism and the Real Cold War," in *Cold War Triumphalism: The Misuse of History after the Fall of Communism* (New York: New Press, 2004), 14; Ann Markusen et al., *The Rise of the Gun Belt: The Military Remapping of Industrial America* (New York: Oxford University Press, 1991). See also Kirkpatrick Sale, *Power Shift: The Rise of the Southern Rim and Its Challenge to the Eastern Establishment* (New York: Random House, 1975). The Soviet people suffered from their own military-industrial complex, which consumed at least 40 percent of the state budget during the Cold War. By the 1980s, about 70 percent of Soviet industrial output was going to the military with even worse consequences for the United States.

13. "Fulbright Speech Charges Defense Contracts Subvert University Services," *Stanford Daily*, January 31, 1968, http://stanforddailyarchive.com; Nick Turse, *The Complex: How the Military Invades Our Everyday Lives* (New York: Metropolitan Books, 2007), 32.

14. Upton Sinclair, *The Goose Step: A Study of American Education* (New York: Albert & Charles Boni, 1922, 1923), 18.

15. Cohen quoted in Christopher Xenakis, *What Happened to the Soviet Union?*

How and Why American Sovietologists Were Caught by Surprise (New York: Praeger, 2002), 165–66. See also Sigmund Diamond, *Compromised Campus: The Collaboration of Universities with the Intelligence Community, 1945–1955* (New York: Oxford University Press, 1992), 55; Bruce Cumings, "Boundary Displacement: Area Studies and International Studies During and after the Cold War," in *Universities and Empire: Money and Politics in the Social Sciences during the Cold War*, ed. Christopher Simpson (New York: New Press, 1998), 159–89.

16. Diamond, *Compromised Campus*, 139. On the CIA and MSU, see Jeremy Kuzmarov, *Modernizing Repression: Police Training and Nation Building in the American Century* (Amherst, MA: University of Massachusetts Press, 2012), chap. 7.

17. See Peter Dale Scott, "North American Universities and the 1965 Indonesian Massacre: Indonesian Guilt and Western Responsibility," *Asia Pacific Journal*, December 14, 2014, http://apjjf.org; Bradley R. Simpson, *Economists with Guns: Authoritarian Development and U.S.–Indonesian Relations, 1960–1968* (Stanford, CA: Stanford University Press, 2008).

18. Joy Rhode, *Armed with Expertise: The Militarization of American Social Research during the Cold War* (Ithaca, NY: Cornell University Press, 2013).

19. Ellen Herman, "Project Camelot and the Career of Cold War Psychology," in *Universities and Empire*, ed. Simpson, 107.

20. Michael Albert, *Remembering Tomorrow: From SDS to Life after Capitalism—A Memoir* (New York: Seven Stories Press, 2006), 97, 99; Stuart W. Leslie, *The Cold War and American Science: The Military-Industrial Academic Complex at MIT and Stanford* (New York: Columbia University Press, 1993).

21. "The Struggle against Army Math," *Science for the People* (January 1974): 27, http://science-for-the-people.org; "Calculus for Conquest," *Science for the People* (March 1973), http://science-for-the-people.org; Tom Bates, *Rads: The 1970 Bombing of the Army Math Research Center at the University of Wisconsin and Its Aftermath* (New York: HarperCollins, 1992).

22. Albert Einstein quoted in Chris H. Gray, *Postmodern War: The New Politics of Conflict* (New York: Guilford Press, 1997), 235.

23. Dwight Eisenhower, "Memo for Directors and Chiefs of War Department, General and Special Staff Division and Bureaus of the Command General of the Major Commands," Subject, "Scientific and Technical Resources as Military Assets," April 30, 1946, Box 11, Stuart Symington Papers, Harry S. Truman Presidential Library, Independence, MO.

24. David Noble, "Academia Incorporated," *Science for the People* (January–February 1983); Jonathan Feldman, *Universities in the Business of Repression: The Academic–Military Complex and Central America* (Boston: South End Press, 1989), 151.

25. Memo for Dr. R. B. Stegmaier Jr., Resources Division Research and Development Board, "List of Glamor Items That Have Emanated from Ordinance R & D Program," January 22, 1952, RG 330 Records of the Office of the Secretary of Defense, Research and Development Board, Box

419; H. N. Worthley, Executive Director, Chemical Warfare Committee, "Committee on Chemical Warfare: Panel on Dissemination," October 28, 1952, RG 330 Records of the Office of the Secretary of Defense, Research and Development Board, Box 365, National Archives, College Park, MD.

26.   Fletcher Knebel, "Remote Control War: Are We Ready for It?" *Look*, November 27, 1950, 33–37.

27.   Norbert Wiener, "A Scientist Rebels," *The Atlantic Monthly*, January 1947, 46. See also Steve J. Heims, *John von Neumann and Norbert Wiener: From Mathematics to the Technologies of Life and Death* (Cambridge, MA: MIT Press, 1982).

28.   Annie Jacobsen, *Operation Paperclip: The Secret Intelligence Program That Brought Nazi Scientists to America* (Boston: Little, Brown, 2014), ix–xii, 7, 104, 353; Linda Hunt, *Secret Agenda: The United States Government, Nazi Scientists and Project Paperclip, 1945–1990* (New York: St. Martin's Press, 1998).

29.   Jacobsen, *Operation Paperclip*, 378–379; Michael Neufeld, *Von Braun: Dreamer of Space, Engineer of War* (Washington, D.C.: Smithsonian Institute, 2007); Herbert F. York, "Nuclear Deterrence and the Military Use of Space," in *Weapons in Space*, ed. Franklin A. Long et al. (New York: W. W. Norton, 1986), 18.

30.   See Ed Regis, *The Biology of Doom: The History of America's Secret Germ Warfare Project* (New York: Henry Holt, 1999), 110, 128; Fred Wilcox, *Scorched Earth: Legacies of Chemical Warfare in Vietnam* (New York: Seven Stories Press, 2011).

31.   Albarelli Jr., *A Terrible Mistake*; Douglas Valentine, *The Strength of the Wolf: The Secret History of America's War on Drugs* (London: Verso, 2004), 222, 223; Lukasz Kamienski, *Shooting Up: A History of Drugs in Warfare* (New York: Oxford University Press, 2016), 155, 156.

32.   Ludo De Witte, *The Assassination of Lumumba* (London: Verso, 2001); Regis, *The Biology of Doom*, 183; Gordon Thomas, *Secrets and Lies: A History of CIA Mind Control and Germ Warfare* (New York: Konecky, Williams & Associates, 2007), 37, 252.

33.   See Annie Jacobsen, *The Pentagon's Brain: An Uncensored History of DARPA, America's Top-Secret Military Research Agency* (Boston: Little, Brown, 2015); Sharon Weinberger, *The Imagineers of War: The Untold Story of DARPA, the Pentagon Agency That Changed the World* (New York: Alfred A. Knopf, 2017). Jacobsen, in *Area 51: An Uncensored History of America's Top-Secret Military Base* (Boston: Little, Brown, 2011), alleges that Vannevar Bush, founder of Raytheon Corporation and director of the Office of Scientific Research and Development in the Second World War, oversaw human experiments to study the effects of the bioweapons lewisite and mustard gas on humans during the early Cold War (382). The *Time Magazine* quote comes from Tim Weiner, *Blank Check: The Pentagon's Black Budget* (New York: Warner Books, 1990), 73–74.

34.   Peter Goodchild, *Edward Teller: The Real Dr. Strangelove* (Cambridge, MA:

Harvard University Press, 2004), 316; Kelly Moore, *Disrupting Science: Social Movements, American Scientists, and the Politics of the Military, 1945-1975* (Princeton: Princeton University Press, 2013), 51.

35. "S.E.S.P.A. Is Nauseated to Present Its Second Annual Dr. Strangelove Award to Edward Teller," *Science for the People Newsletter* 3/10 (February 1971), 10, http://science-for-the-people.org.

36. Letter to the editor, William Palmer Taylor, *Science Magazine*, October 27, 1967, 441.

37. Oliver Stone and Peter Kuznick, *The Untold History of the United States* (New York: Gallery Books, 2012), 257; John W. Dower, *The Violent American Century: War and Terror Since World War II* (Chicago: Haymarket Books, 2017), 28.

38. Stone and Kuznick, *The Untold History of the United States*, 287.

39. Dower, *The Violent American Century*, 37, 38.

40. Matthew Evangelista, *Innovation and the Arms Race* (Ithaca, NY: Cornell University Press, 1988), 262, 263.

41. Frank Kofsky, *Harry S. Truman and the War Scare of 1948: A Successful Campaign to Deceive the Nation* (New York: St. Martin's Press, 1993), xvii.

42. Eric Schlosser, *Command and Control: Nuclear Weapons, the Damascus Accident, and the Illusion of Safety* (New York: Penguin Books, 2013).

43. Jon Wiener, *How We Forgot the Cold War: A Journey across America* (Berkeley: University of California Press, 2012), 109.

44. Richard Rhodes, *Arsenals of Folly: The Making of the Nuclear Arms Race* (New York: Alfred A. Knopf, 2007), 3–15.

45. Dower, *The Violent American Century*, 33; David Vine, *Base Nation: How U.S. Military Bases Abroad Harm America and the World* (New York: Metropolitan Books, 2015), 71, 77.

46. "Bikini Atoll Nuclear Test: 60 Years Later and Islands Still Unlivable," *The Guardian*, March 1, 2014, https://www.theguardian.com.

47. See David Vine, *Island of Shame: The Secret History of the U.S. Military Base on Diego Garcia* (Princeton: Princeton University Press, 2011).

48. Robert Higgs, "The Cold War Economy: Opportunity, Costs, Ideology and the Politics of Crisis," *Explorations in Economic History*, July 1, 1994, http://www.independent.org.

49. *Atomic Audit: The Costs and Consequences of U.S. Nuclear Weapons since 1940*, ed. Stephen Schwartz (Washington, D.C.: Brookings Institute, 1998); Alan Rohn, "How Much Did the Vietnam War Cost?" January 22, 2014, https://thevietnamwar.info.

50. Richard J. Barnet, *The Economy of Death* (New York: Atheneum, 1969), 5.

51. See Stephen Messner and Richard Rosenfeld, *Crime and the American Dream* (Belmont, CA: Wadsworth, 2010); Rhodes, *Arsenals of Folly*, 306.

52. Seymour Melman, *Pentagon Capitalism: The Political Economy of War* (New York: McGraw Hill, 1970), 3.

53. Seymour Melman, "America's Permanent War Economy," in *Warfare Welfare: The Not-So Hidden Costs of America's Permanent War Economy*,

ed. Marcus G. Raskin and Gregory D. Squires (Washington, D.C.: Potomac Books, 2012), 139–65.

54. Ibid., 139–65.

55. Michael A. Bernstein, "Cold War Triumphalism and the Deformation of the American Economy," in Schrecker, *Cold War Triumphalism,* 129; Noam Chomsky, *Failed States: The Abuse of Power and Assault on Democracy* (New York: Metropolitan Books, 2006).

56. Quoted in Nelson Lichtenstein, "Market Triumphalism and the Wistful Liberals," in Schrecker, *Cold War Triumphalism,* 105.

57. Sharon Smith, *Subterranean Fire: A History of Working-Class Radicalism in the United States* (Chicago: Haymarket, 2006), 231, 239; David M. Oshinsky, "Labor's Cold War: The CIO and the Communists," in *The Specter: Original Essays on the Cold War and the Origins of McCarthyism,* ed. Robert Griffith and Athan Theoharis (New York: Franklin Watts, 1974), 120, 121.

58. Joel Kovel, *Red Hunting in the Promised Land: Anti-Communism and the Making of America* (New York: Basic Books, 1994), 12, 147–48; Smith, *Subterranean Fire,* 170; Oshinsky, "Labor's Cold War," 126.

59. Kovel, *Red Hunting in the Promised Land,* 148; Smith, *Subterranean Fire,* 190, 191; Oshinsky, "Labor's Cold War," 158; Nelson Lichtenstein, *Walter Reuther: The Most Dangerous Man in Detroit* (Urbana: University of Illinois Press, 1997). In 1950, the International Longshore and Warehouse Union (ILWU) that Bridges headed was expelled from the CIO.

60. Smith, *Subterranean Fire,* 203, 205, 210; Harry Kelber, "U.S. Labor Reps. Conspired to Overthrow Elected Governments in Latin America," *The Labor Educator,* November 29, 2004, http:www.laboreducator.org.

61. Harry Kelber, "Meany Hired a Former Top Communist to Run AFL–CIO's International Affairs," *The Labor Educator,* November 8, 2004; "U.S. Labor Secretly Intervened in Europe, Funded to Fight Pro-Communist Unions," *The Labor Educator,* November 22, 2004, http://www.laboreducator.org. See also Kim Scipes, *AFL-CIO's Secret War against Developing Country Workers: Solidarity or Sabotage?* (Boston: Lexington Books, 2011).

62. Miles D. Wolpin, *Military Aid and Counterrevolution in the Third World* (Lexington, MA: D.C. Heath, 1972), 136; Kelber, "U.S, Labor Representatives Conspired to Overthrow Elected Governments in Latin America," http://www.laboreducator.org.

63. Ronald Radosh, *American Labor and United States Foreign Policy* (New York: Vintage Books, 1969), 4, 23, 28, 29.

64. Elizabeth Fones Wolf, *Selling Free Enterprise: The Business Assault on Labor and Liberalism, 1945–1950* (Urbana: University of Illinois Press, 1995).

65. J. Edgar Hoover, *Masters of Deceit: What the Communist Bosses Are Doing Now to Bring America to Its Knees* (New York: Pocket Books, 1958), 297.

66. Athan Theoharis and John Stuart Cox, *The Boss: J. Edgar Hoover and the Great American Inquisition* (New York: Bantam Books, 1988), 17; Tim Weiner, *Enemies: A History of the FBI* (New York: Random House, 2012). 149.

67. Schrecker, *Cold War Triumphalism,* 203.

68.   Weiner, *Enemies*, 199.
69.   Ibid.; Douglas M. Charles, *J. Edgar Hoover and the Anti–Interventionists: FBI Political Surveillance and the Rise of the Domestic Security State, 1939–1945* (Columbus: Ohio State University Press, 2007); Frank Donner, *Protectors of Privilege: Red Squads and Police Repression in Urban America* (Berkeley: University of California Press, 1990); Huey P. Newton, *The War Against the Panthers: A Study of Repression in America* (New York: Grove Press, 1980); Arthur M. Eckstein, *Bad Moon Rising: How the Weather Underground Beat the FBI and Lost the Revolution* (New Haven: Yale University Press, 2016).
70.   Gerald Meyer, *Vito Marcantonio: Radical Politician, 1902–1954* (Albany: State University of New York Press, 1989), 6, 42. A protégé of Fiorello LaGuardia, Marcantonio was a champion of working-class interests and his Puerto Rican constituents who had run on a platform of "government control of natural resources and basic industries and public utilities so they could benefit the entire nation and to prevent the exploitation of consumers and the public." (p. 29). He earned the ire of the China lobby as the sole congressman to oppose the Korean War on the grounds of Korea's right to self–determination.
71.   Noam Chomsky, introduction to Nelson Blackstock, *COINTELPRO: The FBI's Secret War on Political Freedom* (New York: Pathfinder, 1988), 6, 27, 47, 73. The FBI worked to undermine the political campaign of SWP leader Clifton DeBerry, the first black man to run for president of the United States in 1964, by engineering his arrest on charges of non-support of his ex-wife and leaking to the press details of previous arrests for labor agitation. For FBI surveillance of a prominent Communist academic who pioneered study of Negro slave revolts, see Gary Murrell, *"The Most Dangerous Communist in the United States": A Biography of Herbert Aptheker* (Amherst, MA: University of Massachusetts Press, 2015).
72   Blackstock, *COINTELPRO*, vii. See also Ward Churchill and Jim Vanderwall, *The COINTELPRO Papers* (Cambridge, MA: South End Press, 2002).
73.   Noam Chomsky and Edward S. Herman, *Manufacturing Consent: The Political Economy of the Mass Media* (New York: Pantheon, 1989).
74.   Marzani, *We Can Be Friends*, 22, 29.
75.   *Life*, July 20, 1945, 20, quoted in Robert Griffith, "American Politics and the Origins of 'McCarthyism,'" *The Specter* (1974), 11, 12.
76.   "Could the Reds Seize Detroit?" in Michael Barson, *Better Dead Than Red! A Nostalgic Look at the Golden Years of Russophobia, Red-Baiting, and other Commie Madness* (New York: Hyperion, 1992).
77.   William Blum, *America's Deadliest Export, Democracy: The Truth about U.S. Foreign Policy and Everything Else* (London: Zed Books, 2015). At different periods in that 1947–77 period the CIA "owned fifty newspapers, news services, radio stations, and periodicals abroad as 'cover' organizations. At least twelve American publishing houses, some 'witting' [and] some not, had printed 250 books . . . paid for by the CIA." More than a hundred U.S.

journalists "worked as salaried CIA operatives (while employed by news organizations) and scores more worked for free. Twelve full–time CIA personnel worked as reporters with writing accreditations from the news-gathering organizations they represented." All in all, the "Propaganda Assets Inventory" of the CIA, "as it was known, encompassed more than eight hundred news and information organizations and individuals." James Aronson, *The Press and the Cold War* (New York: Monthly Review Press, 1970).

78.   Joseph and Stewart Alsop, "The Lessons of Korea," *Saturday Evening Post*, September 2, 1950, 17. "Cape common" apparently refers to the Cape Town area of South Africa.

79.   See Peter Dale Scott, *The War Conspiracy* (Indianapolis: Bobbs Merrill, 1970); William Lederer, *A Nation of Sheep* (New York: Fawcett Crest, 1967), 12–13; Bernard B. Fall, *Anatomy of a Crisis: The Laotian Crisis of 1960–1961* (New York: Doubleday, 1969), 137.

80.   Sulzberger, *New York Times*, March 21, 1946, quoted in Marzani, *We Can be Friends*, 29.

81.   Nancy E. Bernhard, *U.S. Television News and Cold War Propaganda, 1947–1960* (New York: Cambridge University Press, 1999), 1, 2, 107, 122. CBS newsman Edward R. Murrow was censored when he voiced concern about meaningless offensives in Korea that cost hundreds of lives and drained vital supplies and asked what would happen to the people living in the dead valleys whose villages had been put to the torch by Allied troops and whether "our occupation of that flea-bitten land [would] lessen, or increase, the attraction of Communism." CBS Director of the News, Ed Chester, killed the story for violating General Douglas MacArthur's prohibitions on media activity and giving comfort and propaganda to the enemy.

82.   Edward S. Herman, "All the News That's Fit to Print, Part II," *Z Magazine*, May 1998, http://www.thirdworldtraveler.com.

83.   Walter Lippmann and Charles Merz, "A Test of the News," *The New Republic*, August 4, 1920, 19, 20. See also Edward S. Herman, "Fake News on Russia and Other Official Enemies: *The New York Times*, 1917–2017," *Monthly Review*, July–August 2017.

84.   Arthur Copping, "First Story of New Regime at Murmansk Where Russians Flock to Escape Reds," *New York Times*, August 9, 1918.

85.   Arthur E. Copping, "Our Soldiers Fight in Russian Forests: Three Slain in First Encounter with Reds Amid Romantic Surroundings," *New York Times*, October 2, 1918; Arthur Copping, "Bolshevism Dying, Says Tschaikovski," *New York Times*, October 30, 1918.

86.   Dana Adams Schmidt, "The Front in Greece Is Everywhere: Where There Is No Fighting and Destruction There Is Paralyzing Fear of the Next Blow," *New York Times*, December 7, 1947; Anthony Lieviero, "President Warns Communists, Maps New Aid to Greece," *New York Times*, February 17, 1948. Schmidt acknowledges many of the guerrillas were not Communists but said members of left-wing parties had been "duped by the Communists." He said that guerrilla leader Markos Vafiadis, a former tobacco worker, had

as his personal escorts "fanatical Communists." His viewpoint is generally contradicted by recent scholarship. See for example Janet Hart, *New Voices in the Nation: Women and the Greek Resistance, 1941–1964* (Ithaca, NY: Cornell University Press, 1996).

87. "Warning to the West," *New York Times*, June 26, 1950; Matthew E. Mantell, "Opposition to the Korean War: A Study in American Dissent" (PhD diss., New York University, 1973), 85.

88. James Reston, "Washington: A Gleam of Light in Asia," *New York Times*, June 19, 1966. For another biased piece, see Robert P. Martin, "Indonesia: Hope . . . Where Once There Was None," *U.S. News and World Report*, June 6, 1966, 70.

89. Chomsky and Herman, *Manufacturing Consent*, 175–77.

90. Herman, "All the News That's Fit to Print, Part II." The book in question was Tom Gervasi, *The Myth of Soviet Military Supremacy* (New York: HarperCollins, 1987).

5. Truman, McCarthyism, and Domestic Repression

1. Scott Shane, Mark Mazzetti, and Eric Goldman, "Trump Adviser's Visit to Moscow Got the FBI's Attention," *New York Times*, April 19, 2017; Robert Parry, "The McCarthyism of Russia-Gate," *Consortium News*, May 7, 2017, https://consortiumnews.com. Page was branded as a security risk after giving a speech focused on the high level of corruption in Russia resulting from a "hasty transformation" from a command to free-market economy in the 1990s, in which he suggested that corruption also existed in the United States as embodied in the Bernie Madoff and Enron scandals.

2. See Masha Gessen, "How Putin Seduced Oliver Stone—and Trump," *New York Times*, June 25, 2017; Jeremy Kuzmarov, "Spirit of McCarthyism Seen in Attacks on Oliver Stone's Putin Interviews," *Huffington Post*, June 26, 2017, https://www.huffingtonpost.com. Stone actually pointed to Stalin's killing of Trotsky in the film, criticized U.S. policy in Afghanistan rather than Islam as a religion, and asked Putin critical questions such as his enacting a "big brother" law when he had supported Edward Snowden.

3. Robert Parry, "The Did-You-Talk-to-Russians Witch Hunt," *Consortium News*, February 18, 2017, https://consortiumnews.com.

4. See Lance Selfa, *The Democrats: A Critical History* (Chicago: Haymarket Books, 2008).

5. For a good overview, see Richard Fried, *Nightmare in Red: The McCarthy Era in Perspective* (New York: Oxford University Press, 1991).

6. Michael Paul Rogin, *The Intellectuals and McCarthy: The Radical Specter* (Boston: MIT Press, 1969); Richard Hofstadter, *Anti-Intellectualism in American Life* (New York: Alfred A. Knopf, 1963), 41–42; William Appleman Williams, *The Contours of American History*, 50th anniversary ed. (London: Verso, 2011); Peter H. Irons, "American Business and the Origins of McCarthyism: The Cold War Crusade of the United States Chamber of Commerce," in *The Specter: Original Essays on the Cold War*

and the Origins of McCarthyism, ed. Robert Griffith and Athan Theoharis (New York: Franklin Watts, 1974), 78, 79.

7.   Michael Paul Rogin, *Ronald Reagan, the Movie and other Episodes in Political Demonology* (Berkeley: University of California Press, 1987), xiii. See also Ellen Schrecker, *Many Are the Crimes: McCarthyism in America* (Princeton: Princeton University Press, 1998); Tom Engelhardt, *The End of Victory Culture: Post-War America and the Disillusioning of a Generation*, rev. ed. (Amherst: University of Massachusetts Press, 2007).

8.   Maurice Isserman and Ellen Schrecker, " 'Papers of a Dangerous Tendency': From Major Andre's Boot to the Venona Files," in *Cold War Triumphalism: The Misuse of History after the Fall of Communism*, ed. Ellen Schrecker (New York: New Press, 2006), 169.

9.   See Matthew Josephson, *Infidel at the Temple: A Memoir of the 1930s* (New York: Alfred A. Knopf, 1967); Kathryn S. Olmstead, *Right Out of California: The 1930s and the Big Business Roots of Modern Conservatism* (New York: New Press, 2015); Robin D. G. Kelley, *Hammer and Hoe: Alabama Communists during the Great Depression*, rev. ed. (Chapel Hill: University of North Carolina Press, 2015).

10.   Nat Hentoff, *Peace Agitator: The Story of A.J. Muste* (New York: Macmillan Co., 1963), 74–75.

11.   Bruce Cook, *Dalton Trumbo* (New York: Charles Scribner, 1977), 149.

12.   Landon R. Y. Storrs, *The Second Red Scare and the Unmaking of the New Deal Left* (Princeton: Princeton University Press, 2013), 2; Ellen Schrecker, *No Ivory Tower: McCarthyism and the Universities* (New York: Oxford University Press, 1986).

13.   Don E. Carleton, *Red Scare! Right-Wing Hysteria, Fifties Fanaticism and Their Legacy in Texas* (Austin, TX: Texas Monthly Press, 1985), 61.

14.   Quoted in Hajimu Masuda, *Cold War Crucible: The Korean Conflict and the Post-War World* (Cambridge, MA: Harvard University Press, 2015).

15.   Masuda, *Cold War Crucible*, 169.

16.   David Caute, *The Great Fear: The Anti-Communist Purge under Truman and Eisenhower* (London: Secker & Warburg, 1978), 218, 219; Cedric Belfrage, *The American Inquisition, 1945–1960* (Indianapolis: The Bobbs-Merrill Co., 1973), 152; Steve Nelson, James R. Barrett, Rob Ruck, *Steve Nelson American Radical* (Pittsburgh, PA: University of Pittsburgh Press, 1981), 320–79.

17.   Caute, *The Great Fear*, 163; Belfrage, *The American Inquisition, 1945–1960*, 86.

18.   Caute, *The Great Fear*, 35.

19.   Mary S. McAuliffe, *Crisis on the Left: Cold War Politics and American Liberals, 1947–1954* (Amherst: University of Massachusetts Press, 1978), 132.

20.   See Robert Sherrill and Harry Ernst, *The Drugstore Liberal: Hubert H. Humphrey in Politics* (New York: Grossman Publishers, 1968).

21.   Eric Foner, *The Story of American Freedom* (New York: W. W. Norton, 1999), 257; Arthur Schlesinger Jr., *The Vital Center* (Boston: Houghton and Mifflin, 1949), 35–50; McAuliffe, *Crisis on the Left*; Joel Kovel, *Red Hunting*

in the Promised Land: Anticommunism and the Making of America (London: Cassell, 1997), 143. The American Medical Association (AMA) invoked the specter of "socialized medicine" to discredit proposals for national health insurance, and the real estate industry the specter of "socialized housing" to discredit public housing.

22.   Carleton, *Red Scare!*, 93. Dies originated the House Un-American Activities Committee (HUAC) in the 1930s and was reelected to Congress in 1952.

23.   Anthony Summers, with Robyn Swan, *The Arrogance of Power: The Secret World of Richard Nixon* (New York: Viking, 2000), 47.

24.   Storrs, *The Second Red Scare*, 1. See also Colleen Doody, *Detroit's Cold War: The Origins of Postwar Conservatism* (Urbana: University of Illinois Press 2013), which shows wide support for anticommunism in Detroit by businessmen seeking to limit the power of unions.

25.   Ibid, 13. Keyserling, as a legislative aide to Senator Robert Wagner, was a chief draftsman of the 1935 National Labor Relations Act and the U.S. Housing Act. His wife, Mary, who served as an economist in the Department of Commerce, was part of the same investigation during which Leon underplayed his past Socialist ideals. Leon and many contemporaries later became bitter toward the New Left, because it reminded them of how they had sacrificed their youthful idealism for their careers.

26.   See J. Paul Henderson, *Darlington Hoopes: The Political Biography of an American Socialist* (London: Humming Earth, 2005), 126. As a member of the Pennsylvania Legislature in the 1930s, Hoopes led the successful fight to outlaw the use of child labor in factories, textile mills, and coal mines.

27.   Bernard Gordon interviewed by Patrick McGilligan in Patrick McGilligan and Paul Buhle, *Tender Comrades: A Back-History of the Hollywood Blacklist* (New York: St. Martin's Press, 1997), 262.

28.   Thomas L. Friedman, "Cold War Without the Fun," *New York Times*, June 24, 2015.

29.   Gordon's analysis is echoed by Noam Chomsky in *Failed States: The Abuse of Power and Assault on Democracy* (New York: Metropolitan Books, 2006).

30.   This section is drawn from Jeremy Kuzmarov, "Obama Should Exonerate Ethel Rosenberg, A Victim of Red Scare Repression," *Huffington Post*, October 25, 2016, https://www.huffingtonpost; Walter Schneir, *Final Verdict: What Really Happened in the Rosenberg Case* (Brooklyn: Melville House, 2010); Walter and Miriam Schneir, *Invitation to an Inquest*, rev. ed. (London: W. H. Allen, 1966). The third defendant in the case, Morton Sobell, served eighteen years in Alcatraz for espionage. He provided information that assisted Soviet air defense and told the *New York Times* that what Greenglass gave on the atomic bomb "was junk."

31.   Schneir, *Final Verdict*, 155; Schneir and Schneir, *Invitation to an Inquest*, 170, 425. Reflecting the sentiments of the time, a young law clerk named William H. Rehnquist, destined one day to serve as Chief Justice, lamented that "it's too bad that drawing and quartering has been abolished" (Schneir, *Final Verdict*, 157).

32. Jeremy Kuzmarov, interview with Robert and Jennifer Meeropol, October 21, 2016. William Rogers, Deputy Attorney General, admitted the government's strategy in promoting the death penalty was to try to force the Rosenbergs to talk, and that the strategy failed as the Rosenbergs "called their bluff." Sam Roberts, "Figure in Rosenberg Case Admits to Spying," *New York Times*, September 11, 2008.

33. Joan Brady, *America's Dreyfus: The Case Nixon Rigged* (New York: Skyscraper, 2015). The Dreyfus Affair divided France in the aftermath of the Franco-Prussian War, and brought out latent anti-Semitism. Captain Alfred Dreyfus was a Jew accused of leaking military secrets to the German embassy in Paris; he was later exonerated.

34. Ibid., 154.

35. Ibid.; Belfrage, *The American Inquisition, 1945–1960*, 90. On the FBI's role in spying on Hiss's witnesses and sharing of information, see also Curt Gentry, *J. Edgar Hoover: The Man and the Secrets* (New York: W. W. Norton, 2001).

36. Brady, *America's Dreyfus*; Gentry, *J. Edgar Hoover.*

37. Brady, *America's Dreyfus*, 169; Fred J. Cook, *The Unfinished Story of Alger Hiss* (New York: William Morrow, 1958), 168; John Chabot Smith, *Alger Hiss: The True Story* (New York: Holt, Rinehart and Winston, 1976), 273. Nixon claimed that Hiss and Chambers had been introduced by Joszef Peters, "brain" of the entire Communist underground; however, there is no record of this and Peters was deported to Hungary before the trial and said he never met Chambers except possibly once in the early 1930s. A member of the "Ware group," Lee Pressman, testified that this group was actually a Marxist study group, no one pilfered documents, and that Hiss was not a member. Soviet agent Hede Massing was meanwhile threatened with deportation if she did not testify against Hiss. The FBI suppressed a lab report showing that Alger's wife, Priscilla, could not have typed the documents, as was alleged. The Woodcock typewriter serving as key government evidence was also possibly reproduced by the CIA or U.S. military intelligence. Nixon alluded to this when he told Charles Colson (recorded in White House tapes), "The typewriters are always key. We built one in the Hiss case."

38. Kai Bird and Svetlana Chervonnaya, "The Mystery of Ales," *American Scholar*, Summer 2007, https://theamericanscholar.org/the-mystery-of-ales/.

39. Ibid.; Brady, *America's Dreyfus*, 325; S. M Plokhy, *Yalta: The Price of Peace* (New York: Viking, 2010), xxv. General Oleg Kalugin, chief of the KGB foreign intelligence department, stated years after the case that "Russian intelligence service has no documents proving that Alger Hiss cooperated with our service somewhere or anywhere," and General Julius Kobyakov said Hiss "never had any relationship with Soviet intelligence."

40. Brady, *America's Dreyfus*, 333, 334.

41. Robert P. Newman, *Owen Lattimore and the "Loss" of China* (Baltimore: Johns Hopkins University Press, 1992); Owen Lattimore, *Ordeal by Slander* (Boston: Little, Brown, 1950), 7, 175.

42. E. J. Kahn Jr. *The China Hands: America's Foreign Service Officers and What Befell Them* (New York: Viking Press, 1975); Gary May, *China Scapegoat: The Diplomatic Ordeal of John Carter Vincent* (Long Grove, IL: Waveland Press, 1982).

43. James Peck, *Washington's China: The National Security World, the Cold War, and the Origins of Globalism* (Amherst: University of Massachusetts Press, 2006).

44. Errol Morris, *Wormwood*, Netflix Films, 2017.

45. Hal Albarelli Jr., *A Terrible Mistake: The Murder of Frank Olson and the CIA's Secret Cold War Experiments* (Walterville, OR: Trine Day, 2009), 689–93.

46. Ryan Abbott, "CIA Murder Claims Are Credible, but Too Late," *Courthouse News*, July 23, 2013, https://www.courthousenews.com; "A Study of Assassination," http://www.frankolsonproject.org..

47. Albarelli Jr., *A Terrible Mistake*; Morris, *Wormwood*.

48. Albarelli Jr., *A Terrible Mistake*, 637, 654, 699. On Colby, see Zalin Grant, "Who Murdered the CIA Chief? William Colby a Suspicious Death," http://www.pythiapress.com.

49. Gerald Horne, *The Final Victim of the Blacklist: John Howard Lawson, Dean of the Hollywood Ten* (Berkeley: University of California Press, 2006), xiii. According to historian Horne, the fact that Lawson was Communist, Jewish, and affluent "excited the febrile passions of the most dedicated anti-Semites" within HUAC.

50. Ronald L. Davis, *The Glamor Factory: Inside Hollywood's Big Studio System* (Dallas, TX: Southern Methodist University Press, 1993), 350–51.

51. Horne, *The Final Victim of the Blacklist*, 185.

52. Ibid., 111; John Sbardellati, *J. Edgar Hoover Goes to the Movies: The FBI and the Origins of Hollywood's Cold War* (Ithaca, NY: Cornell University Press, 2012), 6.

53. Larry Ceplair and Christopher Trumbo, *Dalton Trumbo: Blacklisted Hollywood Radical* (Lexington: University Press of Kentucky, 2015), 162.

54. Ibid., 242; Dalton Trumbo, *The Time of the Toad: A Study of Inquisition in America* (1949; New York: Harper & Row, 1972), 6. See also Alvah Bessie, *Inquisition in Eden* (New York: Macmillan Co., 1965).

55. Trumbo, *The Time of the Toad*, 36.

56. Herbert Biberman, *Salt of the Earth: The Story of a Film* (Boston: Beacon Press, 1965); Steve Boisson, "*Salt of the Earth*: The Movie Hollywood Could Not Stop," *American History Magazine*, February 2002, http://www.historynet.com.

57. Michael Denning, *The Cultural Front: The Laboring of American Culture in the Twentieth Century* (London: Verso, 1997), xvi.

58. Trumbo, *The Time of the Toad*, 49, 50.

59. Stephen J. Whitfield, *The Culture of the Cold War* (Baltimore: Johns Hopkins University Press, 1997), 35.

60. Leo Cherne, "How to Spot a Communist," *Look*, March 4, 1947.

61. John Joseph Gladchuk, *Hollywood and Anti-Communism: HUAC and*

the Evolution of the Red Menace, 1935–1950 (New York: Routledge, 2007), 72.

62. Tony Shaw, *Hollywood's Cold War* (Amherst: University of Massachusetts Press, 2007), 11. Shaw was discussing the 1985 Columbia Pictures film *White Nights*. A study had found that women behind the Iron Curtain had more orgasms than their counterparts in the West because Communism provided for free child care and gave women more time for leisure. See Kristen R. Ghodsee, "Why Women Had Better Sex under Socialism," *New York Times*, August 12, 2017.

63. Shaw, *Hollywood's Cold War*, 276.

64. Jane Mayer, *Dark Money: The Hidden History of the Billionaires Behind the Rise of the Radical Right* (New York: Doubleday, 2016), 38, 39, 40.

65. Lee Roy Chapman, "The Strange Love of Dr. Billy James Hargis," *This Land Press*, November 2, 2012, http://thislandpress.com/2012/11/02/the-strange-love-of-dr-billy-james-hargis/.

66. Elaine Tyler May, *Homeward Bound: American Families in the Cold War Era* (New York: Basic Books, 1988); Storrs, *The Second Red Scare and the Unmaking of the New Deal Left*, 89.

67. Kate Weigand, *Red Feminism: American Communism and the Making of Women's Liberation* (Baltimore: Johns Hopkins University Press, 2001). On Flynn's career, see Helen C. Camp, *Iron in Her Soul: Elizabeth Gurley Flynn and the American Left* (Pullman, WA: Washington State University Press, 1995). I. F. Stone wrote that he could "not but help admire the courage, the poise, and the gentle firmness with which the elderly woman [Flynn] held her own before the jury and the judge" during her trial for sedition (p. 232).

68. See Daniel Horowitz, *Betty Friedan and the Making of the Feminine Mystique: The American Left, the Cold War, and Modern Feminism* (Amherst: University of Massachusetts Press, 2000).

69. See Penny Von Eschen, *Race Against Empire: Black Americans and Anticolonialism, 1937–1957* (Ithaca, NY: Cornell University Press, 1998).

70. See Kenneth R. Janken, "From Colonial Liberation to Cold War Liberalism: Walter White, the NAACP, and Foreign Affairs, 1941–1955," *Ethnic and Racial Studies*, 21 (6), 1998.

71. Manning Marable, *W. E. B. Du Bois: Black Radical Democrat*, rev, ed. (New York: Routledge, 2004), 20–21.

72. Ibid., 29; Gerald Horne, *Black and Red: WEB Du Bois and the Afro-American Response to the Cold War, 1944–1963* (Albany: State University of New York Press, 1986). 2.

73. Jordan Goodman, *Paul Robeson: A Watched Man* (London: Verso, 2013), 240, 242.

74. Ibid.

75. Ibid.; Martin Duberman, *Paul Robeson* (New York: Alfred A. Knopf, 1989); Jeff Sparrow, "How Paul Robeson Found His Political Voice in the Welsh Valleys," *The Guardian*, July 2, 2017, https://www.theguardian.com.

76. Dr. Martin Luther King Jr., "Beyond Vietnam: A Time to Break Silence:

Declaration of Independence from the War in Vietnam," April 4, 1967, Riverside Church, New York City, available at *Common Dreams*, April 4, 2008, https://www.commondreams.org.

77.   Edward Morgan, *What Really Happened to the 1960s: How Mass Media Failed American Democracy* (Lawrence: University of Kansas Press, 2010), 76; Daniel S. Lucks, *Selma to Saigon: The Civil Rights Movement and the Vietnam War* (Lexington: University Press of Kentucky, 2014), 203.

78.   "Dr. King's Error," *New York Times*, April 7, 1967; Lucks, *Selma to Saigon*, 197.

79.   Will Kaufman, *Woody Guthrie: American Radical* (University of Illinois Press, 2011), 128, 134; Woody Guthrie, "Talkin' Atom Bomb," 1946, Woody Guthrie Archive, Tulsa, Oklahoma. © Woody Guthrie Publications, Inc. All rights reserved. Used by permission.

80.   Kaufman, *Woody Guthrie*, 134.

81.   "I've Got to Know" 1948, Woody Guthrie Archive, Tulsa, Oklahoma. © Woody Guthrie Publications, Inc. All rights reserved. Used by permission.

82.   Woody Guthrie, "Henry Wallace Man," 1948, *Songs for Henry Wallace*, Woody Guthrie Archive, Tulsa, Oklahoma. © Woody Guthrie Publications, Inc. All rights reserved. Used by permission.

83.   Woody Guthrie, "Chiang Kai Shek," July 3, 1946, Woody Guthrie Archive, Tulsa, Oklahoma. © Woody Guthrie Publications, Inc. All rights reserved. Used by permission.

84.   Woody Guthrie, "Mr. Sickyman Ree," November 1952, Words & Music by Woody Guthrie. Woody Guthrie Archive, Tulsa, Oklahoma. © Woody Guthrie Publications, Inc. All rights reserved. Used by permission.

85.   Woody Guthrie, "Hey General Mackymacker," 1952, Woody Guthrie Archive, Tulsa, Oklahoma. Copyright Woody Guthrie Publications, Inc. All rights reserved. Used by permission.

6. A War on the Global South

1.   Jon Wiener, *How We Forgot the Cold War: A Historical Journey across America* (Berkeley: University of California Press, 2012), 31–33.

2.   Odd Arne Westad, *The Global Cold War: Third World Intervention and the Making of Our Time* (New York: Cambridge University Press, 2007).

3.   Noam Chomsky, *Deterring Democracy* (New York: Hill & Wang, 1992), 27, 28.

4.   William Blum, *Killing Hope: U.S. Military and C.I.A. Interventions since World War II* (Monroe, ME: Common Courage Press, 1998); William Blum, "A Brief History of U.S. Interventions, 1945 to the Present," *Z Magazine*, June 1999, http://www.thirdworldtraveler.com; Philip Agee, *Inside the Company: A CIA Diary* (New York: Penguin, 1975); Alfred W. McCoy, *The Politics of Heroin: CIA Complicity in the Global Drug Trade*, rev. ed. (New York: Lawrence Hill Books, 2003); Robert Ramon in "The CIA Assassination of Trujillo," *Soldier of Fortune* 1 (Summer 1975): 17, writes that "U.S. spooks like to work through proxies, puppets, dupes, allies or

whatever you want to call it—and the results are usually unfortunate for the proxies." Ramon, who fought for Chiang Kai-shek, Anastasio Somoza and other U.S. Cold War clients, went on to discuss the fate of Trujillo's intelligence chief, General Arthuro Espillat, who, after assisting in the Trujillo assassination plot, was paralyzed in a mysterious car crash in Lisbon and then committed suicide.

5.   Eqbal Ahmad, "History is a Weapon: The Cold War from the Standpoint of Its Victims," http://historyisaweapon.com.

6.   Marilyn B. Young, "Bombing Civilians: From the 20th to the 21st Centuries," in *Bombing Civilians: A 20th Century History,* ed. Marilyn B. Young and Yuki Tanaka (New York: New Press, 2009), 160; Charles K. Armstrong, *Tyranny of the Weak: North Korea and the World* (Ithaca, NY: Cornell University Press, 2013), 48.

7.   "The Time in Korea," *Time* July 10, 1950, 9.

8.   Armstrong, *Tyranny of the Weak,* 10, 14; James Carroll, *House of War: The Pentagon and the Disastrous Rise of American Power* (Boston: Houghton Mifflin, 2006), 192; Johnson quoted in Michael Parenti, *The Anti-Communist Impulse* (New York: Random House, 1969), 170.

9.   Charles K. Armstrong, *The North Korean Revolution, 1945–1950* (Ithaca NY: Cornell University Press, 2004); Bruce Cumings, *The Origins of the Korean War I: Liberation and the Emergence of Separate Regimes, 1945–1947,* Studies of the East Asian Institute (Princeton: Princeton University Press, 1981).

10. Cumings, *The Origins of the Korean War I,* 370, 380.

11. Dong-Choon Kim, *The Unending Korean War: A Social History,* trans. Sung-ok Kim (Larkspur, Calif.: Tamal Vista Publications, 2000).

12. Walter Sullivan, "Police Brutality in Korea Assailed: Torture, Wholesale Executions of Reds Held Driving People into Arms of Communists," *New York Times,* February 1, 1950, 3.

13. Su-kyoung Hwang, *Korea's Grievous War* (Philadelphia: University of Pennsylvania Press, 2016).

14. Jon Halliday and Bruce Cumings, *Korea: The Forgotten War* (New York: Viking, 1988); Francis Hill, CAO, I-Corps, Headquarters, 8th U.S. Army, BOX 3403, National Archives, College Park MD.

15. Bruce Cumings, *The Origins of the Korean War. II: The Roaring of the Cataract* (Princeton: Princeton University Press, 1990).

16. Halliday and Cumings, *Korea: The Forgotten War,* 117–18.

17. Report of Investigation into Allegations Contained in Letter to International Red Cross from the Two Senior POWs per July 28 to August 11, 1951, RG 554, General Headquarters, Far East Command, Office of the Inspector General, Box 18, National Archives, College Park, MD.

18. Charles S. Young, *Name, Rank and Serial Number: Exploiting Korean War POWs at Home and Abroad* (New York: Oxford University Press, 2014), 40; Wilfred Burchett and Alan Winnington, *Koje Unscreened* (Peking: Britain-China Friendship Association, 1953).

19. Col. Claudius O. Wolfe, UN Zone Staff Judge Advocate and Major Donald C. Young to Commander General, "Review of Report of Proceedings of a Board of Officers Appointed Pursuant to Article 121 Geneva Convention Relative to the Treatment of POWs, August 12, 1949," National Archives, College Park, MD, RG 338, Records of the U.S. Army Commands, 1942–, "Korean Communist Zone, 1951–1952," Box 509.

20. Stephen Endicott and Edward Hagerman, *The United States and Biological Warfare: Secrets from the Early Cold War and Korea* (Bloomington: Indiana University Press, 1989); Davie Chaddock, *This Must Be the Place: How the U.S. Waged Germ Warfare in the Korean War and Denied It Ever Since* (Seattle: Bennett & Hastings Publishers, 2013); Mori quoted in "Dirty Little Secrets: Al Jazeera investigates claims that the US used germ warfare during the Korean War," April 4th, 2010, www.aljazeera.com.

21. Cumings, *The Origins of the Korean War II*.

22. William Manchester, *American Caesar: Douglas MacArthur, 1880–1964* (New York: Laurel, 1978), 776, 780; Richard H. Rovere and Arthur M. Schlesinger Jr., *The General and the President and the Future of American Foreign Policy* (New York: Farrar, Straus and Young, 1951), 12; T. R Fehrenbach, *This Kind of War: A Study in Military Unpreparedness* (New York: Macmillan, 1963), 427–28.

23. John Stockwell, *The Praetorian Guard: The U.S. Role in the New World Order* (Boston: South End Press, 1999), 70; Philip Agee, *Inside the Company* (London: Penguin, 1975).

24. Vijay Prashad, *The Darker Nations: A People's History of the Third World* (New York: New Press, 2007).

25. James Burnham, *The Struggle for the World* (New York: John Day, 1947).

26. Parenti, *The Anti-Communist Impulse*, 239, 240.

27. Ervand Abrahamian, *The Coup: 1953, the CIA, and the Roots of Modern U.S.-Iranian Relations* (New York: New Press, 2013); Stephen Kinzer, *All the Shah's Men: An American Coup and the Roots of Middle Eastern Terror* (New York: Wiley, 2006). See also documents recently published in *Foreign Relations of the United States, Iran, 1952–1954*, ed. James Van Hook (Washington, D.C.: U.S. GPO, 2017), https://history.state.gov.

28. See Stephen Schlesinger Jr. and Stephen Kinzer, *Bitter Fruit: The Story of the American Coup in Guatemala*, 2nd ed. (Cambridge, MA: David Rockefeller Center for Latin American Studies, Harvard University, 1999).

29. Stephen Kinzer, *The Brothers: John Foster Dulles, Allen Dulles and Their Secret World War* (New York: Times Books, 2013).

30. Jonathan Nashel, *Edward Lansdale's Cold War* (Amherst, MA: University of Massachusetts Press, 2005), 40; William Pomeroy, *An American Made Tragedy: Neo-Colonialism and Dictatorship in the Philippines* (New York: International Publishers, 1974), 38; Max Boot, *The Road Not Taken: Edward Lansdale and the American Tragedy in Vietnam* (New York: Liveright, 2018), 139.

31. Peter Kornbluh, *The Pinochet File: A Declassified Dossier on Atrocity and Accountability* (New York: New Press, 2003).

32. Ibid., 28–35.

33. Robert Alden, "Mr. Allende Follows Outline of Speech," *New York Times*, December 5, 1972, http://www.nytimes.com.

34. Naomi Klein, *The Shock Doctrine: The Rise of Disaster Capitalism* (New York: Metropolitan Books, 2007), 79, 80, 82, 85, 49, 50.

35. Jeremy Kuzmarov, *Modernizing Repression: Police Training and Nation Building in the American Century* (Amherst: University of Massachusetts Press, 2012), chap. 5; Lt. Col. Gordon Beach to the Hon. Merle Cochran, "Weapons Delivered to the National Police under MDAP," June 13, 1951, RG 334 MAAG, Indonesia, Box 1, National Archives, College Park, MD.

36. Tim Weiner, *Legacy of Ashes: The History of the CIA* (New York: Anchor Books, 2008), 143, 144; George McT. Kahin and Audrey Kahin, *Subversion as Foreign Policy: The Secret Eisenhower and Dulles Debacle in Indonesia* (New York: New Press, 1995); Peter Gribbin, "CIA in Indonesia: 1965," *Counterspy* (Winter 1980): 25.

37. Wayne Madsen, *The Manufacturing of a President: The CIA's Insertion of Barack Obama Jr. into the White House* (Wayne Madsen, 2012); Marc Curtis, *Web of Deceit: Britain's Real Role in the World* (London: Vintage, 2003); Gabriel Kolko, *Confronting the Third World* (New York: Pantheon, 1988).

38. See David Gibbs, *The Political Economy of Third World Intervention* (Chicago: University of Chicago Press, 1991); Godfrey Mwakikagile, *Western Involvement in Nkrumah's Downfall* (Dar es Salaam, Tanzania: New Africa Press, 2015); "Ghanaian Subversives in Africa," February 9, 1962. For Mac Bundy, State Department Draft Study on Ghana RG 59, Gen. Records of the Department of State, Records of the Bureau of African Affairs, 1958–1966, box 65; Olcott Deming to Mr. Fredericks, "CAS Report on Sabotage in South Africa," January 11, 1962, RG 59.Gen. Records of the Department of State, Records of the Bureau of African Affairs, 1958–1966, box 50; "Nkrumah's Subversion in Africa," October 27, 1966. Joe Matthews was one of the "extremists" who received $10,000 from Ghana for anti-government operations in Basutoland.

39. Richard D. Mahoney, "The Kennedy Policy in Congo, 1961–1963" (PhD diss., Johns Hopkins University, 1980), 266–67; Lawrence Devlin, *Chief of Station, Congo: Fighting the Cold War in a Hot Zone* (New York: Public Affairs, 2008); Sean Kelley, *America's Tyrant* (Washington, D.C.: American University Press, 1993).

40. Piero Gleijeses, *Conflicting Missions: Havana, Washington, and Africa, 1959–1976* (Chapel Hill: University of North Carolina Press, 2002); Ludo de Witte, "The Suppression of the Congo Rebellions and the Rise of Mobutu, 1963–1965," *International History Review* 39/1 (2017): 118.

41. Kuzmarov, *Modernizing Repression*, chap. 8; Kwame Nkrumah, *Dark Days in Ghana* (New York: International Publishers, 1968), 50. Ngendan-dumwe's assassin Gonzalve Muyenzi worked as an accountant in the U.S. embassy in Bujumbura and was allegedly paid three million francs by the CIA.

42. Samuel Farber, *The Origins of the Cuban Revolution Reconsidered* (Chapel Hill: University of North Carolina Press, 2006); Wiener, *How We Forgot the Cold War*, 216.

43. Warren Hinckle and William W. Turner, *The Fish Is Red: The Story of the Secret War Against Castro* (New York: Harper & Row, 1981), 161, 195; Edward Lansdale, "Review of Operation Mongoose," Memo for the Special Group, July 25, 1962, National Security Archives.

44. Keith Bolender, *Voices from the Other Side: An Oral History of Terrorism Against Cuba*, foreword by Noam Chomsky (London: Pluto Press, 2010), 18; Noam Chomsky, "International Terrorism: Image and Reality," in *Western State Terrorism*, ed. Alexander George (Cambridge: Polity Press, 1991), 23.

45. Hinckle and Turner, *The Fish Is Red*, 161.

46. Wiener, *How We Forgot the Cold War*, 220. Goldwater in turn called Kennedy an appeaser.

47. Stephen G. Rabe, *The Most Dangerous Area in the World: John F. Kennedy Confronts Communist Revolution in Latin America* (Chapel Hill: University of North Carolina Press, 1999), 67–68.

48. See Thomas C. Field, *From Development to Dictatorship: Bolivia and the Alliance for Progress* (Ithaca, NY: Cornell University Press, 2014), 168, 196.

49. "Ché Guevara Exposes US Alliance for Progress," *The Militant*, January 20, 2003, http://www.themilitant.com.

50. See Michael Ratner and Michael Steven Smith, *Who Killed Che? How the CIA Got Away with Murder*, with introduction by Ricardo Alarcon (New York: OR Books, 2011).

51. Nick Turse, *Kill Anything that Moves: The Real American War in Vietnam* (New York: Metropolitan Books, 2005); and Paul Shannon, "The ABCs of the Vietnam War," *Indochina Newsletter*, Spring-Summer 2000, 22. This chapter includes material from John Marciano, *The American War in Vietnam: Crime or Commemoration?* (New York: Monthly Review Press, 2016).

52. Michael Parenti, "What Do Empires Do?" *ZNet Daily Commentary*, February 13, 2010, 1–2. https://zcomm.org; and Parenti, *Profit Pathology and Other Indecencies* (Boulder, CO: Paradigm Publishers, 2015), 34. See also H. Bruce Franklin, *Vietnam and Other American Fantasies* (Amherst: University of Massachusetts Press, 2000).

53. Tom Hayden, *The Love of Possession Is a Disease with Them* (New York: Holt, Rinehart and Winston, 1972), 62-65. U.S. ambassador Ellsworth Bunker promoted laws designed to promote foreign investment, and Hayden notes how American corporations like Standard Oil, Shell, and Ford moved into Vietnam along with dozens of other contractors, builders, machine tool companies, and producers of agricultural equipment along with many Japanese businesses.

54. Gareth Porter, *Perils of Dominance: Imbalance of Power and the Road to War in Vietnam* (Berkeley: University of California Press, 2004).

55. McCoy, *The Politics of Heroin*, 229.

56. This material is all drawn from Roger Peace, with John Marciano and Jeremy Kuzmarov, "The Vietnam War," http://peacehistory-usfp.org. See also Marciano, *The American War in Vietnam*.

57. Ibid. See also Rennie Davis, *The New Humanity: A Movement to Change the World* (Las Vegas, NV: Bliss Life Press, 2017), 184. Peace activist Rennie Davis visited the heavily bombed city of Vinh, Vietnam's Dresden, which he said resembled "the moon with crater upon crater, like the aftermath of the atom bomb without radiation." Even though the city was gone, Davis was astounded that many of its residents survived by setting up quarters inside a deep tunnel system, and he was moved by the performance of women singing and dancing for a free and independent Vietnam inside the tunnels.

58. Daniel Ellsberg, *Secrets: A Memoir of Vietnam and the Pentagon Papers* (New York: Penguin Books, 2002), 12–13.

59. In Paul Dickson, *The Electronic Battlefield* (Bloomington: Indiana University Press, 1976), 208.

60. Peace, with Marciano and Kuzmarov, "The Vietnam War."

61. See Fred Branfman, ed., *Voices from the Plain of Jars: Life under an Air War*, 2nd ed., with essays and drawings by Laotian villagers, foreword by Alfred W. McCoy (Madison: University of Wisconsin Press, 2013).

62. Alfred W. McCoy, *A Question of Torture: CIA Interrogation from the Cold War to the War on Terror* (New York: Metropolitan Books, 2006), 5.

63. Ibid., 7, 9. The Communist brainwashing claims were never substantiated. A 1956 Army report stated that "the exhaustive efforts of several government agencies failed to reveal even one conclusively documented case of the actual 'brainwashing' of an American prisoner of war in Korea." Lukasz Kamienski, *Shooting Up: A History of Drugs and War* (New York: Oxford University Press, 2016), 155, 156.

64. Kuzmarov, *Modernizing Repression*; Martha K. Huggins, *Political Policing: The United States in Latin America* (Durham, NC: Duke University Press, 1998).

65. A. J. Languuth, *Hidden Terrors: The Truth About U.S. Police Operations in Latin America* (New York: Pantheon Books, 1978).

66. Kuzmarov, *Modernizing Repression*.

67. See Joanna Harcourt-Smith, *Tripping the Bardo with Timothy Leary: My Psychedelic Love Story* (North Charleston, SC: Creative Space Independent Publishing, 2013), 314.

68. See Jack Nelson-Pallmeyer, *School of the Assassins* (New York: Orbis Books, 1997); Lesley Gill, *School of the Americas: Military Training and Political Violence in the Americas* (Durham, NC: Duke University Press, 2004).

69. Nelson-Pallmeyer, *School of the Assassins*, 32.

70. McNamara, quoted in William Michael Schmidli, *The Fate of Freedom Elsewhere: Human Rights and U.S. Cold War Policy towards Argentina* (Ithaca, NY: Cornell University Press, 2012), 24.

71. See Noam Chomsky and Edward S. Herman, *The Political Economy of Human Rights I: The Washington Connection and Third World Fascism* (Boston: South End Press, 1979).

72. See Jerry Sanders, *Peddlers of Crisis: The Committee on the Present Danger and the Politics of Containment* (Boston: South End Press, 1983).

73. Michael Rogin, *Ronald Reagan The Movie and Other Episodes in Political Demonology* (Berkeley: University of California Press, 1987), xiii, 1–3.

74. Ibid., xiv, xv.

75. John Edwards, *Superweapon: The Making of MX* (New York: W. W. Norton, 1982), 20, 21; James Peck, *Ideal Illusions: How the U.S. Government Coopted Human Rights* (New York: Metropolitan Books, 2010).

76. Daniel Wirls, *Buildup: The Politics of Defense in the Reagan* Era (Ithaca, NY: Cornell University Press, 1992), 42, 44; "The Marsh Years," *Soldiers*, February 1989, 29.

77. See Melvin Goodman, *Failure of Intelligence: The Decline and Fall of the CIA* (New York: Rowman & Littlefield, 2008). Claire Sterling wrote a best-selling book sponsored by the CIA claiming that terrorism was the Soviet Union's ultimate secret weapon against the West, which was based on the unsubstantiated claims of defectors. Claire Sterling, *The Terror Network: The Secret War of International Terrorism* (New York: Berkeley Books, 1981).

78. Frances FitzGerald, *Way Out There in the Blue: Reagan, Star Wars and the End of the Cold War* (New York: Simon & Schuster, 2001); H. Bruce Franklin, *War Stars: The Superweapon and the American Imagination* (Amherst: University of Massachusetts Press, 2008), 200–206.

79. FitzGerald, *Way Out There in the Blue: Reagan*, 23; Robert Scheer, "The Man Who Blew the Whistle on 'Star Wars': Roy Woodrutt's Ordeal Began When He Tried to Turn the Vision of an X-Ray Laser into Reality," *Los Angeles Times*, July 1, 1988; William J. Broad, *Teller's War: The Top-Secret Story Behind the Star Wars Deception* (New York: Simon & Schuster, 1992).

80. Ronald W. Cox, *Power and Profit: U.S. Policy in Central America* (Lexington: University of Kentucky Press, 1994), 97; Norma Stoltz Chinchilla and Nora Hamilton, "Prelude to Revolution: U.S. Investment in Central America," in *The Politics of Intervention: The United States in Central America*, ed. Roger Burbach and Patricia Flynn (New York: Monthly Review Press, 1984), 222.

81. Greg Grandin, *Empire's Workshop: The U.S., Latin America and the Rise of the New Imperialism* (New York: Metropolitan Books, 2005).

82. Mark Danner, *The Massacre at El Mozote: A Parable of the Cold War* (New York: Vintage, 1994), 52. For an eyewitness account of the horror of the El Salvador civil war, see Charles Clements, *Witness to War* (New York: Bantam Books, 1984).

83. Roger Peace, *A Call to Conscience: The Anti-Contra War Campaign* (Amherst: University of Massachusetts Press, 2012), 46, 48; Thomas W. Walker, *Nicaragua: Living in the Shadow of the Eagle* (Boulder, CO: Westview Press, 2003), 114.

84. Holly Sklar, *Washington's War on Nicaragua* (Boston: South End Press, 1999).

85. Robert Timberg, *The Nightingale's Song* (New York: Touchstone Books, 1995); Jonathan Marshall, Peter Dale Scott and Jane Hunter, *The Iran Contra Connection: Secret Teams and Covert Operations in the Reagan Era* (Boston: South End Press, 1987); Daniel Hopsicker, *Barry & 'The Boys': The CIA, the Mob and America's Secret History* (Aurora, CO: Mad Cow Press, 2001).

86. Gary Webb, *Dark Alliance: The CIA, the Contras and the Crack Cocaine Explosion*, rev. ed. (New York: Seven Stories Press, 1999); Noam Chomsky, *Year 501: The Conquest Continues* (Boston: South End Press 1993), 86.

87. Mahmood Mamdani, *Good Muslim, Bad Muslim: America, the Cold War and the Roots of Terror* (New York: Pantheon, 2004).

88. Peter Dale Scott, *American War Machine: Deep Politics, the CIA Global Drug Connection and the Road to Afghanistan* (New York: Rowman & Littlefield, 2010), 11.

89. Alan J. Kuperman, "The Stinger Missile and U.S. Intervention in Afghanistan," *Political Science Quarterly* 114 (1999), http://www.dtic.mil.

90. Robert Dreyfuss, *Devil's Game: How the United States Helped to Unleash Fundamentalist Islam* (New York: Metropolitan Books, 2005); Jeremy Kuzmarov, "Charlie Wilson's War," *Z Magazine*, February 1, 2008, https://zcomm.org/zmagazine/charlie-wilsons-war-by-jeremy-kuzmarov/.

91. Mamdani, *Good Muslim, Bad Muslim,* 137, 138; John Cooley, *Unholy Wars* (London: Pluto Press, 1999), 274–75.

92. Chalmers Johnson, *Blowback: The Costs and Consequences of the American Empire* (New York: Metropolitan Books, 2002).

93. Andrei Tsygankov, *Russophobia: Anti-Russian Lobby in U.S. Foreign Policy* (New York: Palgrave Macmillan, 2009), 55.

94. Tsygankov, *Russophobia,* 55; *The Black Book of Communism,* ed. Stéphane Courtois et al. (Cambridge, MA: Harvard University Press, 1999).

95. Tsygankov, *Russophobia.* For background on the Committee on the Present Danger, which evolved into the Project for the New American Century, see Sanders, *Peddlers of Crisis.*

Conclusion: Avoiding a Third World War

1. C. Wright Mills, *The Causes of World War III* (New York: Ballantine Books, 1958), 66.

2. Andrei Tsyganov, *Russophobia: Anti-Russian Lobby in U.S. Foreign Policy* (New York: Palgrave Macmillan, 2009).

3. John L. Gaddis, quoted in Gabriel Schoenfeld, "Twenty-Four Lies about the Cold War," in *CNN's Cold War Documentary: Issues and Controversy,* ed. Arnold Beichman (Stanford, CA: Hoover Institution Press, 2000), 8.

4. Ruth Leger Sivard, with George F. Kennan, Foreword, *World Military and Social Expenditures, 1981* (Leesburg, VA: World Priorities, 1981), 8.

5. Patrick J. Buchanan, "Who's Really Trolling for War with Russia," *Tulsa World,* June 22, 2016, http://www.tulsaworld.com/opinion/

patrickjbuchanan/patrick-j-buchanan-who-s-really-trolling-for-war-with/
article_fb0facca-c81a-52b9-94aa-ae53e838841f.html.

6. See, for example, Jack Matlock, "Why Do We Want a Cooperative
    Relationship with Russia," April 23, 2017, http://isit2020yet.net/.

7. See Guy Mettan, *Creating Russophobia: From the Great Religious Schism to
    Anti-Putin Hysteria* (Atlanta, GA: Clarity Press, 2017).

8. The propaganda campaign against Wallace was so effective that historians
    still depict him as a pro-Communist dupe and naïve politician. See, for
    example, Thomas W. Devine, *Henry Wallace's 1948 Presidential Campaign
    and the Future of Postwar Liberalism* (Chapel Hill: University of North
    Carolina Press, 2015). Albert A. Woldman, *Lincoln and the Russians* (New
    York: Collier Books, 1952).

9. Zbigniew Brzezinski, *The Grand Chessboard: American Primacy and Its
    Geostrategic Imperatives* (New York: Basic Books, 1998).

10. James Madison, "Political Observations," April 20, 1795, in *Letters and
    Other Writings of James Madison*, vol. 4, (1865; Hard Press Publishing,
    2013), 491.

Selected Bibliography

Abrahamian, Ervand. *The Coup: 1953, the CIA, and the Roots of Modern U.S.-Iranian Relations* (New York: The New Press, 2013).

Agee, Philip. *Inside the Company* (London: Penguin, 1975).

Ahmad, Eqbal. "History Is a Weapon: The Cold War from the Standpoint of Its Victims," http://historyisaweapon.com.

Albarelli Jr., Hal. *A Terrible Mistake: The Murder of Frank Olson and the CIA's Secret Cold War Experiments* (Walterville, OR: Trine Day, 2009).

Albertson, Ralph. *Fighting Without a War: An Account of Military Intervention in North Russia* (New York: Harcourt, Brace and Howe, 1920).

Alperovitz, Gar. A*tomic Diplomacy: Hiroshima and Potsdam* (New York: Vintage, 1996).

_____. *Cold War Essays* (Garden City, NY: Anchor Books, 1970).

Anderson, Godfrey J. *A Michigan Polar Bear Confronts the Bolsheviks: A War Memoir*, ed. Gordon L. Olson (Grand Rapids, MI: William B. Eerdman's Publishing Co., 2010).

Anderson, Perry. *American Foreign Policy and Its Thinkers* (London: Verso, 2015).

Applebaum, Anne. *Iron Curtain: The Crushing of Eastern Europe, 1944–1956* (New York: Anchor, 2013).

Aronson, James. *The Press and the Cold War* (New York: Monthly Review Press, 1970).

Baldwin, Natylie, and Kermit Heartstrong. *Ukraine: Zbig's Grand Chessboard & How the West Was Checkmated* (San Francisco: Next Revelation Press, 2015).

Barson, Michael. *Better Dead Than Red! A Nostalgic Look at Russophobia, Red-Baiting, and Other Commie Madness* (New York: Hyperion, 1992).

Belfrage, Cedric. *The American Inquisition, 1945–1960* (Indianapolis: Bobbs-Merrill Co., 1973).

Bernhard, Nancy E. *U.S. Television News and Cold War Propaganda, 1947–1960* (New York: Cambridge University Press, 1999).

Blackstock, Nelson. *COINTELPRO: The FBI's Secret War on Political Freedom* (New

York: Pathfinder, 1988).

Blum, John Morton, ed., *The Price of Vision*: The *Diary of Henry A. Wallace, 1942–1946* (Boston: Houghton Mifflin, 1973).

Blum, William. *Killing Hope: CIA and US Military Interventions since World War II* (Monroe, ME: Common Courage Press, 1998).

_____. *America's Deadliest Export, Democracy—The Truth about U.S. Foreign Policy and Everything Else* (London: Zed Books, 2015).

Boyd-Barrett, Oliver. *Western Mainstream Media and the Ukraine Crisis: A Study in Conflict Propaganda* (New York: Routledge, 2017).

Brady, Joan. *America's Dreyfus: The Case Nixon Rigged* (New York: Skyscraper, 2015).

Branfman, Fred. *Voices from the Plain of Jars,* rev. ed., with a new foreword by Alfred W. McCoy (Madison: University of Wisconsin Press, 2013).

Browder, William. *Red Notice: A True Story of High Finance, Murder, and One Man's Fight for Justice* (New York: Simon & Schuster, 2015).

Burchett, Wilfred G. *Warmongers Unmasked: History of Cold War in Germany* (Melbourne, Australia: World Unity Publications, 1950).

_____. Koje-do *Unscreened* (Peking: British-China Friendship Association, 1953).

Plokhy, S. M. *Yalta: The Price of Peace* (New York: Penguin Books, 2011).

Carleton, Don E. *Red Scare! Right Wing Hysteria, Fifties Fanaticism and Their Legacy in Texas* (Austin: Texas Monthly Press, 1985).

Caute, David. *The Great Fear: The Anti-Communist Purge Under Truman and Eisenhower* (London: Secker & Warburg, 1978).

Ceplair, Larry, and Christopher Trumbo. *Dalton Trumbo: Blacklisted Hollywood Radical* (Lexington: The University Press of Kentucky, 2015).

Chaddock, David. *This Must Be the Place: How the U.S. Waged Germ Warfare in the Korean War and Denied It Ever Since* (Seattle: Bennett & Hastings Publishers, 2013).

Chomsky, Noam. *Deterring Democracy* (New York: Hill & Wang, 1992).

_____. *Rethinking Camelot: JFK, the Vietnam War, the US Political Culture* (Boston: South End Press, 1993).

_____. *World Orders Old and New* (New York: Columbia University Press, 1994).

_____.*Masters of Mankind: Essays and Lectures, 1969–2013* (Chicago: Haymarket Books, 2014).

Chomsky, Noam, and Edward S. Herman. *Manufacturing Consent: The Political Economy of the Mass Media* (New York: Pantheon, 1989).

_____. *The Political Economy of Human Rights I: The Washington Connection and Third World Fascism* (Boston: South End Press, 1979).

Clemens, Diane Shaver. *Yalta* (New York: Oxford University Press, 1971).

Cohen, Stephen. *Soviet Fates and Lost Alternatives: From Stalinism to the New Cold War* (New York: Columbia University Press, 2009).

_____. *Failed Crusade: America and the Tragedy of Post-Soviet Russia* (New York: W. W. Norton, 2001).

_____. Interview with David Barsamian of *Alternative Radio*, New York, NY, December 3, 2016.

Cudahy, John. *Archangel: The American War with Russia* (Chicago: A.C. McClurg

& Co., 1924).

Culver, John, and John Hyde. *American Dreamer: A Life of Henry A. Wallace* (New York: Norton, 2000).

Cumings, Bruce. *The Origins of the Korean War Vol. I* (Princeton: Princeton University Press, 1981).

_____. *The Origins of the Korean War, Vol. II* (Princeton: Princeton University Press, 1990).

Danner, Mark. *The Massacre at El Mozote: A Parable of the Cold War* (New York: Vintage, 1994).

Davis, Donald E., and Eugene P. Trani. *Distorted Mirrors: Americans and Their Relationship with Russia and China in the 20th Century* (Columbia: University of Missouri Press, 2009).

de Ploeg, Chris Kasper. *Ukraine in the Crossfire* (Atlanta: Clarity Press, 2017).

Diamond, Sigmund. *Compromised Campus: The Collaboration of Universities with the Intelligence Community, 1945–1955* (New York: Oxford University Press, 1992).

Dower, John W. *The Violent American Century: War and Terror since World War II* (Chicago: Haymarket Books, 2017).

Dugin, Alexsander. *Putin vs Putin: Vladimir Putin Viewed from the Right* (UK: Arktos Media Limited., 2014).

Eisenberg, Carolyn. *Drawing the Line: The American Decision to Divide Germany, 1944–1949* (New York: Cambridge University Press, 1998).

Ellsberg, Daniel. *Secrets: A Memoir of Vietnam and the Pentagon Papers* (New York: Penguin Books, 2002).

Endicott, Stephen, and Edward Hagerman. *The United States and Biological Warfare: Secrets from the Early Cold War and Korea* (Indiana University Press, 1989).

Ferell, Robert. *Choosing Truman: The Democratic Convention of 1944* (Columbia: University of Missouri Press, 1994).

Field, Thomas C., Jr. *From Development to Dictatorship: Bolivia and the Alliance for Progress* (Ithaca, NY: Cornell University Press, 2014).

Figes, Orlando. *The Crimean War: A History* (London: Picador, 2010).

FitzGerald, Frances. *Way Out There in the Blue: Reagan, Star Wars and the End of the Cold War* (New York: Simon & Schuster, 2001).

Fleming, Dana Frank. *The Cold War and Its Origins, Vols. I–II, 1917–1960.* (New York: Doubleday, 1960).

Foglesong, David. *The American Mission and the "Evil Empire"* (New York: Cambridge University Press, 2007).

Fones-Wolf. Elizabeth. *Selling Free Enterprise: The Business Assault on Labor and Liberalism, 1945–1950* (Urbana: University of Illinois Press, 1995).

Franklin, H. Bruce. *War Stars: The Superweapon and the American Imagination* (New York: Oxford University Press, 1988).

_____. *Vietnam and Other American Fantasies* (Amherst, MA: University of Massachusetts Press, 2006).

Freedland, Richard M. *The Truman Doctrine & The Origins of McCarthyism: Foreign Policy, Domestic Politics, and International Security 1946–1948* (New York: Schocken Books, 1971).

Friel, Howard and Richard Falk. *The Record of the Paper: How the New York Times*

Misreports US Foreign Policy (London: Verso, 2004).

Gaddis, John Lewis. *The Cold War: A New History* (New York: Penguin, 2013).

Ganser, Daniele. *NATO's Secret Armies: Operation Gladio and Terrorism in Western Europe* (London: Frank Cass, 2005).

Gervasi, Tom. *The Myth of Soviet Supremacy* (New York: Harper and Row, 1986).

Gibbs, David. *The Political Economy of Third World Intervention* (Chicago: University of Chicago Press, 1991).

Goldhurst, Richard. *The Midnight War: The American Intervention in Russia, 1918–1920* (New York: McGraw Hill, 1978).

Goldman, Marshall I. *Petro-State: Putin, Power and the New Russia* (New York: Oxford University Press, 2010).

Goodman, Jordan. *Paul Robeson: A Watched Man* (London: Verso, 2013).

Goodman, Melvin. *Failure of Intelligence: The Decline and Fall of the CIA* (New York: Rowman & Littlefield, 2008).

Grandin, Greg. *Empire's Workshop: The U.S., Latin America and the Rise of the New Imperialism* (New York: Metropolitan Books, 2005).

Graves, William S. *America's Siberian Adventure 1918–1920* (New York: Peter Smith, 1941).

Griffith, Robert, and Athan Theoharis, eds. *The Specter: Original Essays on the Cold War and the Origins of McCarthyism* (New York: Franklin Watts, 1974).

Grose, Peter. *Operation Rollback: America's Secret War Behind the Iron Curtain* (Boston: Houghton Mifflin, 2000).

Heller, Henry. *The Cold War and the New Imperialism: A Global History, 1945–2005* (New York: Monthly Review Press, 2006).

Herman, Edward S. "Fake News on Russia and Other Official Enemies: The *New York Times*, 1917–2017," *Monthly Review*, July-August 2017.

————. *The Myth of the Liberal Media: An Edward Herman Reader* (New York: Peter Lang, 1999).

Hinckle, Warren, and William W. Turner. *The Fish Is Red: The Story of the Secret War Against Castro* (New York: Harper & Row, 1981).

Hogan, Michael *Cross of Iron: Harry S. Truman and the Origins of the National Security State, 1945–1954* (Cambridge: Cambridge University Press, 1998).

————. *The Marshall Plan: America, Britain and the Reconstruction of Western Europe, 1947–1952* (New York: Cambridge University Press, 1987).

Horne, Gerald. *Black and Red: WEB Du Bois and The Afro-American Response to the Cold War, 1944–1963* (Albany, NY: SUNY Press, 1986).

————. *The Final Victim of the Blacklist: John Howard Lawson, Dean of the Hollywood Ten* (Berkeley: University of California Press, 2006).

Horowitz, Daniel. *Betty Friedan and the Making of "The Feminine Mystique": The American Left, the Cold War, and Modern Feminism* (Amherst, MA: University of Massachusetts Press, 2000).

Jacobsen, Annie. *Operation Paperclip: The Secret Intelligence Program That Brought Nazi Scientists to America* (Boston: Little & Brown, 2014).

————. *The Pentagon's Brain: An Uncensored History of DARPA, America's Top-Secret Military Research Agency* (Boston: Back Bay, 2016).

Johnson, Chalmers. *Sorrows of Empire: Militarism, Secrecy, and the End of the Republic* (New York: Henry Holt and Co., 2005).

Kaufman, Will. *Woody Guthrie: American Radical* (Champaign: University of Illinois Press, 2011).

Kennan, George F. *Russia and the West Under Lenin and Stalin* (Boston: Little, Brown, 1960).

_____. "Sources of Soviet Conduct," *Foreign Affairs*, 25 (July 1947).

King, Jr., Dr. Martin Luther. "Beyond Vietnam: A Time to Break Silence: Declaration of Independence from the War in Vietnam," April 4, 1967, Riverside Church, New York City, reprinted in *Common Dreams*, April 4, 2008. http://www.commondreams.org.

Kinzer, Stephen. *All the Shah's Men: An American Coup and the Roots of Middle Eastern Terror* (New York: Wiley, 2006).

Kofsky, Frank. *Harry S. Truman and the War Scare of 1948: A Successful Campaign to Deceive the Nation* (New York: St. Martin's Press, 1993).

Kolko, Gabriel. *Main Currents in Modern American History* (New York: Harper, 1976).

_____. *Confronting the Third World: United States Foreign Policy 1945–1980* (New York: Pantheon Books, 1988).

_____. *The Roots of American Foreign Policy: An Analysis of Power and Purpose* (Boston: Beacon Press, 1969).

_____, and Joyce Kolko. *The Limits of Power: The World and United States Foreign Policy* (New York: Harper & Row, 1972).

Kornbluh, Peter. *The Pinochet File: A Declassified Dossier on Atrocity and Accountability* (New York: The New Press, 2003).

Kovalik, Dan. *The Plot to Scapegoat Russia: How the CIA and the Deep State Have Conspired to Vilify Putin* (New York: Skyhorse, 2017).

Kovel, Joel. *Red Hunting in the Promised Land: Anticommunism and the Making of America* (New York: Basic Books, 1994).

Krainer, Alex. *The Killing of William Browder: Deconstructing Bill Browder's Dangerous Deception* (Monaco: Equilibrium, 2017).

Kuzmarov, Jeremy. *Modernizing Repression: Police Training and Nation Building in the American Century* (Amherst, MA: University of Massachusetts Press, 2012).

_____. *The Myth of the Addicted Army: Vietnam and the Modern War on Drugs* (Amherst, MA: University of Massachusetts Press, 2009).

LaFeber, Walter. *Inevitable Revolutions: The United States in Central America* (New York: W.W. Norton, 1983).

_____. *America, Russia, and The Cold War, Updated Ninth Edition, 1945–2002* (Boston: McGraw Hill, 2002).

Languuth, A. J. *Hidden Terrors: The Truth About U.S. Police Operations in Latin America* (New York: Pantheon Books, 1978).

Lasch, Christopher. *The American Liberals and the Russian Revolution* (New York: Columbia University Press, 1962).

Lattimore, Owen. *Ordeal by Slander* (Boston: Little, Brown, 1950).

Leffler, Melvyn P. *A Preponderance of Power: National Security, the Truman Administration, and the Cold War* (Stanford, CA: Stanford University Press, 1992).

_____. and David S. Painter, eds. *Origins of the Cold War: An International*

History—Second Edition (New York: Routledge, 2005).

Lendman, Stephen. *Flashpoint in Ukraine: How the U.S. Drive for Hegemony Risks World War III* (Atlanta: Clarity Press, 2014).

Lens, Sidney. *The Military-Industrial Complex* (Philadelphia: Pilgrim Press, 1970).

Leslie, Stuart W. *The Cold War and American Science: The Military-Industrial Academic Complex at MIT and Stanford* (New York: Columbia University Press, 1993).

Lippmann, Walter, and Charles Merz. "A Test of the News," *New Republic*, August 4, 1920.

Maddox, Robert J. *The Unknown War with Russia: Wilson's Siberian Intervention* (San Rafael, CA: Presidio Press, 1977).

Mamdani, Mahmood. *Good Muslim, Bad Muslim: America, the Cold War and the Roots of Terror* (New York: Pantheon, 2004).

Marable, Manning. *W. E. B. DuBois: Black Radical Democrat*, rev ed. (New York: Routledge, 2004).

_____. *Race, Reform and Rebellion: The Second Reconstruction and Beyond in Black America*, 3rd Edition (Oxford, MS: University of Mississippi Press, 2007).

Marciano, John. *The American War in Vietnam: Crime or Commemoration?* (New York: Monthly Review Press, 2016).

Marshall, Jonathan, Peter Dale Scott, and Jane Hunter. *The Iran Contra Connection: Secret Teams and Covert Operations in the Reagan Era* (Boston: South End Press, 1987).

Marzani, Carl. *We Can Be Friends* (New York: Tropical Books Publishers, 1952).

Masuda, Hajimu. *Cold War Crucible: The Korean Conflict and the Post War World* (Cambridge, MA: Harvard University Press, 2015).

McAuliffe, Mary S. *Crisis on the Left: Cold War Politics and American Liberals, 1947–1954* (Amherst: The University of Massachusetts Press, 1978).

McCoy, Alfred W. *A Question of Torture: CIA Interrogation from the Cold War to the War on Terror* (New York: Metropolitan Books, 2006).

_____. *The Politics of Heroin: CIA Complicity in the Global Drug Trade*, rev ed. (New York: Lawrence Hill Books, 2003).

McGilligan, Patrick, and Paul Buhle. *Tender Comrades: A Back-history of the Hollywood Blacklist* (New York: St. Martin's Press, 1997).

Melman, Seymour. *Pentagon Capitalism: The Political Economy of War* (New York: McGraw Hill, 1970).

Mettan, Guy. *Creating Russophobia: From the Great Religious Schism to Anti-Putin Hysteria* (Atlanta, GO: Clarity Press, 2017).

Meyer, Gerald. *Vito Marcantonio, Radical Politician, 1902–1954* (Albany: State University of New York Press, 1989).

Mills, C. Wright. *The Power Elite* (New York: Oxford University Press, 1956).

_____. *The Causes of World War III* (New York: Ballantine Books, 1958).

Moore, Capt. Joel H., Lieut. Harry H. Mead, Lieut. Lewis E. Jahns. *The History of the American Expedition Fighting the Bolsheviki: Campaigning in North Russia 1918–1919* (Nashville: The Battery Press, 2003).

Moore, Kelly. *Disrupting Science: Social Movements, American Scientists, and the Politics of the Military, 1945–1975* (Princeton: Princeton University Press,

2008).

Nelson-Pallmeyer, Jack. *School of the Assassins* (New York: Orbis Books, 1997).

Oglesby, Carl. "Vietnam Crucible: An Essay on the Meanings of the Cold War," in Oglesby and Richard F. Schaull, *Containment and Change: Two Dissenting Views of American Foreign Policy* (New York: Macmillan, 1967).

Overy, Richard. *Why the Allies Won* (New York: W.W. Norton, 1997).

Parenti, Michael. *Against Empire* (San Francisco: City Lights Books, 1995).

_____ .*The Anti-Communist Impulse* (New York: Random House, 1969).

Pauwells, Jacques. *Myth of the Good War: The USA in World War II* (Toronto: Lorimer, 2002).

Peace, Roger, with John Marciano and Jeremy Kuzmarov. "The Vietnam War," http://peacehistory-usfp.org.

Peace, Roger. *A Call to Conscience: The Anti-Contra War Campaign* (Amherst, MA: University of Massachusetts Press, 2012).

Peck, James. *Washington's China: The National Security World, the Cold War, and the Origins of Globalism* (Amherst, MA: University of Massachusetts Press, 2006).

_____ . *Ideal Illusions: How the U.S. Government Coopted Human Rights* (New York: Metropolitan Books, 2010).

Perry, William J. *My Journey at the Nuclear Brink* (Palo Alto: Stanford Security Studies, 2015).

Prados, John. *Safe for Democracy: The Secret Wars of the CIA* (Chicago: Ivan R. Dee, 2006).

Prashad, Vijay. *The Darker Nations: A People's History of the Third World* (New York: The New Press, 2007).

Rabe, Stephen G. *The Most Dangerous Area in the World: John F. Kennedy Confronts Communist Revolution in Latin America* (Chapel Hill: University of North Carolina Press, 1999).

Radosh, Ronald. *American Labor and United States Foreign Policy* (New York: Vintage Books, 1969).

Ratner, Michael, and Michael Steven Smith. *Who Killed Che? How the CIA Got Away with Murder* (New York: OR Books, 2011).

Reed, John. *Ten Days That Shook the World.* (New York: New American Library, 1967).

Regis, Ed. *The Biology of Doom: The History of America's Secret Germ Warfare Project* (New York: Henry Holt, 1999).

Rhode, Joy. *Armed with Expertise: The Militarization of American Social Research during the Cold War* (Ithaca: Cornell University Press, 2013).

Rhodes, Richard. *Arsenals of Folly: The Making of the Nuclear Arms Race* (New York: Alfred A. Knopf, 2007).

Richard, Carl J. *When the United States Invaded Russia: Woodrow Wilson's Siberian Disaster* (New York: Rowman & Littlefield, 2012).

Rogin, Michael Paul. *The Intellectuals and McCarthy: The Radical Specter* (Boston: The MIT Press, 1969).

_____ . *Ronald Reagan The Movie and Other Episodes in Political Demonology* (Berkeley: University of California Press, 1987).

Rositzke, Harry. *The CIA's Secret Operations: Espionage, Counter-Espionage and*

Covert Action (New York: Reader's Digest, 1977).

Saunders, Frances Stonor, *The Cultural Cold War: The CIA and the World of Arts and Letters* (New York: The New Press, 2013)

Sanders, Jerry. *Peddlers of Crisis: The Committee on the Present Danger and the Politics of Containment* (Boston: South End Press, 1983).

Sakwa, Richard. *Frontline Ukraine: Crisis in the Borderland* (London: I.B. Tauris, 2016).

Schlesinger, Stephen C., and Stephen Kinzer. *Bitter Fruit: The Story of the American Coup in Guatemala*, 2nd ed. (Cambridge: David Rockefeller Center for Latin American Studies, Harvard University, 1999).

Schlosser, Eric. *Command and Control: Nuclear Weapons, the Damascus Accident, and the Illusion of Safety* (New York: Penguin Books, 2013).

Schmitz, David. *The United States Support for Right Wing Dictatorships, 1921–1965* (Chapel Hill: University of North Carolina Press, 1999).

Schneir, Walter and Miriam. *Final Verdict: What Really Happened in the Rosenberg Case* (New York: Melville House, 2010).

Schrecker, Ellen. *Many Are the Crimes: McCarthyism in America* (Princeton: Princeton University Press, 1998).

_____. ed. *Cold War Triumphalism: The Misuse of History after the Fall of Communism* (New York: The New Press, 2006).

Schuman, Frederick L. *American Policy towards Russia since 1917* (New York: International Publishers, 1928).

Scott, Peter Dale. *The American Deep State: Wall Street, Big Oil and the Attack on U.S. Democracy* (New York: Rowman & Littlefield, 2014).

_____. *The War Conspiracy: JFK, 9/11, and the Deep Politics of War*, rev. ed. with foreword by Rex Bradford (New York: Skyhorse, 2008).

Shaw, Tony. *Hollywood's Cold War* (Amherst, MA: University of Massachusetts Press, 2007).

Shoup, Lawrence, and William Minter, *Imperial Brain Trust: The Council on Foreign Relations and United States Foreign Policy* (New York: Authors Choice Press, 2004).

Simpson, Christopher. *Blowback: The First Full Account of America's Recruitment of Nazis, And Its Disastrous Effect on Our Domestic and Foreign Policy* (New York: Weidenfeld & Nicolson, 1988).

Smith, John Chabot. *Alger Hiss: The True Story* (New York: Holt, Rinehart & Winston, 1976).

Smith, Sharon. *Subterranean Fire: A History of Working Class Radicalism in the United States* (Chicago: Haymarket, 2006).

Stewart, George. *The White Armies of Russia: A Chronicle of Counter-Revolution and Allied Intervention* (New York: The Macmillan Company, 1933).

Stockwell, John. *The Praetorian Guard: The U.S. Role in the New World Order* (Boston: South End Press, 1999).

Stone, Oliver, and Peter Kuznick. *An Untold History of the United States* (New York: Gallery Books, 2012).

Storrs, Landon R.Y. *The Second Red Scare and the Unmaking of the New Deal Left* (Princeton: Princeton University Press, 2013).

Theoharis, Athan, and John Stuart Cox. *The Boss: J. Edgar Hoover and the Great*

American Inquisition (New York: Bantam Books, 1988).

Thomas, Gordon. *Secrets and Lies: A History of CIA Mind Control and Germ Warfare* (New York: Konecky, Williams & Associates, 2007).

Tirman, John. *The Deaths of Others: The Fate of Civilians in America's Wars* (New York: Oxford University Press, 2011).

Tsygankov, Andrei P. *Russophobia: Anti-Russian Lobby and American Foreign Policy* (New York: Palgrave McMillan, 2009).

Turse, Nick *Kill Anything that Moves: The Real American War in Vietnam* (New York: Metropolitan Books, 2005).

Vine, David. *Base Nation: How U.S. Military Bases Abroad Harm America and the World* (New York: Metropolitan Books, 2015).

Von Eschen, Penny M. *Race Against Empire: Black Americans and Anticolonialism, 1937–1957* (Ithaca: Cornell University Press, 1998).

Wallace, Henry. *Toward World Peace* (New York: Reynal & Hitchcock, 1948).

Walton, Richard. *Cold War and Counter-Revolution: The Foreign Policy of John F. Kennedy* (New York: Penguin Books, 1973).

Warriner, Doreen. *Revolution in Eastern Europe* (London: Warriner Press, 1950).

Weiner, Tim. *Enemies: A History of the FBI* (New York: Random House, 2012).

_____. *Legacy of Ashes: The History of the CIA* (New York: Anchor Books, 2008).

Westad, Odd Arne. *The Global Cold War: Third World Intervention and the Making of Our Times* (New York: Cambridge University Press, 2007).

Whitfield, Stephen J. *The Culture of the Cold War* (Baltimore: The Johns Hopkins University Press, 1991).

Wiener, Jon. *How We Forgot the Cold War: A Journey across America* (Berkeley: University of California Press, 2012).

Williams, William Appleman. *American Russian Relations 1781–1947* (New York: Rinehart & Co., 1952).

_____. *The Contours of American History.* (London: Verso, 2011).

_____. *Empire as A Way of Life: An Essay on the Causes and Character of America's Present Predicament along with a Few Thoughts about an Alternative.*

Wittner, Lawrence. *American Intervention in Greece, 1943–1949: A Study in Counter-Revolution* (New York: Columbia University Press, 1982).

_____. *Cold War America: From Hiroshima to Watergate* (New York: Praeger, 1974).

Woldman, Albert A. *Lincoln and the Russians* (New York: Collier Books, 1952).

Wolfe, Alan. *The Rise and Fall of the Soviet Threat: Domestic Sources of the Cold War Consensus* (Boston: South End Press, 1984).

Zinn, Howard. *The Bomb* (San Francisco: City Lights, 2010).

_____. *On War* (New York: Seven Stories Press, 2011).

Index